J. L. STYAN

THE DARK COMEDY

THE DEVELOPMENT OF
MODERN COMIC TRAGEDY

Second edition

CAMBRIDGE UNIVERSITY PRESS

CAMBRIDGE

LONDON · NEW YORK · MELBOURNE

Published by the Syndics of the Cambridge University Press
The Pitt Building, Trumpington Street, Cambridge CB2 1RP
Bentley House, 200 Euston Road, London NW1 2DB
32 East 57th Street, New York, NY 10022, USA
296 Beaconsfield Parade, Middle Park, Melbourne 3206, Australia

Library of Congress catalogue card number: 68-23185

ISBN 0 521 06572 0 hard covers
ISBN 0 521 09529 8 paperback

First published 1962
Second edition 1968
Reprinted 1974, 1979

First printed in Great Britain
at the University Press, Cambridge
Reprinted and bound in Great Britain by
Weatherby Woolnough, Wellingborough, Northants

PREFACE TO THE SECOND EDITION

In the short time since this book was written, the sense that we are witnessing something of a dramatic renaissance has been confirmed. Labels like 'the theatre of the absurd' and 'the theatre of cruelty' have been selected and partly discarded as too limiting. Drama of importance has been written by new playwrights like Edward Albee, John Arden, Saul Bellow, Harold Pinter and Peter Weiss. Older playwrights like Jean Anouilh, Samuel Beckett, Jean Genêt, Eugène Ionesco and Tennessee Williams have continued to write major works. Earlier playwrights like Chekhov, Shaw, Pirandello, O'Casey and Brecht are being increasingly recognized for their contribution to the resurgence of tragicomedy and the direction it has taken. The theatre has become, more than it ever was, an international marketplace.

I have therefore taken the opportunity offered by a new edition to bring the book up to date and to expand the reading list, to modify or reinforce earlier judgments, and to include extended illustrative analysis (of the kind which was found helpful in the first edition) from *Mother Courage* and *Waiting for Godot*, two plays of seminal influence in the 1960s and, no doubt, for the future.

J. L. S.

UNIVERSITY OF MICHIGAN
April 1967

v

PREFACE TO THE FIRST EDITION

I hope that the title chosen for this book, *The Dark Comedy*, will not mislead readers into thinking that the drama of the twentieth century is dull, or necessarily gloomy: it is anything but this for the spectator. When it is stimulating, it is because it refuses to allow us to respond with preconceived notions of the tragic or the comic. I have therefore been at pains to lose in my title the associations belonging to the spurious term 'tragicomedy', which invites us to measure a play by two widely different yardsticks simultaneously, regardless of their possible irrelevance.

Once again I owe my very sincere thanks to Professor G. E. T. Mayfield, Mrs Pat Roberts and my wife for their most valuable suggestions and assistance. Grateful acknowledgment is also made to the owners of copyright material quoted in this book.

J. L. S.

UNIVERSITY OF HULL
June 1961

CONTENTS

vii

I cannot immediately determine whether or no I am dignified by the Title you have graciously conferred on me. You cannot but recollect the difficulties that have unceasingly arisen to prevent my discerning whether your Angels are black, white, or grey.

THOMAS BUTTS *to* **WILLIAM BLAKE**

I

ON TEARS AND LAUGHTER

DELMONTE. I play everything, classical and modern plays, tragedies and comedies.

ISABELLE. And you never get them muddled, mix them up at all?

DELMONTE. Never used to in the old days! Comedy was comedy and tragedy was tragedy! But with the plays we get served up nowadays, of course...

JEAN ANOUILH, *Dinner with the Family*

FORM OR FORMULA?

García Lorca is reported by his brother as saying, 'If in certain scenes the audience doesn't know what to do, whether to laugh or to cry, that will be a success for me.'[1] Such a statement by a playwright could not easily have been made in any century but our own. We know that several great plays from the past have called for an equally vacillating response from their audiences, yet not until now, confronted by a prolific line of modern plays which refuse to be pigeon-holed as comedies or tragedies, are we being forced to re-think some of the long-accepted categories which have traditionally helped us to evaluate the play.

Over recent years, comments from critics have grown increasingly ambivalent and paradoxical, and we now flounder in the near-meaningless terminology of the farcical tragedy and the pathetic comedy, the *drame comique* and the *pseudo-drame*, the 'charade' and the 'extravaganza'. The term 'tragicomedy' was equivocal enough in the past. On the other hand, the enigma is far from resolved when a contemporary writer, Ronald Peacock, states forthrightly, 'In the midst of more intricate details of aesthetic analysis it is well to state a simple truth. Drama must be one of two things: either comic or

[1] Francisco Lorca, introduction to *Three Tragedies of Federico García Lorca*, trans. Graham-Luján and O'Connell (New York, 1955), p. 13.

intensely moving.'¹ It is partly to discuss how far such embarrassing words as 'comic' and 'moving' in themselves beg important questions that this book is written.

Drama, as a structure of shifting relationships between character and spectator, today ranges over largely uncharted fields of feeling; and it reveals itself in infinite variety. A traditional nomenclature is just no longer serviceable for the description or analysis of the relationships developed by Chekhov, Pirandello, Jean Anouilh, Brecht and Samuel Beckett. These are the playwrights who best exemplify a new direction in the twentieth-century theatre.

It is time to call a halt to the Polonius-like mobilization of genres and sub-genres. Our standard is still to be the intensity of the reflection and the incisiveness of the comment the play calls up. But we shall recognize that a play may legitimately refuse to be a failed tragedy or a failed comedy—because the response it wants may be of neither kind, and the forms and conventions it uses may bear no relation to either. Ambiguous plays like *Hamlet* and *Major Barbara* are unique ways of speaking, devised to satisfy the demands of their own subjects, not to conform to preconceived patterns of thought or feeling explored elsewhere.

As early as 1775, Goethe saw the distraction of caring for form when it was merely fashion: 'It is well nigh time that people ceased talking about the form of dramatic compositions, about their length and shortness, their unities, their beginning, middle, and end, and all the rest of it; and that we now begin to go straightway to their contents, which hitherto, it seems, have been left to take care of themselves.'² We are but a step away from Coleridge. His reiterated demand was for our awareness of the relevance of the part to the whole, for our appreciation of the total pattern as it takes shape from within the work itself. The creative impulse which fixes the unity of the piece may take no account of fashion.

Ibsen's *An Enemy of the People* is an angry pamphlet play about a half-comic, hot-headed individualist, Dr Thomas Stockmann, who

¹ R. Peacock, *The Art of Drama* (London, 1957), p. 189.
² Goethe, quoted by B. H. Clark, *European Theories of the Drama* (Cincinnati, 1918), p. 339.

sacrifices everything in his fight against 'the compact majority'. It narrowly misses tragedy, and Ibsen admitted that he was not sure whether the play was comedy or drama: 'It partakes of the nature of either, or lies half-way between.'[1] *An Enemy of the People*, as is well known, was written in haste as an urgent personal statement: this accounts for its polemics, and also for its uncertain form, which Ibsen did not preconceive. He was instinctively tilting against the formal frontiers of drama in his imaginative effort to find a public analogy for his private battle.

Or consider *The Silver Tassie*, O'Casey's play about the callousness of war, which he calls uncomfortably a 'tragicomedy'. It develops from farce to tragedy, adopting in turn the conventions of pseudo-realism and expressionism, in order to smite us with the grotesque ironies of the last act in which we see young Harry the ex-footballer soldier sitting helplessly in a wheel-chair. As O'Casey felt the need to regulate our response in the audience, so he called into play first one, then another, expedient. Only the vehement drive of the play's theme fuses its several parts. We must recognize a distinction between form and formula.

Eliot's *The Family Reunion* is a more deceptive example. It is too easy to see this play in the pattern of tragedy: it invites our sympathy with a central figure, Harry, Lord Monchensey, who cannot understand his agony of mind; this 'hero' in human suffering traces a course through and beyond a universal human predicament; it incorporates elements of the *Oresteia* of Aeschylus, deriving its energy from the Greek concept of the curse, merged with a Freudian concept of heredity; Harry's impulse towards 'atonement' may even be taken as an equivalent to that intangible, the cathartic effect of classical tragedy. Audiences might be forgiven for faintly hoping to apply standards acquired from Sophocles' *Oedipus Rex* or Shakespeare's *King Lear*.

Second thoughts confirm that these elements of the 'tragic' are quite lost in another pattern which makes a stronger impression. This pattern is marked by differing manners of speech, by indicative

[1] Ibsen, letter to Jonas Lie, 1882, quoted by J. Lavrin, *Ibsen: an Approach* (London, 1950), p. 85.

3

action on the stage, by contrasting levels of characterization. These present an argument on two levels: the world of Harry and Agatha, his favourite aunt, is set against the lower level of the family chorus. The chorus persists vividly throughout the play even when not speaking as a formal group. It does not have the traditional function of explaining, anticipating, exciting, but, in a new way, it ironically accentuates the spiritual problems of Harry. The family is the negative to Harry's positive. Here is one view of an older generation who live and move in a narrow orbit of the past, who

> tighten the knot of confusion
> Into perfect misunderstanding,

who are 'ridiculous in some nightmare pantomime', who do not 'understand'.

In organizing this second pattern, Eliot has done more than write the 'tragedy' of Harry, Lord Monchensey: he has, perhaps inadvertently, written the melancholy comedy of those whose 'ordinary day isn't much more than breathing'. Amy, his mother, and the aunts and uncles together take our attention as much as Harry does, and Eliot has written neither tragedy nor comedy. The tensions between the two constituents present us with a *tertium aliquid*, and the author rightly calls *The Family Reunion* 'a play', simply. Central to the play, as to *The Cocktail Party*, is the conception of the monstrous discrepancies between human minds.

More recently, the attack on Anouilh's play of St Joan, *The Lark*, is rooted in the wish to see the play as tragedy when it was conspicuously intended to be nothing of the kind, any more than was Shaw's *Saint Joan*. It is not considered that the 'scaling-down' process of Anouilh's treatment is important for our fresh response to a well-worn theme, and to help us to recognize man as a creature doing evil and doing good, created by God, as Anouilh says in the person of Joan, 'in that contradiction to make his difficult way'. Joan is presented to us in modest, human terms, not as the idealized saint of legend, nor as a Shavian and rationalized symbol; to say this, of course, does not mean that she is not also a fit subject for tragedy or for comedy in other hands. Is this humanizing treatment of Anouilh's

4

really an attempt to introduce 'a form of realism which belongs to bourgeois comedy and drama, and which is completely out of place in this context and has no relevance to the theme'?[1] Within a patently simple theatrical convention, with the trial presented detachedly as a play-within-a-play, thus having a far from naturalistic impact, we are shown a Joan who is not a religious mystic, but a child in pigtails who *might have been* beaten by her father, as a girl who *might have been* easy in the company of earthy soldiers on their own level, who *might have been* mocked by other women and seduced by men like Baudricourt. Not a mystic, not a tragic, but a naïve, Joan is offered to us by mixing her with a selfish and pompous sensualist, a good-humoured brute, a fanatical psychopath, and other types of the 'experienced' beside whom Joan's simplicity glows. The transfiguration of Joan at the final curtain is not the ascension of Joan to heaven, but the coronation of the Dauphin; it is not there to send us off happily, not a misplaced attempt at a tragic irony, but an irony to impress upon us the presence of the mystery, the phenomenon of Joan, like 'the phenomenon', as Anouilh remarks in a programme note, 'of a daisy or of the sky or of a bird', of a lark uncaged.

The argument against *The Lark* is reinforced by formal preconceptions about tragedy which are commonly held:

Who ever heard of jesters or clowns at the foot of the Cross at the moment when the world rent itself in an eternal wound? Clowning and tumbling can certainly be moving homages to God, but they cannot take place at the foot of Calvary. The death of a saint, a hero or a myth-maker is part of the revelatory process of the very essence of life through death, and in order to be effective it can only take place in a setting of austere grandeur, which may include irony but not snivelling or tearful jocularity. A tragedy must have a style, a form or ritual which cannot include barracks life.[2]

But clowning and tumbling *can* take place at the foot of Calvary, and in as sober a Mystery Cycle as that from York there is evidence enough that the pinners took very much to heart the idea of the

---

[1] J. Chiari, *The Contemporary French Theatre: the Flight from Naturalism* (London, 1958), p. 189.
[2] *Ibid.* pp. 194-5.

mockery of Jesus by the soldiers who crucified him, as the Gospel suggested. It appears first as a direct sarcasm:

> 1 KNIGHT. And since he claimeth kingdom with crown,
> Even as a king here have it shall he.[1]

During the action of a very protracted crucifixion, the men quarrel among themselves with a fair sprinkling of comedy:

> 1 KNIGHT. Why chat ye so? Fasten on a cord,
> And tug him to, by top and tail.
> 3 KNIGHT. Thou commands lightly as a lord;
> Come help to haul, with an ill hail.
> 1 KNIGHT. Now certes that shall I do,
> Full surely as a snail.[2]

After a natural modicum of advertisement to the crowd of their skill and trade, the business of casting lots for the garments while Christ is in his agony is abruptly concluded by the leader in this way:

> 3 KNIGHT. I rede we draw cuts for this coat;
> Lo, see how soon all sides to save.
> 4 KNIGHT. The short cut wins, that well ye wot,
> Whether it falls to knight or knave.
> 1 KNIGHT. Fellows, ye need not take offence;
> This mantle is my gain.[3]

The real interest of this drama lies in what these apparent contradictions contribute to the theatrical experience. Anouilh is ostensibly refusing us the austere grandeur of tragedy; the author of the York play seems to be testing us by including barracks life. By oblique means these plays yield their meaning, and, unless we choose to read their attempts as ignorant structural errors and to ignore their effect on an audience, they bring sharply into question the so-called 'rules' that must be followed by the dramatist.

Before we consider the inadequacy of traditional theories of tragedy and comedy to identify and explain the characteristic tone of modern drama in general, we should remind ourselves quickly of

---

[1] *The York Cycle of Mystery Plays*, version by J. S. Purvis (London, 1957), p. 284.
[2] *Ibid.* p. 285.   [3] *Ibid.* p. 289.

those great, intuitive playwrights of earlier years who have upset the theories. Notably, these are Euripides, the anonymous authors of the English Mystery plays, Marlowe and, pre-eminently, Shakespeare and Molière.

EURIPIDES, MEDIEVAL MYSTERY PLAYS, MARLOWE

It is no part of the argument to suggest that dark comedy is a new vogue, only that it has had its fullest expression in the last sixty years. It would be surprising should we fail to find a mixture of moods, comic and pathetic, and of responses, critical and sympathetic, at times earlier than the twentieth century, especially since the mixture can so well reflect the multicoloured world of society or the soul. We do in fact find the dark note making itself heard subversively at particular moments in earlier ages of the drama. How far an unstable public or private temper, an uncertain climate of opinion or an uneasiness in the spirit of the writer from disturbing personal experiences, was responsible for the troubled drama we are describing, is for others to decide. Athens' declining years, England at the turn of the sixteenth century, Molière's France under Louis XIV, Russia at the turn of the nineteenth century, and Western Europe as a whole after the two world wars seem to have in common that mood of unrest that permits a Judas drama.

Towards the end of Euripides' long life, Athens, previously confident and secure as the commercial centre of the Greek world, was a creature spent and frustrated by the exhausting Peloponnesian wars. After the fatal Sicilian expedition of 415 B.C. she was torn by factions at home. At the same time, scepticism of the old beliefs was undermining the Athenian sense of moral security; and rationalism, pervasive as scepticism is in educated society today, encouraged the fruition of an iconoclastic theatre, notably in Euripides and Aristophanes. With his comic eye, Aristophanes chose the way of burlesque, mercilessly satirizing the man whom one would have thought closest to his own mind.

As far as we know, Euripides, the restless Socratic questioner, chose to write largely within the given tragic form he inherited from

7

Aeschylus and Sophocles, and it proved the more powerful weapon for that. Within the limits of tragedy he tried to depict the truth about the people of the old legends as he saw it. He makes a gesture, for example, towards showing two sides of Jason, towards explaining Clytaemnestra's sin, towards querying the popular religion that could find the matricide Orestes at once right and wrong. In Aristophanes' *The Frogs*, Euripides is made to explain that he taught men to talk with freedom, 'to fall in love, think evil, question all things'. And he adds,

I put things on the stage that came from daily life and business,
Where men could catch me if I tripped; could listen without dizziness
To things they knew, and judge my art.

A little later we hear,

I mingled reasoning with my art,
And shrewdness, till I fired their heart
To brood, to think things through and through;
And rule their houses better, too.[1]

In some of his plays Euripides is at moments within an ace of creating something of dark comedy by his modernity, and its presence may account for the arguments that have surrounded him in the past.[2] Thus although his first extant play, the *Alcestis*, was probably a type of satyr-play, as Gilbert Murray argued,[3] we can recognize its contradictory nature. In it the story is told of the loyal wife Alcestis, who agrees to die in lieu of Admetus, not the best of husbands. Meanwhile Heracles, receiving hospitality in the palace of Admetus, has apparently got himself roaring drunk at the very time when Alcestis' funeral procession is moving off. So much so that the butler makes a complaint about him; but also, in order to shame him, the butler has told Heracles all about Alcestis. This information not only sobers the reveller, but inspires

---

[1] Aristophanes, *The Frogs*, trans. G. Murray (London, 1908), pp. 72–3.
[2] These positions are reviewed by A. R. Thompson, *The Dry Mock* (Berkeley, 1948), ch. 8.
[3] See the Introduction to *The Alcestis of Euripides*, trans. G. Murray (London, 1915).

him to go and rescue her forthwith, and thus the play ends as a 'comedy'.

The *Helen*, of *c.* 412 B.C., is a high comedy, satirical to the point of undermining the glory of the Trojan War itself, hallowed repository of the greatest among the Greek legends. The *Ion*, of about the same time, tells of the princess Creusa who was seduced by the god Apollo and bore him the child Ion. This child is exposed to die, only to be saved by Hermes. The play ends with a conventional recognition scene between mother and son, but in the meantime Apollo the seducer has been smoothly debunked.

The wit in this author was working against the greater single-mindedness of his famous predecessors, but also towards a greater resourcefulness in drama. As Murray suggested so long ago, 'Greek drama has always suffered from a school of critics who approach a play with a greater equipment of aesthetic theory than of dramatic perception.'[1]

Even more difficult to disentangle are the contradictory springs of feeling present in the popular drama of medieval times in England. We saw how the soldiers who are set to crucify Christ in the York 'Pinners' and Painters' Play' performed their task well 'in character' as broad, insensitive sadists. The guilds' actors obviously also saw their function as one of amusing their audience with horseplay, in spite of the grim seriousness of the moment. This element of near-blasphemy is common to all the medieval Mysteries. Herod, the slayer of the Innocents, is the prize clown of the show; the devils and Satan himself contribute to the fun at the very moment when the sinners are thrown into the jaws of Hell, and especially when Hell is being harrowed. Years later, in Marlowe's *Doctor Faustus*, 'shaggy-haired devils' were still to be seen 'roaring over the stage with squibs in their mouths'.

The reader may not need reminding of the joy evident at other, less pressing, times. The introduction of a wife for Noah in the Chester *Flood* is one of those happy opportunities for the male actor in his skirts to caricature some wifely aberrations, and in so doing un-avoidably present God's chosen one as a poor pathetic creature easily

---

[1] *The Alcestis of Euripides*, trans. G. Murray, p. vi.

led by the nose. Having teased Noah for as long as the farce will stretch, the wife is finally carried into the Ark by force:

> NOYE. Welckome, wiffe, in to this botte.
> NOYES WIFFE. Have thou that for thy note!
> NOYE. Ha, ha! Marye, this is hotte!

Mrs Noah's blow as she passes him, however, is abruptly forgotten as the Ark begins to float, and we hear from her no more.

Of most unusual interest, Joseph in the York Mysteries supplies a very earthy comment on the Immaculate Conception, for Joseph is the unsophisticated peasant of medieval England. He makes his entry primarily to establish for the spectator that Jesus will shortly be born, but he speaks like the old cuckold who cannot trust his young wife:

> For shame what shall I say,
> That thusgates now in my old days
> Has wedded a young wench to my wife,
> And may not well stride over two straws?[1]

So Mary for a brief instant is delightfully seen as a 'wench', with all the connotations of the word.

The story of Mak and Gyll in the notorious Second Shepherds' Play from Wakefield undoubtedly parodies the birth of Jesus in the manger. The play is jolly with the coarseness of the clowning of Mak, the *extra* shepherd who turns out to be a sheep-thief, and with the raucous groaning of Gyll who hides the stolen sheep in the cradle by her assumed childbed. After Mak's crime has been discovered and he has been suitably tossed in a blanket, it is not surprising if we are today startled to hear a ready Angel break into a 'Gloria in Excelsis'. But the play must go on. This example is in no way explicable as illuminating by contrast the holy event. Nor would one think that any 'restlessness' in the audience of this time could in this case account for such strange phenomena in the drama. These instances, however, do strongly suggest that it is natural and human for an unfettered popular audience to be willing to undergo surprising contrasts of feeling and to joke about what is deeply revered.

[1] 'The Pewterers' and Founders' Play' in *The York Cycle of Mystery Plays*, trans. J. S. Purvis (London, 1957), p. 86.

The medieval Christian life was one of optimism, which invited a certain necessary contempt for the sufferings of common existence. For the devout Christian, happiness lay in the next world. Thus poverty, bad weather, bad crops, bad wives, or hate, cruelty, murder and crucifixion were part of the divine comedy. In a divine order of things the incongruity of man's baseness and stupidity was part of the sacred pattern. The human world of littleness and sin is set on the same stage with the emblems of heaven, and is all part of the same story. In play after play, the link with the earthly reality of the audience is emphasized in direct address by the actor from pageant to street: it may be by Cain's curse on the spectators or Jesus' injunctions. The soldiers who nail a man to the Cross *are* the pinners of medieval York: they are of the same world as the audience, not only seen in contemporary medieval dress, but representing the cruelty familiar to all who watch. It is not in simplicity, but in a satisfying perspective, a unified drama of recognition and confirmation of belief, that grotesque farce and human comedy are present in the English mystery plays. Mrs Noah and Mak can jest, sin and be saved—it is all part of the divine sense of humour.[1]

The mixture of 'hornpipes and funerals', to use Sir Philip Sidney's phrase, was very much to the public taste. As if to spite the exertions of Renaissance critics, English drama of the sixteenth century brazenly flourished the peculiar tragicomic legacy of medieval drama. In *Doctor Faustus* Marlowe made an incomplete attempt at comic parody in the subplot of the servant Wagner, with whom Faustus makes a mock compact of seven years to echo his own of twenty-four with Lucifer. However, the set-piece scenes of Faustus' jests with the great and the not-so-great belittle the hero and detract from the dignity of his impending doom. The clowning makes for a heterogeneous play: it hardly controls the light and shade of the drama of the soul in its hell on earth. Not until Marlowe's *The Jew of Malta* does the racy temper of the age translate itself effectively into drama. In this play in particular, its author's own wild, robust temperament added a special unity of spirit to the whole; this unity has been

---

[1] The author is indebted to discussions with Dr Edith Gold for the development of this argument.

difficult to recognize, probably for the simple reason that the play is never seen on the stage. We remember T. S. Eliot's firm diagnosis in 1918 of the play's piquancy:

If one takes *The Jew of Malta* not as a tragedy, or as a 'tragedy of blood', but as a farce, the concluding act becomes intelligible; and if we attend with a careful ear to the versification, we find that Marlowe develops a tone to suit this farce, and even perhaps that this tone is his most powerful and mature tone. I say farce, but with the enfeebled humour of our times the word is a misnomer; it is the farce of the old English humour, the terribly serious, even savage comic humour.[1]

It was perhaps typical of the time to choose a Jew to be at the centre of a blood-curdling play, but it was especially typical of Marlowe to work so hard to make the Barabas we first meet as sympathetic as he is. Barabas has much of Tamburlaine's vast vitality and faultless logic:

> What, bring you Scripture to confirm your wrongs?
> Preach me not out of my possessions,

he answers to the Governor who is robbing him. His hatred of the Christians is justified, and he stands upright amid his calamities. But quite early on, hints are supplied for another, more farcical, view of him, as when with the help of his daughter Abigail he manages to recover his wealth from his house, requisitioned as a nunnery. As she throws his money-bags down to him, he cries, 'O girl! O gold! O beauty! O my bliss!' In this attitude he repels us, till the figure of heroic stature is steadily dwarfed to the caricature of a 'bottle-nosed knave'.

The character of Barabas is also instinct with Marlowe's evident delight in the outrageous conduct of a monster:

> As for myself, I walk abroad a nights
> And kill sick people groaning under walls:
> Sometimes I go about and poison wells,

which suggests Marlowe's grotesque, teeth-dripping interest in the fascination of fear. Our sympathy does not long survive Barabas'

---

[1] T. S. Eliot, 'Christopher Marlowe', in *Selected Essays* (London, 1932), p. 123.

cruel use of Abigail's feelings and the sacrifice of her lovers for the sake of his revenge, however just, but the defiant note of a superman warring against inevitable defeat is heard even to the end when he curses his enemies from his boiling cauldron: 'Die, life! fly, soul! tongue, curse thy fill and die!'

Marlowe's 'acid humour', as F. S. Boas calls it,[1] remains strong in *The Massacre at Paris*, his tale of the Duke of Guise and the murky slaughter of the Huguenots. 'The Guise' is yet another Tamburlaine and very like Barabas; all are men of 'policy'. He commits a short series of gruesome murders on stage, giving a quick impressionistic view of the general massacre supposedly taking place off-stage. But each killing is conducted with a grim mockery of the victim and a short parody of his belief. Thus he mimics a Protestant preacher with 'Dearly beloved brother—thus 'tis written' as he thrusts his dagger home. The horror is streaked with a vein of perverse humour, and farcical cruelty is a mood we do not truly feel again, after the Jacobean drama of Marston, Tourneur, Webster, Jonson and Middleton, until Jean Anouilh and Samuel Beckett arrive in the theatre three hundred years later.

SHAKESPEARE

So to Shakespeare, the most intuitive writer of them all. So much has been written about his tragicomic spirit that a cursory view of his position as a whole would seem useful. The simple fact is inescapable that Shakespeare's exploration of his experience in terms of the stage led him quite often, though of course not always, to touch his comedy with the tragic and his tragedy with the comic. Especially in the relatively new fields we are pleased to call 'histories' and 'problem comedies', he obeyed his most profound impulses to mix the two. In Dr Johnson's words, he 'caught his ideas from the living world', and it was this that produced his exciting results.

Shakespeare could draw a broad comic character and situation with the best of them. But again and again we notice that special power of his to observe, reflect and reassess which sets in motion a

---

[1] F. S. Boas, *Christopher Marlowe* (London, 1940), p. 159.

conflicting, even sobering, undercurrent. It is this which restrains our unharnessed submission to the potential comedy of Shylock and Jaques. In little, we see the process at work in our picture of the justices Shallow and Silence, for example. On one level they are comic because they are utterly serious about themselves. But on another they are serious for us too because we know we have that within us which can find two pathetic old men comic. In these two creations Shakespeare displays his delicious sense of people growing old and thinking of their lusty youth; but they are also aware that their acquaintances are dying, and that 'we shall all follow'. However, punctuating these troubled thoughts on the great eternal verity are other more material troubles like the price to be fetched by 'a good score of ewes'. As when King Hal's procession passes Falstaff by and the old man turns to his friend with an ambiguous 'Master Shallow, I owe you a thousand pound', so in the Shallow and Silence exchanges Shakespeare touches exquisitely a true nerve of comedy.

In another department of comic pleasure we must place, for example, the rare portrait of Rosalind on which so much of our enjoyment of *As You Like It* hangs. Rosalind lacks the single-minded strength of a Célimène or a Millamant, the larger-than-life creatures of Molière's and Congreve's comedy; it is her weaknesses that make her more compassionate and warm than either of these. Our moments for laughing at her are balanced by the times when we laugh with her. Thus, caught in the stutters and hesitations of romantic love, she cannot drag herself away from Orlando's presence, for all an embarrassed Celia pulls at her sleeve:

> ROSALIND. He calls us back: my pride fell with my fortunes,
>   I'll ask him what he would: did you call sir?
>   Sir, you have wrestled well, and overthrown
>   More than your enemies.
> CELIA. Will you go coz?
> ROSALIND. Have with you: fare you well.

When she hears that Orlando is there in the forest with her, her agitation is that of an articulate canary:

ROSALIND. Nay, but the devil take mocking: speak sad brow, and true maid.

CELIA. I'faith, coz, 'tis he.

ROSALIND. Orlando?

CELIA. Orlando.

ROSALIND. Alas the day, what shall I do with my doublet and hose? What did he when thou saw'st him? What said he? How look'd he? Wherein went he? What makes he here? Did he ask for me? Where remains he? How parted he with thee? And when shalt thou see him again? Answer me in one word.

Yet this same Rosalind can advise her Orlando when in a similar condition that 'men have died from time to time, and worms have eaten them, but not for love', and describe the meeting of brother Oliver and Celia with the perceptive diagnosis of a wise old aunt:

For your brother, and my sister, no sooner met, but they look'd: no sooner look'd, but they lov'd: no sooner lov'd, but they sigh'd: no sooner sigh'd, but they asked one another the reason: no sooner knew the reason, but they sought the remedy...

As a result of this treatment, the spectator is placed in the position of one who feels sympathy with the chicken that might have been hatched from the egg he is relishing.

The dramatic pattern of *As You Like It* as a whole exemplifies those qualities of comic balance found in *A Midsummer Night's Dream*, *Much Ado About Nothing* and *Twelfth Night*. The play's pattern is again one of the frivolous pulling against the serious, felt in the opposition between the picture of social disruption and the affairs of the heart, between the 'desert inaccessible' of 'melancholy boughs' and the concept of 'the golden world' of Arden. The love stories themselves explore the 'tyranny' of the pretty passion, Phoebe teasing Silvius, and Rosalind teasing Orlando, while the harmony brought by Hymen may only descend after the trials and torments of harsh experience. Already a Pirandellian questioning of earthly values is felt in this most gentle of comedies, where we are invited to see, in the words of old Corin the bystander, 'a pageant truly play'd' by those who wear their masks quite lightly. In the structure of his scenes Shakespeare conceals another of his mysteries. The contrast and continuity of mood and tone forbid and welcome us by turns;

and for us to pass between the worlds of Silvius, the absurd lover, and of Corin, the plain man, from Orlando's noble but rather rhapsodical sentiments to Audrey's slap-and-tickle substantiality and Rosalind's bright sanity, to pass from Jaques the pessimist to Touchstone the realist, is to build rhythmically within the mind the balanced image of a unique play.

This oblique approach to dramatic meaning found in the earlier comedies marks that salty style that defies final analysis. Though we would not say that such roseate comedy contains more than a tinge of grey, the manner of its keeping its equilibrium is recognizably that of other Shakespearian comedy in which the complexion is darker. The last comedies, and in particular *The Winter's Tale*, stagger us with a more brazen disregard of 'form'. This tragedy of Leontes' jealousy is turned face-about, and yet remains extraordinarily stable for its sheer vitality. In his effort to translate a portrait of ugly human caprice into one of regeneration and hope, Shakespeare uses a series of outrageously successful tricks of theatre: planting an ironic Paulina at the heart of the tragedy, introducing clowns into the emotional storm into which the child Perdita is cast, having the irresistible realist Autolycus take our whole attention with his delightful 'coney-catching', inviting us to jump from one generation to another that is young and infinitely lovable, and demanding daring leaps in tone that make the sheep-shearing feast of IV. iv the enduring piece of legerdemain it is.[1]

How far is such a technique truly distinguishable from that which Shakespeare introduces with extraordinary effect into some of the tragedies? In a tragic context rarer and deeper passions are plumbed by the presence of the commonplace and the trivial, the comic and the absurd. We are confronted by a tragedy like *King Lear*, the peak of Shakespeare's achievement, at whose point of crisis is conceived the scene of the mad trial. 'The core of the play', writes Wilson Knight, 'is an absurdity, an indignity, an incongruity.' Webster's *The Duchess of Malfi* and Middleton's *The Changeling*, at whose climax

---

[1] An interesting analysis of the tragicomic mixture in this play will be found in S. L. Bethell, *The Winter's Tale: a Study* (London, 1944). See especially 'Antiquated Technique and the Planes of Reality', pp. 47 ff.

madmen touch off the mordant mood of the drama, and Marston's *The Malcontent* and Tourneur's *The Revenger's Tragedy*, which close with an indecorously medieval Dance of Death, seem to have borrowed some of *King Lear*'s feverishness for the next generation. The peculiar tensions of Shakespearian tragedy arise not only from the total irony of the events in their course, but as well from the many and detailed moments misleadingly called comic 'relief', moments carefully thrust into the tragic action to make the pain the more acute.

The facilities offered by Shakespeare's neutral stage lent themselves to his special dramatic rhythm of ironic contrasts. A virtual absence of scenery encouraged an exceptional fluidity in the structure of scenes, affecting the pattern of responses demanded from the spectators. A possible intimacy between the actor and his audience permitted a wide and flexible range of playing, from rhetorical declamation to the naturalistic confidence of a whisper, affecting the pattern of tone in speech, scene and sequence of scenes. These patterns are especially likely to be missed in reading: in performance we become immediately aware that a scene in Shakespearian tragedy is written always as a stage in the cumulative extortion of feeling from an audience, a well-planned turning of the screw.

The simply constructed, early apprentice tragedy of *Romeo and Juliet* may serve as our example. In this play Shakespeare tested the scope of his stage, and explored the powers of tragedy by balancing scene against scene. He found that by mixing the spectators' moods within the continuity of the narrative line of the story, he could add immensely to our sense of the lovers' isolation and the poignancy of their difficulties. The lovers meet after the hostile presentation of the civil unrest in Verona, and the ominous threat from Tybalt in the ballroom scene is felt against the gay galliard danced in the background. Shakespeare prepares us for the balcony scene, otherwise surely one of the sweetest of saccharine love-scenes in drama, by the coarseness of Mercutio's ribaldry:

> I conjure thee by Rosaline's bright eyes,
> By her high forehead, and her scarlet lip,
> By her fine foot, straight leg, and quivering thigh,
> And the demesnes, that there adjacent lie...

In jest Mercutio invites Romeo to 'cry but ay me': 'ay me' is the very note we hear echoing joyfully from Juliet a moment later. 'Pronounce but love and dove,' cries Mercutio, mocking the hollow clichés of the love-songs: soon after, we hear the soft exquisite music of 'Oh speak again bright Angel'. So the beauty of the love-scene is itself enhanced by contrast, while the total dramatic flavour we retain is that of a bittersweet prelude to the more distasteful action to come. Similarly, the Nurse's banter to Juliet about the preparation of her 'bird's nest' to receive her lover echoes in the mind long after the old shrew has left the stage, sounding right through the frightening and portentous scene in which Tybalt is killed and Romeo banished.

The play moves towards its climax of feeling. The lovers are to have their last secret assignation 'at the window', but not before old Capulet and the County Paris, Juliet's betrothed, boorishly plan the wedding below:

> CAPULET. ...bid her, mark you me? on Wednesday next.
> But soft, what day is this?
> PARIS. Monday my Lord.
> CAPULET. Monday, ha ha, well Wednesday is too soon,
> O' Thursday let it be, o' Thursday tell her,
> She shall be married to this noble Earl:
> Will you be ready? Do you like this haste?
> ...what say you to Thursday?
> PARIS. My Lord, I would that Thursday were tomorrow.
> CAPULET. Well get you gone, o' Thursday be it then.

Nudging his future son-in-law in the ribs, Capulet exudes his vulgar *bonhomie*, casting over the succeeding love-scene a finer feeling of purity and simplicity than it would otherwise have, but nevertheless leaving us with the ominous impression that time is hounding its victims. We come finally to the controversial 'burlesque' of mock-mourning, the simultaneous expression of the comic and the tragic, performed by the quartet of Lady Capulet, the Nurse, Paris and Capulet, with their awkward concatenation of apostrophes to the 'woeful day' and the rest of it. This is of a piece with, and perhaps a tiresome introduction to, the farce of Peter (the Second Quarto has 'Enter Will Kemp', who was the company's clown) and his request to the musicians to play 'Heart's Ease'. Here Shakespeare is, if less successfully, attempting another and bolder withdrawal of sensation before the onset of his catastrophe.

Who can doubt that it was a trial of this kind that led him, with a subtler pen, to introduce into the mature tragedies scenes like those of Macbeth's Porter, Hamlet's Gravediggers in their discussion over Ophelia's grave, Lear's Fool, Cleopatra's Clown? In these tragedies, however, Shakespeare was careful to make the comic element less obtrusive.

Only faintly does the quality of parody and burlesque appear in these plays, in, for example, the verbal insistence of Mercutio's mockery, in Lear's mad trial of his absent daughters, in the disrespectful love-play of Charmian and Alexas which follows the heroic exchanges of Antony and Cleopatra themselves: 'Lord Alexas, sweet Alexas, most anything Alexas, almost most absolute Alexas...' But parody was the likeliest form of mockery for the less trammelled 'history' plays, in which not a tragic but a narrative form was uppermost in the author's mind in the writing, and in which a lucky balance was struck between the comedy of Eastcheap and the noble deliberations and enterprises of the kings and princes of the realm.

Falstaff and Eastcheap, one can guess, were first introduced to mark the point of departure from which the audience was to trace the development of Prince Hal from rogue to monarch, and for more fashionable reasons than to provide meaningful parody of the glorious by the inglorious. Falstaff, who can move freely among both, grows to represent more than the common clown before his death in *Henry V*: he is felt to embody a common humanity. This function of a unique character creation has been excellently stated elsewhere, and D. A. Traversi makes the point succinctly:

At one time, in his account of his own exploits at Eastcheap, he parodies the heroic boasting to which the more respectable characters in their weaker moments are given; at others, he provides a comic version of the moral lectures addressed by Henry IV, not without a strong hint of political calculation, to his son (1 *Henry IV*, II. iv) or comments bitingly at Shrewsbury (v. i and iii) on the true meaning of the word 'honour' so freely invoked by dubious politicians to urge others to die in their interest.

Working sometimes through open comment, sometimes through parody, his is a voice that lies outside the prevailing political spirit of the play, drawing its cogency from an insight that is the author's own and expressing itself in a flow of comic energy.[1]

It remains only to estimate for ourselves the joy with which the Elizabethan spectator of *Henry IV, Part I*, must have heard the bright irony of 'Honour pricks me on. Yea, but how if honour prick me off when I come on? how then?...', and the mixed feelings with which he heard the lugubrious irony in *Part II* of 'Peace, good Doll! do not speak like a death's-head; do not bid me remember mine end'.

The so-called 'problem' comedies, *Troilus and Cressida*, *Measure for Measure* and *All's Well that Ends Well*, are dramas of such romantic form that in them Shakespeare feels himself even more at liberty to swing between the *pièce rose* and the *pièce noire*. They are plays demonstrating as original a dramatic exploration of experience as anything in the canon. Each has, too, a special interest as an experiment in controlling an audience's quality of attention; it may be that this is one of the reasons why so many playgoers declare roundly how much they dislike them. Few of their characters are endearing; their behaviour is less so. Yet the force of their drama is irresistible, and the peculiar pungency of dark comedy is strong within them.

We no longer bother to face the impossible task of deciding whether *Troilus and Cressida* is a tragedy, a comedy or a history. Nowhere in Shakespeare are riotous gyrations of style so complete as in this play. The swinging of the tone between tragedy and mockery persists throughout, though it is not introduced to intensify its potential tragedy, but to extract that special flavour of bitterness we associate with it.

The acrid taste of the play is partly due to its anti-romantic subject, which is the disintegration of social and personal values under certain stresses; it is partly due to its ugly imagery; and partly to a deliberate confounding of the audience—the play sets the classical heroes of traditional romance over against the coarseness of Thersites and Achilles, and contrasts our romantic ideal of Helen

---

[1] D. A. Traversi, *An Approach to Shakespeare*, 2nd ed. (London, 1957), pp. 30–1.

and her world with the crude reality of Pandarus and Cressida. In the outcome, Cressida finds another lover and Troilus loses both Cressida and his horse. But the particular quality of our dramatic experience arises from the range of styles and juxtapositions through the play, deliberately kneading our every reaction, in spite of the jocularity of the Prologue's

> Like, or find fault, do as your pleasures are,
> Now good, now bad, 'tis but the chance of war.

The keynote is struck at the outset of the play, where we meet a despondent and introspective Troilus wallowing in his love, but under fire from a bantering Pandarus—it is clear we are not to take this Trojan hero seriously. In this same spirit of mockery we are invited to watch the chieftains at their counsels. So through to the end, where Pandarus, our irresponsible guide through the play, walks downstage like Laudisi in Pirandello's *Right You Are If You Think So*, and half laughs, half spits at the spectator to whom he says he will 'bequeath' his 'diseases'. There can be no mistaking that we are to respond in a mood of acute scepticism.

This scepticism is enacted in the language of the play: the poetry directs the inflexion of our mind. Thus we are prepared for the scene in which Cressida is to play her part as 'daughter of the game' by, of all things, a conventional expression of sentiment in a Petrarchan manner from Troilus. Troilus, it seems, has spent a last impassioned night with her, though we may have noticed that 'the busy day/ Wak'd by the lark' also 'hath rous'd the ribald crows'. But Troilus' romantic rhetoric is set sharply against Cressida's keen psychological naturalism and Pandarus' coarse prose. So, too, after the fine public speeches of the Greek politicians, we drop with startling frankness into Ulysses' private tone, and have our misgivings clinched by the unequivocal voice of Thersites. When Cressida is finally handed over to the Greek camp, she finds herself a woman alone in a male circle of armed and brutal soldiery, and the notorious 'kissing scene' reflects more disgrace upon her captors—and especially upon Ulysses, who organizes the game out of contempt for anyone who shares the sex of Helen of Troy—than it does upon Cressida's own realistic attempt to handle the situation. The conflict and uncertainty in the spectator's mind are thus given shape and authority. Changes in the language of this play anticipate amazingly those changes in convention more commonly met with in twentieth-century drama.

Measure for Measure tells the story of the chaste Isabella, who is invited to sell herself, sinning to save her brother Claudio, himself under sentence of death for a sin of the flesh. This is a situation we should declare today to be of pure Pirandellian irony: a seduction for a seduction. This raw and grotesque plot is further coloured by the garish presence of a gang of comic supers, who coarsely restate the moral points of the theme throughout.[1] Thus the words of the wit Lucio, spoken to his friend Claudio who has just expressed his somewhat belated regrets at finding himself in prison, are spliced with ambiguity: 'I had as lief have the foppery of freedom, as the morality of imprisonment.' The comic bawd Pompey, upon being apprehended by the comic lord Escalus, asks gently, 'Does your worship mean to geld and splay all the youth of the city?' The macabre interlude before the anticipated execution of Claudio is taken up, first, with a light-hearted discussion between the executioner Abhorson and the bawd, here become the gruesome figures of Death and the Jester, on the 'mystery' of hanging, then in pointedly direct address to the audience with Pompey's merry comments on the assortment of criminals he finds with him in the prison, and, third, with a clown's performance from Barnardine who, because he is drunk, 'will not consent to die this day, that's certain'. Though this fooling may have assured the Elizabethan audience that a happy end was to be anticipated,[2] we cannot fail to hear in Barnardine's indifference to death the distorted echo of Claudio's own agonized

> Ay, but to die, and go we know not where;
> To lie in cold obstruction and to rot...

In this profound and constantly engrossing play, Shakespeare compels us to weigh in one scale the meaning of life, as illuminated

---

[1] In the problem comedies the chorus characters have noticeably proliferated, in order to 'distance' and set in perspective their inflammable subjects.

[2] M. Lascelles, *Shakespeare's Measure for Measure* (London, 1953), p. 111.

by death both tragic and comic, against, in the other, the meaning of 'honour', as illuminated by lechery both tragic and comic; then he coolly asks us whether it is God or man who holds the scales. Having posed an insoluble problem, he promptly cuts the knot with a facile *dénouement*: he scandalously and contemptuously has the Duke of Vienna marry Mariana and Julietta to their seducers Angelo and Claudio. Mary Lascelles comments on the easy intervention of the Duke that, when a writer of tragicomedy 'propounds a situation from which no happy issue seems possible', he 'then deploys a power strong enough to avert the expected ill'.[1]

The matter of *All's Well that Ends Well* offers a similarly cold analysis, without solution, of the problem of the battle of the sexes in relation to class. Can the woman who loves a man of higher rank than herself chase him, and remain virtuous? Can she chase him knowing that he loves her not, and remain virtuous? Even though she is technically married to him, can she substitute herself in bed for her husband's mistress, and remain virtuous? It seems she can; and live happily ever after. But to accept this, we are asked to question the precepts on the nature of honesty in woman that we previously held dear. That Shakespeare, in approaching the technical problems of this interesting task, faced insuperable difficulties, is clear from the awkward mixture of the real and the unreal among the characters. Thus the Countess, mother of Bertram the rake of a husband, is sympathetically real, while Bertram himself is ugly and unnatural. Helena, the embarrassing lady who initiates the problems of the play, is both real and unreal: like Cressida and like Isabella, she must behave as a puppet when Shakespeare is not warming her to life by his poetry.

In this play again there is a running *badinage*, this time from Parolles, Bertram's self-opinionated follower, and from Lavatch, clown to the Countess; and again the calculated mixing of scenes and styles. Thus, as Helena plans her campaign to sleep with Bertram against his wishes, stressing the 'wicked meaning in a lawful deed' and suggesting the ambivalent values in the trick, Bertram is simultaneously preparing to ambush his friend Parolles to test his

[1] *Ibid.* p. 146.

valour and prove him a liar in a scene reminiscent of the baiting of Falstaff. With these two scenes juxtaposed in performance, we receive an oblique mockery of our objections to the motives behind Helena's action. The moral pattern of the play is thus defined. The honest justice in deflating Parolles is scaled against Helena's instinctive and justifiable immodesty in deflating Bertram.

The degree of horseplay and the casual and irresponsible endings of these 'romantic' plays seem to belie their seriousness. Is it that Shakespeare did not quite know what he was about, taking up popular stories in haste and finding too late that their form was unsuitable? Their poetic strength denies uncertainty in their tone, though an uncertainty might have been presupposed from a recapitulation of their plotting. The tone is as deliberate and serious as any in Shakespeare. Mary Lascelles should have the last word for the moment when she says that 'the logic of tragicomedy may seem slack', but 'it is capable of gratifying a natural and proper desire to ruminate modes of human experience other than our own'.[1] But: *other* than our own? The Jacobean drama is uneasy with doubt, and its troubled heart reflects its feelings about a questionable world. Significantly, there has been a marked revival of interest in the problem comedies since 1946.

MOLIÈRE

Having adopted the comic form and made it delightfully his own, Molière was quick to find that any comic character and any comic situation pressed hard enough can turn a comedy towards tragedy. At times he seems to slip into the limbo inadvertently; but at his best he is working consciously to secure that fine balance of attraction and repulsion, that partial identification of the spectator with a character who would otherwise be viewed detachedly. In doing this, he roused a new excitement in the theatre of his time which survives today, and at times he touched depths of painful feeling which put *The Misanthrope*, for example, in a class far above the more farcical comedies deriving from the *commedia dell'arte*. The intimate back-

---

[1] M. Lascelles, *Shakespeare's Measure for Measure*, pp. 157–8.

stage reasons for his special understanding of the enormous potential and the enduring fascination of a comic-pathetic picture of life have been repeatedly traced to the misery and uncertainty of his private life with Armande Béjart, his young leading actress. More attention is needed now, not upon the causes, but upon the effects in the auditorium, of his dramatic wisdom.

Molière's own statements of his intentions indirectly offer some little help in this. There are the well-known comments of Dorante–Molière in *La Critique de l'école des femmes*. With eminent common sense, it is suggested that the dramatist should make his final reference to nature rather than to forms and rules. Dorante declares,

When you portray heroes, you may treat them as you please: they are imaginary portraits in which one does not look for a likeness, and you have only to follow the promptings of a soaring imagination, which often abandons the truth in order to attain the miraculous. But when you portray men, you must paint from nature.[1]

Again and again in Molière's art, it is nature which sharpens the edge that cuts deeper into our sensibilities.

Nature takes a firm hand in *The School for Wives*, the prototype for Anouilh's *Colombe* and other plays of innocence betrayed. Beginning as an exercise in pure comedy, the presence of natural forces introduces that inescapable note of tragedy which makes it the first of Molière's great dramatic *causes célèbres*. Arnolphe has tried to educate his young ward Agnès to be the perfect wife for himself. He has kept her in ignorance to ensure her innocence. The point of the play becomes plain after a few moments; this same ignorance must leave a void which may be filled by bad as well as good, and her sweet inexperience of life lays her especially open to impulses over which Arnolphe can have no control. What is more, we are completely won over by her spontaneous joy when she innocently tells Arnolphe of her encounter one warm evening with the charming Horace: 'Such a handsome young man. When he saw me he immediately gave me a deep bow. I didn't want to seem less polite, so I curtsied in return. So promptly he gave me another bow; then I did the same again...' Under the lyrical influence of the simplicity

---

[1] Trans. A. Tilley, in *Molière* (Cambridge, 1936), p. 93.

and the poetry, we are ready to see Arnolphe as the comic villain of the piece and Horace as the knight errant, and we respond lightly. But with the crisis of the last act our mood is changed for us. Agnès tells how much she loves her Horace, and cannot love the angry Arnolphe:

AGNES. Don't blame me. Why didn't you make yourself loved like him? I didn't try to stop you as far as I know.
ARNOLPHE. I did the best I could, but I've been wasting my time.
AGNES. Then it's clear he knows more about such matters than you, since he had no difficulty at all in making himself loved.

So Arnolphe discovers, too late, that he is really devoted to her, and in a speech full of pathos we are given a glimpse of the other side of the coin. The play hovers for an instant on the brink of a precipice, one we approach frequently in dark comedy; then Molière quickly resolves the difficulty. Arnolphe is made to sheer over to safety with the 'rolling eyes, ridiculous sighs and childish tears' of Pantalone from the *commedia dell'arte*. With this and a facile *dénouement*, Molière saves the play, spares his audience and avoids the issue.

In the second half of *Tartuffe* the action totters crazily between farce and tragedy. If we feel discomfort, it derives largely from the conception of the central character and the impossibility of his actor's keeping a balance in performance. Is Tartuffe a clown or a monster? At first 'his red ears and his red face' of Dorine's description, his manifest hypocrisy, his greed and his piety, would seem to stamp him as a buffoon. For him to hurt others would stifle our sense of comedy, but the laughable fanaticism of Orgon helps us feel that no great harm could come to such a patron. Yet as the play progresses, the true Tartuffe emerges to show himself a vile and sinister scoundrel, determined upon marriage to the guileless daughter Mariane, ready to insult Orgon's wife, resolved to turn his benefactor and his family penniless into the street. The spectator watching this rugged and unlovely play must feel that Molière's sense of congruity has been sacrificed for an ulterior motive. His desire to make a reckless frontal attack on sanctimonious cant rends his comedy from top to bottom. Boileau may well have had a point when he suggested that Molière was forced to make Tartuffe a viper to ensure that we recognized the evil in him in time to correct earlier misjudgments, but the artistic failure seems unmistakable in every performance.

Don Juan, like *Tartuffe*, swings between farce and tragedy. We laugh when Juan makes love simultaneously to Charlotta and Mathurine; we laugh when he flatters and out-talks M. Dimanche, who comes to ask for the repayment of Juan's debts. But his scurvy desertion of his wife Elvire and the cheating of Don Luis his father leave him a despicable and far from romantic hero. He is merely the atheist whose appropriate end is for the earth to open and swallow him with rolls of thunder and flashes of lightning. The Statue is a *deus ex machina* who serves only to bring down the curtain on a dramatically purposeless mixture.

In *Amphitryon, Georges Dandin, The Miser* and *The Imaginary Invalid* the case is different again. In each the initial 'humour' of the central character makes for broad comedy, and though in excess it is always ready to slip into pathos, the tone of the play is kept largely under control. Indeed, a submerged pathos tends to strengthen our response. Amphitryon's jealousy of the king of the gods who seduces his wife is mixed with his shame as a dishonoured husband. Dandin is another unhappy husband presented in terms of explosive farce, but whose despair is just allowed to show itself. The miser Harpagon, in the pursuit of his love of money, runs the risk of hurting his family, and the exchanges between Harpagon and his son Cléante repeatedly introduce a strong suspicion of serious comment into the broad comedy of the plot. Thus, because of the oscillations of feeling in this play particularly, we cannot be as sure of the direction in which Molière is taking us, or that the contrary elements of the play have been blended with assurance. The story of Argan the hypochondriac might have been the tragedy of a man whose carefully preserved life is hardly worth preserving anyway. But the element of tragedy is almost completely hidden. Only in the brief moment when his daughter thinks him dead is there any hint of another point of view. Rightly, the plays in this group are generally performed with all the weight on the farce, in the confidence that this will outweigh our doubts.

The Misanthrope justly deserves its place at the head of Molière's work, if only for the reason that nowhere else does his writing display so beautifully that comic-pathetic poise which has us rooted to our seats. Those who think with Bergson that comedy is more like life than tragedy because the latter must sublimate life, might think that here at least is the justification of that loose remark. The truth is that *The Misanthrope*, in touching life more closely, has run the risk of ceasing to be comedy. It successfully remains a comedy, but then it is a very exceptional play.

Alceste is a bear and a prig; yet we love him for his faults. Without moderation and without that indispensable sense of humour needed to ease the rigours of social life, he will not tolerate the insincerity and cheap flattery he hears about him; yet our conscience tells us he is right. Thus the direction of sympathies in the auditorium is carefully prescribed in the first place by the ambivalence in the central character. He is weighed against his friend Philinte, who seems shallow by comparison. He speaks his mind fiercely about the poor sonnet of the poetaster Oronte, and this honesty is justified in our eyes to a great extent, not only because the verses are bad, but also because that same sonnet is addressed to the lady Alceste loves. In all this we are with him in spirit. But he is also in love with an enchanting creature, Célimène, and as soon as he is seen to apply his rigid standards of social morality to her, we know that the man is impossible.

Célimène's part is the second key to our understanding of the complexity of the piece. She is admittedly the queen of coquettes, and by Alceste's standards she deserves more than censure; we may even pity his infatuation. Nevertheless we love her too, because we know that there are qualities in *nature* again that justify such behaviour in a young girl. Though she lacks the sincerity of her rival Eliante, she is contrasted cleanly with the prudish Arsinoé to exemplify her truly feminine merits, and her wit and her engaging ease in society—the pleasure she gives us as social beings ourselves—must plead her cause. Molière has arranged it that the man who hates the ways of society is hopelessly in love with the idealized woman who has them all. The situation is a nice development from that of *The School for Wives*, where Arnolphe in his way also mistrusts society, and his inflexibility is similarly belied by our common sense; but both Alceste and Célimène lack the innocence of Arnolphe and Agnès, and their more human errors accentuate the more human problem, stressing the conflict between heart and head and between the male and the female principle.'

Elasticity and compromise are the secret of happy human relations; without them, as Bergson suggested, there inevitably follows either laughter or tears. The great scene of the play, Act IV, scene iii, calls up both, because it is alive with the vitality of two characters, perfectly balanced, whose natural opposition we have been made to feel and understand. Like Strindberg's eternal query, 'Man or woman, who is master?', like Shaw's life force in *Man and Superman*, like the inevitable opposition of Marcel and Albertine in Proust's great novel, this quality elevates the scene to become symbolic of the battle of the sexes itself.

In the face of Alceste's blind rage at having discovered her letter to Oronte, Célimène remains completely in command of herself. At first she calmly comments, 'This is certainly a remarkable method of love-making.'[1] Her frankness continues to disarm: 'Why should I blush?...Why should I disown a letter in my own hand?' She begins to draw our sympathy in spite of the justness of Alceste's accusations. She suggests that the letter might have been written to a woman—but she is careful to avoid saying that it has. Then, in apparent anger herself, she encourages him to believe what hurts him most, that the letter was addressed to Oronte, but again she concedes no secrets:

No, it's to Oronte. I'd rather you thought that. I delight in his attentions, enjoy his conversation, esteem his qualities—I'll agree to anything you like. Go on, pursue your quarrel, don't let anything deter you...so long as you plague me no longer.

She shows her strongest weapon, but we are less in sympathy with her for this feline subterfuge, though we cannot avoid some momentary amusement at her craft. Célimène now has him in thrall, and he pleads with her to relieve him of his doubts in passionate words which win us completely.

[1] Trans. J. Wood, from *Molière, the Misanthrope and Other Plays* (London, 1959).

Yet to keep the equilibrium, Molière has her answer ready: 'You are mad when you are in these jealous fits, and don't deserve the love I have for you. . . I ought to bestow my affections elsewhere and give you reason for legitimate complaint.' Incensed, Alceste goes so far as to declare his feelings in outrageously paradoxical terms characteristic of the man we know:

ALCESTE. Ah! My love is beyond all comparison! Such is my desire to make it manifest to all the world that I could even wish misfortune might befall you—yes, I would have you unloved, reduced to misery or born in indigence, without rank or birth or fortune so that I might in one resounding act of loving sacrifice repair the injustice of your fate and enjoy the love and satisfaction of knowing that you owe everything to my love.

CELIMENE. A strange way of showing your goodwill! . . .

Which promptly thrusts her back where she previously stood in our esteem. So the balance is re-established and the only 'uproarious' scene in the play, the farcical interlude with the servant Du Bois, consolidates the position.

In the following act Molière repeats these tricks at the expense of the spectator. The reading of another communication from Célimène reduces her in our eyes to a scandalmonger who respects no one. This time she pathetically admits her guilt, but in spite of Alceste's confession that he loves her still, it is he who rights the balance of our affections once again by condemning himself out of his own mouth. Du Bois had planted the idea in his mind that, as a result of a lost lawsuit, he should decamp. Thus he now offers to forgive her everything, 'provided you'll agree to join me in my plan of fleeing from all human intercourse and undertake to accompany me forthwith into the rustic solitude to which I have sworn to repair'. Her reply is the one we might have made ourselves: 'Me? Renounce the world before I'm old and bury myself in your wilderness!. . . The mind shrinks from solitude at twenty. . . ' She sweeps out and is gone for ever. The separation of these two was the only 'happy ending' for both, and the growth of our image of the play's meaning has been marvellously held in check for the last twenty minutes of the play.

In the last analysis, however, there are no shocks in Molière. The eruption of savage farce always possible with his predecessors dies down during the seventeenth century; it belongs to a less classical age, and is not felt again until the licence of our own. Wyndham Lewis reaches the conclusion about Molière that 'we realize from the beginning that he is on our side',[1] and the truth is that we are reasonably safe in distinguishing the villain from the victim. With the possible exception of *The Misanthrope*, we are largely at ease with ourselves, and we in the audience who share Molière's common sense and humanity need to fear little for our personal security, compared with the risks we run when we watch, say, Pirandello's dark comedy of the twentieth century. To say this is in no way to discredit a dramatist who primarily offers other things; it is only to stress that the ancestry of Chekhov's muddled families, Pirandello's introspective fanatics and Beckett's helpless clowns, if traceable at all, is certainly hybrid and probably illegitimate.

TRAGEDY AND TRAGICOMEDY

It is understandable if today we are inhibited in our diagnosis of tragedy and comedy. The vexed question of what properly constitutes the tragic is accentuated by our often muddled preoccupation with an appropriate dramatic formula and correct playing convention for the play. We may too readily anticipate as the form for a tragedy what should grow out of the content of the play and not be imposed upon it: recent efforts to resurrect the ancient Greek tragic chorus on the modern stage, or to find a verse pattern for the lines, or to contrive a modern equivalent for the soliloquy and other conventional devices, or to employ a mythological framework within which to work, are symptomatic. The elements by which we tend to identify tragedy are generally conventional ones: verse, in preference to prose, that the diction may be suitably 'heightened'; kings, princes, heroes and their rarefied circumstances providing the characters and their situations, that the play may be suitably elevated in tone; the plot leading remorselessly towards disaster, that the

[1] D. B. Wyndham Lewis, *Molière: the Comic Mask* (London, 1959), p. 205.

spectator shall be properly edified, sometimes by pity, sometimes by fear, sometimes by both. Each of these agencies is artistically equivocal.

Drama is not to be heightened by verbal dexterity alone—burlesque gains some of its peculiar force by being grand with the words when the situation or the character explicitly lacks grandeur. The words take their substance from the action to which in turn they give rise, and prose dialogue which is functioning fully within the play may be reinforced as well by the action on the stage as verse is. The unaffected language and the exquisitely simple expression of Lear's grief in the lines,

> Why should a dog, a horse, a rat, have life,
> And thou no breath at all? Thou'lt come no more,
> Never, never, never, never, never!
> Pray you, undo this button. Thank you, sir,

gather power chiefly because of the context: it comes quietly at the end of a great rush of feeling and it marks the reversal of the King's former attitude and his complete humility. Nor could the magnificent appeal of Lear's

> O, reason not the need; our basest beggars
> Are in the poorest thing superfluous...

reach its intended degree of poignancy out of the mouth of the Fool or of Edgar.

The heroic character is dependent for its dignity upon the world in which it moves: Hamlet grows taller in our eyes in proportion as Ophelia, Gertrude, Claudius or Laertes by their presence raise him and in consequence grow smaller themselves. But the commonplace world can have its relative nobility too, and can be equally fearful and pitiful, just as a man can attain heroic proportions in his own circle or in his own eyes. Provided that circle is recognizable and brought close enough to us, and provided his eyes are our eyes, with our absorption in the play intense and complete, the character can be exalted for us too. For the quality of the heroic on the stage must always lie within the imagination of the audience: Nora, the child-wife of Ibsen's *A Doll's House* who defies the world of respectability, or Maurya, the fisherwife of Synge's *Riders to the Sea* who faces nature itself, can rise above her littleness to the solemnity and grandeur of a queen; Willie Loman, Arthur Miller's salesman in his tough territory, can have the temporary dramatic stature of a king on his uncertain throne. Theatrical convention dictates that the stature of the hero is relative to the setting in which he is placed, and if the dramatist is capable of passing a character into our experience, that character may also be capable of assuming tragic proportions.

A sense of 'the remorseless' in the drive of the plot towards the dethronement of man in his pride by forces beyond his control is what induces the emotion characteristic of tragedy. This remorselessness is felt by ironic implications which must lie within the structure of the play: a snare is set by the dramatist for the protagonist, and we wait breathlessly for the trap to be sprung. Yet the spectator must not feel that the trap is there by accident, that it is arbitrarily planted to rouse his excitement: his natural sense of unfairness must not betray his dramatic sense of the just subjugation of his deputy on the stage. Whether Fate, Necessity, or the Gods, or the short-sightedness of the hero himself, shall set and spring the trap, punishment must be in one sense explicable: it must be justifiable. Here too convention plays its part. If any audience is to declare, 'Yes, this outcome is fitting', it must have some moral presuppositions; by common assent there must be some scale of judgment. Thus, unless we are prepared to share imaginatively the convictions of the Greek world, we may doubt whether we can today know the catharsis of which Aristotle speaks after we witness, for example, the *Oedipus Rex* of Sophocles. Nor is the glory of Thomas à Becket's martyrdom in Eliot's *Murder in the Cathedral* likely to be fully meaningful outside Christendom. This is not to say, of course, that the pity or fear felt about our mortality, which is common to ancient Greek, modern Christian and all men alike, may not persuade us to an emotional response in the theatre satisfying in itself.

Today the ethical conventionalism of tragedy seems impossible to adopt. If an implicit moral valuation must contribute to the understanding and enjoyment of the play, the dramatist must share it with his audience, and a homogeneous theatre seems a prerequisite for successful tragedy. In his researches as a playwright since the war in plays like *The Cocktail Party*, Eliot has trusted his audience less and less: he does not deploy religious counters about his play; he merely implies a vaguely Christian reference which may be felt or not felt only after the characters have suffered a particular secular experience. Writing in France during the same period, Sartre sets up his own framework of values in order to lend moral significance to the events of his play. But the obsessive inevitability of tragedy is lost in *Men Without Shadows*, his play about men of the French Resistance who discover an existentialist meaning in their sufferings, or *Crime Passionnel*, the play which invites us to question whether its hero has acquired existentialist grace, because we are too busy questioning first premises to attend to conclusions; we think too much to be passionate. The important 'universal human predicament' may exist within Celia Coplestone of *The Cocktail Party*, the society girl who suffers a change of heart sufficient to sacrifice herself as a missionary, or within Hugo Barine of *Crime Passionnel*, the new party member who asks to be allowed to kill a traitor in order to prove himself a man; but the universal impact is dangerously softened by our asking with simple pagan sentiment whether Celia has not wasted her talents, or whether Hugo did not die a rather selfish death.

The Elizabethans had no need to ask whether Romeo and Juliet died worthwhile deaths: they defied the irrepressible powers of society to the glory of a greater cause, and a limited sexual encounter became a spiritual triumph in an age which admitted individualistic experiment. Tragedy, like any drama, should be a reflection and interpretation of life—on this it stands or falls; but it may argue from a silly philosophical standpoint even though it may have much of 'life' in it. If Eliot's philosophy is too narrow, or Sartre's incomplete, there is no reason why it may not be dramatized successfully, though this may yet not prove the value of the philosophy: it merely proves that it may be dramatized. Tragedy may escape. Both Eliot and Sartre have nevertheless done us a service by implying within the body of the play a code by which to reason and evaluate its meaning; they have shown again that it is possible to evolve a serious drama, given meaning by what may be a selected, fantastic and subjective ethic, in a play which is, however, neither tragedy nor comedy.

In these ways at least 'tragedy' is precariously balanced on variously ephemeral conventions of theatre or audience, and it is not surprising that the tragic of one age may not easily be revived in another with any assurance. Especially where the appositeness of earlier conventions is in doubt, a parochial near-tragedy is likely to follow. Thus Arthur Miller's *Death of a Salesman* is arguably a lesser creation than the *Agamemnon* of Aeschylus; but if criticism, in order to make sense of such a play as Miller's, continues to employ a term associated with a set of conventions no longer in use, it invites confusion.

Perhaps the most tiresome instance in modern times has been the drama of Ibsen. Those who missed the ritualistic heroism in his mature plays found it necessary to say he was writing a solemn form of satirical domestic tragicomedy based on personal psychology but having social reference. Oh, dear. We see more clearly now that the movement towards realism of subject and manner in the nineteenth century was one which simply modified the conventions of classical tragedy and produced another kind of play. The tragic individual superseded the tragic hero, but had the power to be no less moving and no less significant. Ibsen was raising important issues for drama: What are the near limits of the tragic world? May the spectator's intelligence be used with his emotions to help rationalize his interest and yet allow the flow of the play to be preserved? Dare the dramatist risk hearing us laugh when he would wish us to weep? Can he risk diminishing the stature of his hero in order to ensure his individuality, as happens with Dr Stockmann of *An Enemy of the People*, whom Ibsen variously declared to be 'muddle-headed' and 'an extravagant immature fellow and a hothead'? Might not the narrowing of the frame and setting of the play limit the width of its appeal as seems to have happened with *A Doll's House*, but not with *The Master Builder*, concerned with those who will not accept the limitations of middle age, and so touching us all? As Desmond MacCarthy justly said of Hjalmar Ekdal of *The Wild Duck*, Hjalmar the small man and our representative of illusory happiness, 'Hjalmar is a wide shot that hits half the world.'[1] We may sense tragedy here, but we may not find it: we may be looking for the wrong evidence.

Thus tragedy 'in the full sense of the word' is missing today. Our present-day mongrel conventions, interbred with the spirit of naturalism, can better do other things, and do not encourage the exclusive consistency of purpose we ask of tragedy. Twentieth-century currents of contradictory thought and the mood of audiences do not permit it; the laws of tragedy belong to a world which is religious in its affirmation of human greatness. Today we hear only the uncertainty and the whimper of the ending of Jean Cocteau's Oedipus story, *The Infernal Machine*, as Creon and Tiresias watch the blinded king led away by his daughter Antigone and the ghost of his wife Jocasta:

CREON. And even supposing they leave the town, who will look after them, who will admit them?
TIRESIAS. Glory.
CREON. You mean rather dishonour, shame...
TIRESIAS. Who knows?

Curtain.[2]

The play slips imperceptibly into 'tragicomedy'. In an age when tragedy is submerged in moral indifference, we may expect a kind of tragicomedy to come into its own.

The line between tragedy and its hybrid partner tragicomedy is often difficult to draw, and is a central concern in this essay. A technical point, however, invites attention here. The ironies which enforce the dialectical conflict of tragedy are simple in formula: each step the hero takes towards a supposed triumph is a step nearer his death, each step one which strengthens the audience's sense of a necessary end. The spectator, knowing or feeling this outcome, is wholly in the confidence of the author and the secret of the play; the characters are not. The spectator stands where the Gods themselves

---

[1] D. MacCarthy, 'The Wild Duck', 1905, reprinted in *Specimens of English Dramatic Criticism, XVII–XX Centuries*, selected P. C. Ward (London, 1945), p. 237. In his essay on 'Tolstoy: Tragedian or Comedian?', 1921, Shaw later suggested that 'Ibsen was the dramatic poet who firmly established tragicomedy as a much deeper and grimmer entertainment than tragedy'.
[2] J. Cocteau, *The Infernal Machine*, trans. C. Wildman (London, 1950).

stand, in a happy position of omniscience. Therefore his excitement during the performance does not arise from a simple chemical mixture, as it were $x+y$, where x is each decision arising from the hero's wish to assert his personal responsibility, the positive element, and y is the tightening of the net of inevitable destruction, the negative element; but its source is in an active chemical compound, where the resulting passion is xy, imaginatively irreducible, a new substance with fierce properties of its own. It has even been given a name of its own: 'tragic irony'.

Yet its counterpart, 'comic irony', is not very different in kind. It may indeed merge at times into the more easily recognizable irony of tragedy. The spectator is equally omniscient, able by his presence in the comic theatre to perform a chemical experiment like his fellow in the tragic theatre. Within his mind he mixes the positive image of a character wishing to be and to assert himself, x, with another aspect of necessity's power to destroy—its power to belittle and undermine by suggesting commonplaceness and triviality, y. Comic irony, however, can prick with a thousand pins in the course of a play, and in its way be as all-pervading and relentless and irresistible in its effect as tragic irony itself. Nor need we assume that such tragicomedy as emerges carries less weight than tragedy, is any the less moral, or bears any the less relationship to the society which promotes it. Its philosophy may come equally from profound laws of feeling and understanding, just as important in themselves for our apprehension of the quality of life.

Both experience of life and familiarity with the best of twentieth-century drama constantly compel us to be aware of the blood relationship of the tragic and comic senses, of the interbreeding of tears and laughter. In an earlier essay, Ronald Peacock had declared with more justice that both tragedy and comedy 'spring from the tension between our imperfect life and our ideal aspirations. They exist together in their dependence on the contradictions of life. They are parallel expressions, in different keys, of our idea of what is good.'[1]

---

[1] R. Peacock, *The Poet in the Theatre* (London, 1946), chapter on 'Tragedy, Comedy and Civilization', p. 126.

We may gladly defer to the sound judgment of Dr Johnson in his familiar defence of Shakespeare's tragicomedy:

> Shakespeare's plays are not in the rigorous and critical sense either tragedies or comedies, but compositions of a distinct kind; exhibiting the real state of sublunary nature, which partakes of good and evil, joy and sorrow, mingled with endless variety of proportion and innumerable modes of combination; and expressing the course of the world, in which the loss of one is the gain of another; in which, at the same time, the reveller is hasting to his wine, and the mourner burying his friend; in which the malignity of one is sometimes defeated by the frolick of another; and many mischiefs and many benefits are done and hindered without design.[1]

Dr Johnson is of course the last man to invite anarchy in literary or dramatic standards: the play must disclose its design if life will not. But even he allows that 'there is always an appeal open from criticism to nature': we must be well prepared to admit an endless variety of proportion and innumerable modes of combination.

TYPES OF COMEDY

The recognized theories of comedy do not help us any the more to understand the characteristic drama of the twentieth century. Ideas about the comic have never been expressed as abundantly as those about tragedy, both because the seriousness of comedy has not been as evident to writers as its more impressive high-toned counterpart, and because the ways and intentions of comedy may be more tiresome to explain. Up to the beginning of this century, comedy suffered a hardening in its arteries, and its critics had grown further and further away from the practice on the stage. Certainly, no theorist seemed capable of putting forward an explanation sufficiently all-embracing, and the philosophical and the psychological approaches have both been wanting.

The diagnosis of comedy presents many difficulties. Laughter, a recurring and therefore an evidently important ingredient, seems to arise from a great variety of sources: we laugh at other people's bad

---

[1] Johnson, *Preface to Shakespeare*, ed. W. Raleigh (London, 1908), pp. -5-16.

luck, or at relief from embarrassment, or at a little flattery, or even when we do not want to laugh. We laugh heartily, or smile gently, or at some comedy we may not laugh at all. There are so many uses to which laughter can be put, from the promotion of a cold vindictive sarcasm to that of the empty gaiety of knock-about. There is considerable discrepancy between the things we find comic in life and those contrived on the stage: a man falling on his face in the street may be an object of pathos, but on the stage an object of derision. There is confusion between the techniques of comedy designed to raise laughter and the use to which the laughter is put: why should an anticlimax make us happy, or a clown make us sad? There are too many 'types' of the comic, and we plague ourselves by trying to sort comedy from burlesque, satire and farce, notwithstanding that in Shakespearian comedy elements of each seem to be present, and the points where they overlap are none too clearly defined. We are often at a loss to assess a total impression: even where in Molière the play's parts have been largely sweet and farcical, the whole when swallowed can leave a bitter taste in the mouth.

We find that when a joke is dissected, it abruptly ceases to be funny, which is disconcerting to say the least. It is also notorious that a 'sense of humour' is an unreliable quality, and what will seem laughable to an English audience will not necessarily seem so to a Scottish. As a psychologist has written, 'If members of a social group observe that their own objects of laughter do not produce laughter in another social group they are inclined to express this fact by saying that the second group has "no sense of humour".'[1] From the world of the theatre we might add that what will seem laughable on Monday may be damned on Tuesday. It is, moreover, a nuisance that what is comic to one age is not to another: Shylock was a butt for the Elizabethans, but not for the Victorians; Richard III was played for comedy by Irving, but for pathos by Olivier. Fashions in laughter change too readily, and we are in some doubt today whether to laugh at or sympathize with a Falstaff or a Tartuffe or a Sir Peter Teazle. Furthermore, should we begin by studying crowd psychology or the particular successes of a particular writer? And if we

[1] R. H. Thouless, *General and Social Psychology* (London, 2nd ed. 1937), p. 209.

are to set our standards by one author, who shall it be?—Aristophanes, Shakespeare, Molière, Shaw?

For Hazlitt[1] the essence of the laughable was 'the incongruous', a distinction between 'what things are and what they ought to be'. This happily enough explains what we may call 'satirical' laughter, the laughter by which the spectator refuses to acknowledge the propriety of the fop and the coquette in Restoration comedy, when he recognizes the affectation in their gesture and speech, or by which he knows to ridicule the seriousness with which the characters in *The Importance of Being Earnest* pursue their absurd ends. But Hazlitt lets fall a damning admission: 'It is perhaps the fault of Shakespeare's comic muse that it is too good-natured and magnanimous. We sympathize with his characters more often than we laugh at them.' It is a *fault*!

For Meredith[2] 'the test of true Comedy is that it shall awaken thoughtful laughter', but he too can only comfortably explain the *raison d'être* of the 'high' comedy of intellect: 'The laughter of Comedy is impersonal and of unrivalled politeness... It laughs through the mind, for the mind directs it.' And though in another place he suggests, attempting to distinguish between comedy and humour, that 'the stroke of the great humourist is world-wide, with lights of Tragedy in his laughter', he will not admit that this quality can also appear in the greatest forms of comedy. Shakespeare is again the stumbling-block: because Shakespeare paints 'humanity' rather than 'manners', he does not begin to explain Shakespeare's eye for the comic. 'Jaques, Falstaff and his regiment, the varied troop of Clowns, Malvolio, Sir Hugh Evans and Fluellen—marvellous Welshmen!—Benedick and Beatrice, Dogberry, and the rest, are subjects of a special study in the poetically comic.' So we move on to safer ground with Molière, some of whose success he can account for.

After Meredith has named this glittering variety of the ostensibly comic, should he not have tried to understand them? Neither Hazlitt nor Meredith can explain the warm comic success of these and

[1] Hazlitt, Introduction to *The English Comic Writers* (1818).
[2] Meredith, 'On the Idea of Comedy and of the Uses of the Comic Spirit', a lecture delivered in 1877.

others like Rosalind and Touchstone and Quince and Bottom and that great host of Shakespeare's comic creation which reflects so closely the 'English' sense of humour. Moreover, they cannot help us to sense the nature of the achievement in plays like *The Wild Duck*, *The Cherry Orchard*, *Major Barbara* and *Waiting for Godot*, ambiguous plays of the modern theatre which challenge our laughter, as we shall see.

Bergson,[1] with every good intention, turned to example after example to establish his precepts, but concerned himself too much with first causes and with the detail of technique rather than the odd results produced in the theatre. He further remained rather parochial in drawing too much on the kind of comedy which has so admirably set the standard for the French comic stage, that of Molière. It is noticeable that his examples are drawn chiefly from the farces and farcical moments of Molière and Labiche (author of such plays as *Le Voyage de M. Perrichon* and *Un Chapeau de paille d'Italie*) or the comical-absurd of such works as *Don Quixote*. He diagnoses comedy as arising from the incongruity of 'something mechanical encrusted on the living': 'The attitudes, gestures, and movements of the human body are laughable in exact proportion as that body reminds us of a mere machine.' He thus cites as laughable the forms and movements of the puppet, and in the same way Molière's Sganarelle and his kind. Sganarelle, *The Doctor in Spite of Himself*, is enjoying his new-found power as a man of medicine when he is accused by Géronte of reversing the position of the heart and the liver:

GÉRONTE. ...the heart should be on the left side, and the liver on the right.

SGANARELLE. Yes, it used to be so, but we have changed all that.

Likewise, Dr Bahis, of *Love's the Best Doctor*, provides an excellent example of professional automatism when he advises that 'it's better [for a patient] to die through following the rules than to recover through violating them'. This argument of course helps us to explain the fun in much of Molière, and the comedy of snobbery in Lady Bracknell, and how in Fry's *The Lady's Not For Burning* Tyson's

[1] Bergson, *Laughter, an Essay on the Meaning of the Comic*, trans. C. Brereton and F. Rothwell (London, 1921), first French ed. 1889.

pomposity as mayor is belied by his having a frightful cold in the head. It explains all manner of caricature in character and action on the stage. It explains the prohibition of much emotionality from the comic theatre. It does not explain the force of its *presence*, and emotion is often present to great purpose in comedy. Bergson declares rigidly that 'laughter is incompatible with emotion', when we know well enough from experience, if not from countless moments on the comic stage, that we *do* have the faculty of laughing and feeling at one and the same time. It must exclude Shakespeare once again, and, what is more, it cannot approach our true sense of Molière's greatest achievement, *The Misanthrope*. Bergson's laughter is a 'social corrective', as Meredith's was an 'agent of civilization', but it trades on the debased and degraded in human nature and cannot respond to the warmth of comic humanity which remains after the eccentricities have been skimmed off.

The argument was not quite over. Freud[1] arbitrarily narrowed his field to include only what he pleased to call 'wit', and satisfactorily explains to us, after much belabouring, that wit serves as an escape from authority just as nonsense serves as an escape from critical reason (with occasional help from alcohol). Having said this at great length, he has said little that we did not know already. Others have since taken up the challenge, and J. B. Priestley's essay on humour[2] was a hopeful advance on his predecessors. Where Freud started from minimal instances, with little wish to move into the wider world of comedy, Priestley saw all the limitations and difficulties and perhaps would embrace too much. He would admit Shakespeare into the ranks, and goes some way to explaining his humour as the product of the close observation of human character and behaviour in its incongruities.

Among all the hints offered by these writers, certain recurring elements in the comic stand out. A sense of incongruity, with a resulting release of tension, is felt within the mind. Whether by the laughter of success or of failure, whether arising from the recognition of a friend or a tune, or from Santayana's 'little triumph' of the

[1] Freud, *Wit and its Relation to the Unconscious*, trans. Brill (London, undated, ?1906).
[2] J. B. Priestley, *English Humour* (London, 1929).

mind when it receives an illumination, whether by the laughter that
follows upon bathos or upon the loss of a lady's dignity when her hat
is blown off by the wind, some bulwark of our natural resistance,
little or big, is broken down, and a weapon of unquestionable power
is in the hands of the one who can effect this artificially. The
comedian is suddenly free to pour his shafts through the gap, re-
buffing us with mockery or drawing us with tears. Whatever the
technique he employs he has his audience captive.

On the other hand, that a comedy *should* make you laugh is not
admissible as an argument: incongruity is not necessarily laughable.
There are too many plays, patently not tragedies, which clearly
evoke no laughter, or little that is perceived as laughter; too many
fine plays end in questions and by sobering us, from *Troilus and
Cressida* and *The Misanthrope* to the comedies of Pirandello. The
interested reader should look into that excellent discussion initiated
by L. J. Potts in a more recent essay on our subject.[1] Where it does
arise laughter can be a means to a greater end than itself, creating the
conditions for the dramatic achievement of other things. The values
of the comic attitude appear only when we measure the *uses* to which
it is put. Nor should we deceive ourselves into thinking that its uses
are not infinitely variable. The evidence suggests that the conventions of the comic stage readily admit an admixture of seemingly
extraneous elements like the tragic and the pathetic, whereas tragedy
has its fabric dangerously stretched to admit the comic or the farcical.
What then are the traditional uses of comedy?

Broad comedy had contrived the release of laughter for partly
satirical purposes by a relatively uncomplicated incongruity. Just as
we laugh at the clown who sacrifices his self-respect by wearing
trousers that are excessively too big for him, or at Charlie Chaplin
for his exaggerated delight in a 'house' whose wall afterwards
collapses when he leans on it, so we laugh at Harpagon, grotesque
in his avarice, faced with the costly processes of being in love; or we
laugh at the newly honoured Lord Foppington's airs and graces as
he incongruously rehearses his part for the evening's *levée* while still
in his nightgown: 'Well, 'tis an unspeakable pleasure to be a man of

[1] L. J. Potts, *Comedy* (London, 1948), esp. pp. 18–22.

43

quality—Strike me dumb—My Lord—Your lordship—My Lord Foppington...' Of course, it is the situation which the dramatist may complicate, and the wink at the audience can be very much more subtle when, say, Lady Bracknell finally succumbs to hard cash in lieu of the desirable attributes of an elegant lineage, or when Volpone the fox out-foxes himself. The bookworm is funnier and more like a bookworm on a dance-floor than in a library, the flirt funnier and more of a flirt in a library than on a dance-floor.

Even at the level of the near-farcical, where the merely physical sensationalism of the laugh is uppermost in the playwright's mind, such drama can sometimes justify itself morally by being acutely pointed in its object of derision. The contrivance of derisive laughter by the exaggeration of some affectation of human behaviour is a time-honoured method used since the days of Aristophanes. Thus the learned Meton of *The Birds* arrives in Cloudcuckooland to 'subdivide the air into square acres':

> METON. Observe:
> The conformation of the air, considered as
> a total entity, is that of a conical damper.
> Very well. At the apex of this cone we apply
> the ruler, bracketing in the dividers to allow
> for the congruent curve. Q.E.D....

But his notions are not received as gratefully as he expected:

> PISTHETAIROS. ...we've passed a law
> that charlatans shall be whipped in the public square.
> METON. Oh. Then I'd better be going.
> PISTHETAIROS. You're almost too late.
> Here's a sample, God help you! (*Knocks him down.*)
> METON. My head! My head![1]

One would not, of course, think that there was a majority of learned mathematicians in the Greek audience to make the satirical and corrective point of this very far-reaching. Nor would Molière have expected to find too many hypochondriacs like Argan in the court of Louis XIV. These comedies can nevertheless give us,

---

[1] Aristophanes, *The Birds*, version by D. Fitts (London, 1958).

44

perhaps incidentally, many tiny and momentary insights into human nature through the agency of puppets like Meton and Argan. We all share a little of Meton's desire to make order of fantasy, to stiffen what should be flexible. Even if we would not confess to being, each of us, a little of the hypochondriac with a natural fear for our health, we must feel just a touch of fellow-feeling for Argan when M. Purgon the doctor wreaks his rage like this:

M. PURGON. I foretell that within four days you'll be in an incurable condition.

ARGAN. Oh mercy!

M. PURGON. You'll fall into a state of bradypepsia.

ARGAN. M. Purgon!

M. PURGON. From bradypepsia into dyspepsia.

ARGAN. M. Purgon!

M. PURGON. From dyspepsia into apepsia.

ARGAN. M. Purgon!

M. PURGON. From apepsia into diarrhoea and lientery.

ARGAN. M. Purgon!

M. PURGON. From lientery into dysentery.

ARGAN. M. Purgon!

M. PURGON. From dysentery into dropsy.

ARGAN. M. Purgon!

M. PURGON. And from dropsy to autopsy that your own folly will have brought you to.

ARGAN. Oh my God! I'm dying.[1]

Here character, situation and dialogue are 'artificial' and the playing demands a special degree of stylized speech and movement, all apparently earnest in manner. The characters' behaviour tends to puppetry, and the situations, though still recognizable, may be outrageous: the ways of the actors are deliberately shown at some 'distance' from normal behaviour in order that the spectator can freely laugh across the gap at what he believes different from his own. The classical methods of comedy, whether broad and low, romantic and pastoral, or high and mannered, have always been anti-naturalistic. A stage extravagant in word and deed permitted those excesses which still compel us to deride certain characters and their

[1] Molière, *The Imaginary Invalid*, in *The Misanthrope and Other Plays*, trans. J. Wood (London, 1959).

attitude to life. To talk of 'stylization' equally to cover *As You Like It*, *Volpone*, *The Way of the World*, *The School for Scandal*, *The Importance of Being Earnest* and *Man and Superman* is perhaps an impertinence, but in each of these plays the dramatist invented a world to different degrees fantastic the better to compare our own. Artificial characters in an artificial situation gained him more freedom and more force for his dramatic effects. It is only after we have laughed spontaneously that we perhaps perceive that the laugh has rebounded upon us, and that the artificiality was all a snare. In the same way a simple verbal witticism can leave some permanent mark upon us—if it includes some quality of illuminating humour too.

Thus the best comedy teases and troubles an audience; it *can* be painful. Comic method can serve to create an imaginative but dispassionate attitude; to create the conditions for thinking; to free the dramatist in his attempt to tap certain rational resources of mind in his audience. Derisory laughter may be used for this and it may arise from this; it may not. Clearly it must do so in mannered comedy like Shaw's *Arms and the Man* or *Heartbreak House*, where we are encouraged for the most part to keep our critical distance from the central characters Raina and Ellie the better to recognize their whole significance. It may do so in surrealistic comedy like Samuel Beckett's *Waiting for Godot*, where the slapstick convention of the play deceives us most of the time into thinking that we are not looking at ourselves. It probably will not do so in *King Lear*, where an ironic joke from the Fool, laughable out of its context, is the more caustic in context because we feel our sympathies are too directly its butt. The urgent fact remains that, whether we laugh or not, the 'comic' attitude may be present in any genre of play. The best jokes are not only compatible with the most solemn intention, but are likely to be the best jokes for that reason.

As the gap narrows so that what remains incongruous is still funny, but too close to the bone to laugh at, then we move swiftly across the frontier into the realms of the tragic. We have seen that plays with large measures of sympathy felt through the laughter, like Shakespeare's romantic comedies, were inconvenient to the theorists. Similarly, plays which came near to closing the gap between the normality of the audience and the abnormality of the stage, plays like *Measure for Measure* or *The Misanthrope*, have been regarded as on the suspect fringe of the comic tradition, unwelcome exceptions to the rule. The presence of the comic eye in the midst of tragedy, as in *King Lear* or *Hamlet*, was put down to the licence of genius. Now, in the work of Chekhov, Pirandello, Anouilh, Brecht and Beckett, it is the rule and not the exception to mingle the laughter and the tears; large numbers of plays today merely *use* the mechanism of laughter without granting its expected release of tension.

For our overall understanding of the comic in drama today, we should turn, not to Hazlitt and Meredith, nor to Bergson and Freud, but to Pirandello, whose essay *L'Umorismo* offers the key to the comedy of our own times. In this he suggests a brilliant example, which demonstrates among other things how flexible and serviceable for serious purposes is the comic attitude once the dramatist can evoke it. Imagine, he says, an elderly lady: we are immediately predisposed to be sympathetic. But she is overdressed, her face painted, her hair dyed like a girl's: we find this comic and we are ready to laugh. Yet suppose she is aware of the figure she is cutting, and is behaving in this way in order to hold the affections of her husband: we are sobered. The old lady seems pathetic again, and the laugh is 'on us'. The comic may be no laughing matter.[1]

Pirandello in 1908 was feeling for those qualities demanded by the modern stage in acknowledging with some finality the flexible nature of the theatre as a medium. Through it an audience could, and should, be drawn, repelled and drawn again, the 'gap' closed,

[1] Pirandello, *L'Umorismo*, 2nd ed. (Florence, 1920), p. 179. The original reads, 'Vedo una vecchia signora, coi capelli ritinti, tutti unti non si sa di quale orribile manteca, e poi tutta goffamente imbellettata e parata d'abiti giovanili. Mi metto a ridere. *Avverto che quella vecchia signora è il contrario di ciò che una vecchia rispettabile signora dovrebbe essere.* Posso così, a prima giunta e superficialmente, arrestarmi a questa impressione comica. Il comico è appunto un avvertimento del contrario. Ma se ora interviene in me la riflessione, e mi suggerisce che quella vecchia signora non prova forse nessun piacere a pararsi così come un pappagallo, ma che forse ne soffre e lo fa soltanto perchè pietosamente s'inganna che, parata così, nascondendo così le rughe e le canizie, riesca a trattenere a sè l'amore del marito molto più giovine di lei, ecco che io non posso più riderne come prima, perchè appunto la riflessione, lavorando in me, mi ha fatto andar oltre a quel primo avvertimento, o piuttosto, più addentro: da quel primo avvertimento *del contrario* mi ha fatto passare a questo *sentimento del contrario.* Ed è tutta qui la differenza tra il comico e l'umoristico' (Pirandello's italics).

opened and closed again. Since the comic view has always been instinctively felt to be an indispensable, if not quite respectable, prophylactic in drama as in life, so the methods of broad and artificial comedy were devised to make the comic view presentable. Now Pirandello insists that the comic view is a powerful and essential element in the effective control of an audience and an immensely serviceable corrective for its image of the play in the process of its formation. The fidelity of the drama to truth of feeling, and its accuracy of understanding in its handling of life on the stage, may depend upon the command the author has of the comic view and the keenness of his comic eye. How the comic may make of the drama a world living and flexible, and yet one unnaturally confined within the strict bounds of the stage, is also our concern in this study.

A simple short example for analysis is chosen to demonstrate the way impressions flow from actor to spectator with the kind of ironies most typical of the drama of recent times. In *The Rose Tattoo*, Tennessee Williams is catching at the incongruities of life by overtly setting them on the stage in their barefaced opposition. The scene is the home of Serafina delle Rose, who lives in a Sicilian colony on the coast between New Orleans and Mobile. The cottage is presented as a sectional 'frame', set in the semi-tropical vegetation of the place and in 'extremely romantic' lighting; this method of stage-setting is one that Williams has practised carefully both in order that we should retain a sense of environment throughout the play by actually seeing it, and that we should feel some initial detachment from the persons of the play. The characters are to be both typical and particular: we are to spy on them without joining them, and Serafina is to be 'a strange beast in a cage'.

Against the romantic setting and lighting we see the odd details of the living-room, introducing both Serafina and the incongruities of feeling that are to ensue. Serafina takes in sewing, and in a room cluttered with 'at least seven' dressmaker's dummies 'in various shapes and attitudes', as the author's production notes tell us, we see

an interior that is as colourful *as a booth at a carnival*. There are many religious articles and pictures *of ruby and gilt*, the *brass* cage of a *gaudy* parrot, a large bowl of *goldfish*, cutglass decanters and vases, *rose-*

patterned wallpaper and a *rose-coloured* carpet...There is a small shrine against the wall between the rooms, consisting of a prie-dieu and a little statue of the Madonna in a *starry blue* robe and a *gold* crown. Before this burns always a vigil light in its *ruby* glass cup. [The italics are mine.]

This is the passionate but limited world of the heroine of the play, bold in its contradictions. Williams significantly adds the comment, 'Our purpose is to show these gaudy, childlike mysteries with sentiment and humour in equal measure, without ridicule.'

Serafina, fiercely in love with her truck-driver husband, learns in the course of the play that not only has he been killed, but that he was, in spite of her love, unfaithful to her. She has regarded her marriage with the same kind of reverence that she reserved for the Madonna, and now her worship of her dead Rosario is turned to bitter grief, in its expression a kind of blasphemy. This little tragedy is presented to us against the incongruous details of her ordinary life, which include the chase of a symbolic goat around the house by Serafina dressed in high-heeled slippers and a tight silk skirt, frequent screaming matches with the neighbours and their children, and the grotesque intrusion of the two prostitutes, Flora, 'tall and angular', and Bessie, 'rather stubby'. It is these who reveal the husband's infidelity against a background noise of a Souza march indifferently played by the band of her daughter's high school. Every ironic impression is a signal to the audience to revalue its estimate of Serafina's importance. Curiously she grows more weighty the more her simple dignity is undermined, and the strength of the ironic method Williams uses carries the play through many of the crudities of the theme's heated overstatement.

In the second act, the man who is to replace the magnificent Rosario arrives: 'He is short in stature, has a massively sculptural torso and bluish-black curls. His face and manner are clownish; he has a charming awkwardness.' Serafina's first comment upon him when she is alone sums up the whirling mixture of our own image: 'Madonna Santa!—*My husband's body*, with the head of a *clown*! (*She crosses to the Madonna.*) O Lady, O Lady! (*She makes an imploring gesture.*) Speak to me!' But Alvaro Mangiacavallo, for that is indeed his name, is, we learn, hardly sincere in his feelings for Serafina in the way that she wants him to be.

The following, finally, is the kind of sequence with which the play impresses itself upon its audience. The last act begins with both the widow and the wooer prepared ludicrously for their assignation. Serafina has put on an intolerably tight girdle, which she has only just managed 'with much grunting' to strip off again before the arrival of her lover. Alvaro has soaked rose oil in his hair and has had a rose tattooed upon his chest, reminder of the dead Rosario, and the better to appeal, as he thinks, to Serafina's sensibilities. Now—horror!—a contraceptive drops from his trousers' pocket—their ludicrous passions thus merging into the repulsive.

SERAFINA. . . . You think you got a good thing, a thing that is cheap!
ALVARO. You make a mistake, Baronessa! (*He comes in and drops to his knees beside her, pressing his cheek to her flank. He speaks rhapsodically.*) So soft is a lady! So, so, so, so, so *soft*—is a lady!
SERAFINA. Andate via, sporcaccione, andate a casa! Lasciatemi! Lasciatemi stare!
(*She springs up and runs into the parlour. He pursues. The chase is grotesquely violent and comic. A floor lamp is overturned. She seizes the chocolate box and threatens to slam it into his face if he continues towards her. He drops to his knees, crouched way over, and pounds the floor with his fists, sobbing.*)
ALVARO. Everything in my life turns out like this!
SERAFINA. Git up, git up, git up!—you village idiot's grandson! There is people watching you through that window, the—strega next door . . .

So Alvaro is humiliated, though not as much as Serafina herself.

If we examine the impressions passed to us by the actors within this short space of time, we may begin to feel something of the way modern dark comedy operates. First, any sympathy we felt for Serafina in her grief is taken up and strengthened by her new agony, much as she had brought it upon herself. Her implication that she is not a 'thing' to be bought so cheaply, spoken with all the ferocious dignity of her Sicilian birth, is entirely as we would have her speak. To this extent we are self-composed, a relaxed audience, and Alvaro's abasement in his half-drunken state, with Serafina's spitting and lashing abuse of him, comforts us in our need to raise the widow as someone worthy of our commiseration. She has been outraged enough already.

But at this point in the play, Serafina's own baser instincts begin to emerge, though she cannot this time begin to elevate her new relationship to the holy level of her intimacy with her late husband. In all her self-righteous fury, she is already unbending a little, and in her 'Lasciatemi stare', 'let me be', we hear the old note re-enter her voice. We feel some of her willing pity for this fool who presumes to take the place of Rosario. And in her one ironic gesture of *running* from him, inviting his pursuit, our composure is shattered by a contradictory impression, and our image of the play once again turns turtle. Instead of growing to a nobility, Serafina, with the incongruous rose in her hair, shrinks to be another clown with Alvaro: 'The chase is grotesquely violent and comic.' She fights with the box of chocolates he had brought her, he drops to the floor sobbing like a frustrated child: 'Everything in my life turns out like this!' We might say that here an incipient tragic convention has become a comic one by inversion.

This is the way that Serafina's romantic obsession is punctured. We know her humiliation more than she knows it herself, since we have the complete situation in view and the whole counterpoint of the action violently registered in our minds. And it seems even Serafina has some sense of objective appearances, feeling her indignity, when she draws attention to the 'witch' next door: 'There is people watching you.' As she says this she knows the eyes are on herself.

This is a play about human illusions, about a simple woman who believes too much in herself; it is about her sin of pride. It is not about the man Mangiacavallo, who has few illusions and no pride. He is introduced into the action, this man with the head of a clown, simply as an agent of destruction, not so much to destroy Serafina as to destroy our image of human worth. But, oddly, the heroine in her simplicity and in spite of her littleness and nakedness, is given by this author an ineluctable stature by her very weaknesses, warmly comprehensive and curiously close to us. The summation of the individual ironies of the play's action is the huge particular irony of the total image the play leaves with us. We do not now deal in tragedies, nor in comedies, nor indeed in the nondescript 'tragi-comedy'. There flourish—what?—dramas of 'mood'. These are not necessarily plays calling up a peculiar atmosphere, but plays which attempt to control the exceptionally disparate audiences of modern times by teasing the mind and the emotion this way and that, making the one deceive, encourage and contradict the other.[1]

What follows is not intended as a history of modern drama, nor indeed can it deal justly, if at all, with individual playwrights of major status, like Ibsen, Hauptmann, Shaw, O'Neill, Eliot and Sartre, writers who do not always display to advantage the dark characteristics of twentieth-century dramaturgy. But it may illuminate some of the drama that has flourished in the theatre of paradox, and trace a development in this most disturbing technique of dramatic communication which is recognizably of our time.

[1] Friedrich Dürrenmatt, in a lecture delivered in Switzerland in 1954, emphasized that this was a problem of dramatic form: 'The task of art, in so far as art can have a task at all, and hence also the task of drama today, is to create something concrete, something that has form. This can be accomplished best by comedy. Tragedy, the strictest genre in art, presupposes a formed world. Comedy—in so far as it is not just satire of a particular society as in Molière—supposes an unformed world, a world being made and turned upside down, a world about to fold like ours.' *Problems of the Theatre*, trans. G. Nellhaus (New York, 1958), p. 30.

2

NATURALISTIC SHADING

Choose something ordinary and greyish, without bright colours
and superfluous noises. In general construct your life in a stereotyped way. The more grey and monotonous the background the
better.   IVANOV *to* DR LVOV

Incidentally, as we're not likely to meet again, I'd like to give you
a bit of advice, by way of farewell: stop throwing your arms
about! Try to get rid of that habit of making wide, sweeping
gestures!   TROFIMOV *to* LOPAKHIN

EARLY NATURALISM

Naturalism in the theatre is hardly the invention of Ibsen, Strindberg and Chekhov, but its vigorous exploitation by these great
dramatists marks the resuscitation of European drama in the second
half of the nineteenth century. With its emergence and astonishing
progress over a short period, the dark tones are heard again for the
first time since the seventeenth century.

'Naturalism' as a dramatic convention should be distinguished
from 'realism', the content of the drama.[1] Euripides, in trying to
reproduce more commonplace human feelings, lays claim to being a
great realist, though his plays are founded on the most artificial set
of stage conventions Western drama has known. *Hamlet* investigates
the mind and spirit of man with deeper psychological realism than
the theatre had known before, but only because the free Elizabethan
pattern of action and the supremacy of the soliloquy permitted it.
Shaw is an outstanding realist in the sense that he directs all his
art against the romantic attitudes of his contemporaries, but he

---

[1] In this discussion, of techniques rather than themes, we should not confuse the issue
with the concept of naturalism borrowed from criticism of the nineteenth century
post-Darwinian novel. In this concept, 'naturalism' is used to describe an historical
purpose, revealing factors of environment acting upon human life (education, poverty,
riches) and of biology (heredity, sexual differences and needs). This concern does not
necessarily affect the style and experience of the work.

53

nevertheless writes as mannered a comedy as he pleases. It is clear that realism bears no direct relation to the manner of performance.

On the other hand, it is very questionable whether some 'realists' of their own time, like Eugène Scribe in France and Arthur W. Pinero in England, playwrights very advanced by their own standards in the skills of uncovering skeletons in private cupboards,[1] succeeded in fact in getting any closer to the flavour of human life and its social relations. Pinero at the close of *The Second Mrs Tanqueray* composes dialogue like this:

AUBREY. Curse him! My poor, wretched wife! My poor, wretched wife! (*The door opens and Ellean appears. The two men turn to her. There is a moment's silence.*)
ELLEAN. Father...father...!
AUBREY. Ellean?
ELLEAN. I—I want you. (*He goes to her.*) Father...go to Paula! (*He looks into her face, startled.*) Quickly—quickly! (*He passes her to go out, she seizes his arm, with a cry.*) No, no; don't go!
(*He shakes her off and goes. Ellean staggers back...*)

Actors 'hurl' things to the floor, actresses 'faint' upon convenient ottomans, and it is apparent that those who are given the task of embodying such clichés of thought and feeling can do little more than 'register' the improbable emotions of improbable beings. Meanwhile a self-satisfied, if titillated, audience is unlikely to respond with the kind of anguish dark comedy provokes.

Realism, or truth to life, is therefore always the legitimate end for a good playwright; naturalism intends truth to life only as a method of presentation, using what is likely to be said and done as a way of reaching out to us. Naturalism, as a technique and a convention in its own right, does not necessarily imply realism. If it did, we should soon find unbearable the slaughters sustained by cowboys and Indians or by cops and robbers as seen on the cinema or television screen. Naturalism is serviceable for drama, but only as the stylizing of the Greek or Elizabethan theatre is serviceable. Indeed, 'naturalis-

---

[1] The reader is recommended to read Shaw's formula for the 'well made' play in his preface to *Three Plays by Brieux* (London, 1911), p. xxiii. He suggests that 'the situation of an innocent person convicted by circumstances of a crime may always be depended on. If the person is a woman, she must be convicted of adultery, etc.'

tic drama' is a fine contradiction in terms, since drama can never reproduce life with complete fidelity; in the end it must always cheat us to serve some ulterior purpose. The stage must always supply meaning and form to what is otherwise meaningless and formless, and it does this knowing that we are quite willing to be cheated.

The advent of *realistic* naturalism brought with it many new problems for the writer, and placed many new pressures on the actor and his audience. The play's dialogue had to do all it had done before, carrying character and movement, exposing the past and furthering the plot, but it had to do this while seeming casual and conversational. Elements of triviality and a lightness of touch had to be presented together with elements of importance and seriousness, if the illusion was to be sustained. Instead of distracting the attention of the spectator from the true aims of the play, paradoxically such dialogue tended to intensify and hold the attention by supplying the gentle ironies implicit in everyday intercourse. Even more striking changes appeared in dramatic construction. Because of the shape and structure of naturalistic plays, events followed one another more reasonably and less theatrically, and dramatists quickly discovered the enormous asset of a scene or a portrait rendered with the contrasting lights and shades of nature. All the great naturalists found it helpful to equate stage time more with chronological time, telescoping the action to start the play near the crisis of events. Here again, they tended to cause new and unexpected juxtapositions of feeling. But the sharpest changes occurred in the depiction of ˜haracter. For a character to be sufficiently rounded, his background and past had to be granted a more detailed history; he needed a memory and he needed roots; his relationships with others had to be implicit in every speech and action. Thus the actor found himself a student of psychology, and devised elaborate systems to aid him in his art. But, notably, a three-dimensional creature like the central character of a dark comedy showed more than one side of his nature: if comic, he could also be serious; if serious, he could also be comic. He was especially comic if he lacked a sense of humour.

It followed that audiences, in reconstructing the image of a naturalistic play from a great wealth of impressions, found themselves compelled to supply a newly sensitive response. The new drama was not only complicated for them by demanding an honesty of assessment and judgment: they found themselves more and more having to ask the question 'why?' of the events of the play. Interest became centred on causes and not effects, and in the best of the naturalistic plays that old cliché 'the irony of life' acquired the reality it deserved. Reality became the test of the play and the audience, and cast the grey shadows characteristic of the labyrinth of ordinary experience. Yet a microscopic view of experience which was also a prismatic one was to reveal a surprisingly full range of colour within the small areas of domestic life, as it had previously done in the novel.

The new playwright tried to keep to conventions suggested by ordinary behaviour, carefully eschewing the unnatural in his stage devices.[1] This policy left great voids to be filled where, for example, a more direct expression of feeling had been possible before. Alternative tricks, of the inoffensive stage letter, the casually adroit use of servant or telephone, the innuendo in conversational dialogue, even tell-tale properties deposited about the stage and persuasive suggestions in costume and *décor*, became the unnatural clichés of the naturalistic theatre in their turn. Nevertheless, the general suppression of rhetorical language and the striking gesture left a surface so smooth and unruffled that the gentlest emphasis broke the calm with an illuminating splash. Like the parent bird brooding over her family, the spectator was expected to be eagle-eyed for signs of unrest, and he was prompt with laughter and ready with compassion. Effects were possible which might have passed unnoticed in the boisterous theatres of other times. The toning down of feeling, the merging of farcical and tragic exaggeration, in fact required the spectator to be more alert to overtones of tragicomedy. Admittedly the switches in mood and feeling in modern naturalistic drama, moving as it must

---

[1] We do not discuss the effects on the naturalistic playwright of the proscenium-arch playhouse, which was developed to a high degree in this period. The reader may care to notice that this playwright is compelled to draw the spectator into the illusion inside the arch in order to overcome the loss of spatial immediacy in this type of theatre, and at the same time, for a comic perspective, to undercut the identification of audience with character which results. This nice ambivalence is to be seen practised at its best by Chekhov, and adds to the ambiguities of feeling created by his plays.

through narrower channels of expression, will be less bold and colourful. But more delicate effects may be none the less impressive and efficient in agitating our mental image of the play's meaning if they are woven into an appropriately fine-spun texture. The ironic effect when Hedda Gabler subtly destroys Lövborg is as exciting in the close context of Ibsen's play as when Iago succeeds in destroying Othello in the openwork pattern of Shakespeare's.

The naturalistic playwright wished to point the incongruities he observed, but without having to distort the truth of life as he saw it. He aimed, therefore, at avoiding the cardinal principle of the old comedy—that of exaggeration, which had guided the creation and presentation of comic characters from Bottom and Harpagon to Lady Wishfort, Mrs Malaprop and Miss Prism. As a result of this, he was not able entirely to exclude the audience's tearful response as writers had done before. Nor perhaps did he wish to; but he could command it at will. Essentially, only the details of life as it was lived were to be his raw material: he chanced upon a variety of the so-called 'domestic comedy' which has since his time been vastly abused by the countless dramatists who wrote a melodrama spiced with a handful of cardboard characters drawn from artificial comedy: sniffling maids, pompous aunts, well-bred fiancés, absent-minded grannies and comic policemen.

By a constant reference back to life, the good naturalistic playwright had us appreciate the chaotic emotions and the feel of life beneath the surface of his drama. It remained for him only to perfect a method whereby incongruities could be presented intelligibly in the theatre. We meet an acquaintance in the street: 'How nice to see you,' we say; while we think, 'What wretched luck to meet him at this moment!' We come down to breakfast with the conventional early morning greeting and comment; we would perhaps be happier to say nothing at all at such a time. From one point of view this duplicity can be pathetic, but from another it is very funny.

The microcosm of everyday life was the ground over which a drab tragicomedy seemed to be most fruitfully worked. In this the drama received many stimuli from the novel, particularly its nineteenth-century achievements, and Mario Praz has written illuminatingly of the 'democratization of the heroic'.[1] Since Chaucer, the domestic world had provided unlimited sources for the exciting details which go to make up life, but with the work of Jane Austen, Flaubert, Tolstoy and others, the novel had deliberately used this apparently restricted field in order to reveal the ways of humanity at large. The worst of the novelists narrowed their subject by so doing; the best infinitely widened it. The worst made the novel mean and bourgeois; the best made it universal. For already the novelist had faced the problem which twentieth-century dramatists have not yet completely solved: how to make what might otherwise sink into domestic cosiness or sordidness rise to be representative. Professor Praz wrote of Trollope,

Just as the seventeenth century Dutch painters, in their *genre* pictures, did not so much tell stories as present types of men and women who were in no way exceptional, just as they presented pictures of social life, constantly repeating themselves, so also does Trollope obtain his results through a slow accumulation of little pictures of ordinary life, with nothing spectacular about them—often, in fact, varied by only slight alterations. And both the Dutch painters and the English novelist knew how to make monotony lively, and how to bring a universal character into the portraiture of everyday things.

The novel provided a direction, even supplied a pressure, for the dramatist, but it did not solve the distinctive dramatic problem of turning reality to significant theatrical account. Eventually, many dramatists adopted symbolism as their aid to greater expression, but many, like Ibsen, Strindberg and Chekhov, who resorted to symbolic methods themselves, in fact spent much time in perfecting the typical reaction, the typical behaviour, in reproducing the typical tempo of life in given circumstances, in order to solicit our attention. They discovered that their plays had to create what is a verisimilitude rather than an exact replica of life.

A quick comparison between the function of Natasha in *Three Sisters*, the young lady who succeeds in marrying brother Andrey and eventually in taking over the family home, and that of Lopakhin in *The Cherry Orchard*, the embarrassed overseer who almost accidentally buys up the family estate, may show how a correct

[1] M. Praz, *The Hero in Eclipse in Victorian Fiction*, trans. Davidson (London, 1956).

balance in the structure of a naturalistic comedy can help it to suggest its universal quality.

In the first act of *Three Sisters* it seems that Chekhov does not wish us to make up our minds about Natasha. We meet her first only through Masha's eyes: 'The way she dresses herself is awful!... And her cheeks look as though they've been scrubbed, they're so shiny! Andrey's not in love with her—I can't believe it; after all, he has got some taste...'[1] But do we accept at face value the criticisms of one woman of another? Natasha with her scrubbed cheeks may be out to deceive Andrey, but, we tell ourselves, this is his jealous sister speaking. So now we anticipate her entrance, prepared to scrutinize every detail of her behaviour to confirm or deny Masha's statement. Thus we see her wearing a pink dress with a green belt... but, after all, isn't she a young girl? She preens herself before the mirror...but isn't this what all women do before a party? She gives Irena an ostentatious kiss...but isn't Irena of her own age, and isn't it her saint's day? May not all these things be an expression of her nervousness? Then Olga cruelly criticizes her clothes, and the company teases her at dinner: Natasha may have no sense of humour, but we are prepared to sympathize with the little outsider, even to the point of hoping she will capture brother Andrey. Thus at the end of Act I we remain neutral and uncommitted: Chekhov's character-drawing is brilliant, like his control of our sympathies.

After this the control relaxes. For the rest of the play Natasha treats her new husband Andrey abominably, ruthlessly takes charge of the household, puts on superior airs, uses her child as a whip to dominate the family, abuses the old servant Anfisa, persuades Andrey to mortgage the house and herself holds the money. She even has a child by another man. By the end of the play she has completely turned the tables and is incarnate selfishness. By this time the character has so nettled us that, rather than conclude that the sisters' own lethargy has brought this upon themselves, we place her in our picture no longer as the 'balanced' character of Act I, nor as the comic *Hausfrau* of Act II, but as an insensitive amorality, even an unmotivated evil; in Andrey's own words, 'a mean blind

---

[1] Chekhov, *Three Plays*, trans. E. Fen (London, 1951).

thick-skinned animal'. For this reason this play is a lesser achievement than *The Cherry Orchard*: the play tends to be small without becoming a microcosm. True, there are such women as Natasha, and perhaps Chekhov is right to emphasize that the less sensitive, the less imaginative, people usually win the day. True, the sisters and their brother Andrey make a substantial, human and universal core for the play. But such a Natasha in this particular framework of helplessness risks toppling the play into melodrama.

By contrast, Chekhov is careful to remove any sense of evil from *The Cherry Orchard*, which followed. His only potential villain is Lopakhin, who buys up the house and the orchard rather out of a mistaken sense of duty, through a failure to realize the propriety of the situation, than through any desire for revenge. His forebears had been serfs on the estate, and the tables are as effectively turned by Lopakhin as by Natasha; but we feel sympathy for both parties in the transaction. The family lose their beloved orchard because they are themselves, and no external moral pattern of malevolence is introduced into the structure of the play to distract us.

Thus by excluding the cliché, Chekhov extends his *Cherry Orchard* to include 'all Russia'. Even the largely farcical characters, Epihodov, Charlotta, Pishchik and Gaev, have their sympathetic side. Everyday life is permitted to carry its own message by his careful adjustment of our critical with our sympathetic faculties throughout the play, balancing laughter and tears. The great discovery of modern drama was that an arrangement of the tiny elements of life could do this. Says Maddy Rooney, the old Irishwoman in Beckett's *All That Fall*, realistic in conception if nonrealistic in convention, 'Oh I am just a hysterical old hag I know, destroyed with sorrow and pining and gentility and church-going and fat with rheumatism and childlessness. . .' This little catalogue of human ills epitomizes that ironic alertness required of today's audience; we are to weep at the sorrow and pining, but laugh at the gentility and church-going; laugh at the fat and rheumatism, but weep at the childlessness. The little things are mixed with the bigger, the social pressures with the personal agonies. The irony of the whole is the overwhelming insight we take away with us.

Naturalism on the stage gave great impetus to the creation of a fresh structure of character, and thereby made a powerful assault on one of drama's indispensable agencies for affecting its audience. The dark comic hero has an inner life of great and contradictory variety. In naturalistic drama it is more a case of representing outward behaviour and events in order to point to this confusion and complexity than one of shaping a character in order to exemplify a particular sequence of events. The outer world of events loses interest for us and gives place to an inner world with which we live in intimacy. Events sink into the background when the drama of human personality is shifted into the spotlight. Naturalistic drama is less concerned to illustrate external ethical and religious values and more to analyse and evaluate personal worth. In proposing the personal view in terms of the particular instance, it permits a new freedom to express an individual vision; in this sense an indeterminate and unstable Peer Gynt or Miss Julie has as much to offer us as an Orestes or a Tamburlaine. We may not go so far as to say, as Strindberg does, that 'the naturalist has abolished guilt by abolishing God', but we may well agree that, in the naturalistic theatre, God assumes no importance and holds no interest unless a character specifically admits Him.

In the preface to *Miss Julie* of 1888, an astonishingly precocious statement of the aims of naturalism for its time, Strindberg distinguishes between 'character' as an expression for 'automaton', and 'character' as an expression for a 'soul-complex':

An individual who had once for all become fixed in his natural disposition, or had adapted himself to some definite role in life—who, in fact, had ceased to grow—was called a 'character'; while the man who continued his development, the skilful navigator of life's river who does not sail with sheets set fast, but veers before the wind to luff again, was called 'characterless'. In a derogatory sense, of course, since he was so difficult to catch, to classify, and to keep guard over.

He goes on,

I do not believe, therefore, in simple characters on the stage. And the summary judgments on men given by authors: this man is stupid, this one brutal, this one jealous, this one stingy, etc., should be challenged by naturalists, who know the richness of the soul-complex, and recognize that 'vice' has a reverse side very much like virtue...My souls (characters) are conglomerations from past and present stages of civilization; they are excerpts from books and newspapers, scraps of humanity, pieces torn from festive garments which have become rags—just as the soul itself is a piece of patchwork.[1]

The chameleon character is now installed and domesticated.

In the characters of some dramatists, like Strindberg and Chekhov, the variegations are less apparent to the eye. In others, like Pirandello and Anouilh, the colour without may vary with the colour within. Thus every character in *The Cherry Orchard* of Chekhov, whether more or less comic to the beholder, suffers inwardly and has a sense of isolation. Lopakhin knows the value of money, works hard, is an efficient overseer and keeps a close eye on the clock, but he is also delighted and troubled by trees and fields and poppies in bloom, and cannot possibly cope with a girl in tears. Charlotta the governess is full of fun and parlour tricks, and eats cucumbers as though they were bananas, but she declares that she aches with loneliness for a family and a home she cannot remember. And so on through the long list of parts in this play.

A character in Pirandello, on the other hand, finds that his inner self can rarely communicate with the person he shows to the world at large. Pirandello has his Cecè, in the play of the same name, say, 'Is it not tormenting to think that you live diffused into a hundred thousand individuals who know you and whom you do not know?' Again, 'I am sure that you agree with me that we are not always the same. According to our humour, moments, relations, we are now one way and then another; happy with one, sad with another, serious with this man, funny with that one.'[2] In his sequence of great plays in the 1920s, Pirandello puts this principle of personality to dramatic use many times. Thus Ersilia Drei in *Naked* tries by attempted suicide to clothe her dull life in a dress of her own making, while every one of those about her accepts only his own view of her personality until in despair she decides for a second time to take her

[1] Strindberg, preface to *Lady Julie*, trans. C. D. Locock, in *International Modern Plays* (London, 1950), pp. 8–9.
[2] Quoted from D. Vittorini, *The Drama of Luigi Pirandello* (New York, 1935), p. 76.

own life. In the age of Freud and Joyce and Pirandello we explore more deeply into human personality, and have come up against one of the immediate frontiers of drama.

The last attribute of dark comedy in naturalistic drama would seem to be something more than universality, something closer to timelessness. It would seem to exist in direct contradiction to the particularity of naturalistic and trivial detail, which would tend to limit the subject, individualize the character, identify the moment in time. But, in making the play infinitely immediate, the very normality of behaviour extends the application of the play's theme. While its highest common factor remains human, it demonstrates the simple arithmetic of all ages. Thus Shaw thought he found twentieth-century England in Chekhov's nineteenth-century Russia: 'Just as Ibsen's intensely Norwegian plays exactly fitted every middle and professional class suburb in Europe, these intensely Russian plays fitted all the country houses in Europe...'[1] In one sense Shaw was right. Halvard Solness and Uncle Vanya, like Willie Loman and Maddy Rooney and Archie Rice, are permanently amongst us.

Pirandello in his early phase expresses the doubts of the naturalist about his chances of capturing and communicating the timelessness of his subject. He said that 'art, too, like all ideal or illusory creations, tends to fix life: it fixes it into one moment or into various definite moments: the statue in one gesture, the landscape in one momentary aspect, unchangeable. But what of the perpetual movement of its successive aspects? What of the continuous fusion in which life is found?'[2] One can guess that such doubts encouraged Ibsen, Strindberg and Chekhov to introduce suggestive symbolism more and more into their plays. The Master Builder's steeple, which he must climb in spite of his years, for example, takes on a life of its own and becomes the prototype of all foolhardy aspirations and ugly refusals

---

[1] Shaw, preface to *Heartbreak House*.

[2] Pirandello, *L'Umorismo*, 2nd ed. (Florence, 1920), p. 222. The original reads, 'Anch'essa l'arte, come tutte le costruzione ideali o illusorie, tende a fissar la vita: la fissa in un momento o in varii momenti determinati: la statua in un gesto, il paesaggio in un aspetto temporaneo, immutabile. Ma, e la perpetua mobilità degli aspetti successivi? e la fusione continua in cui le anime si trovano?'

to know thyself. A cherry orchard binds us all to the beauty we like to find in our past and blinds us to the realities of the present. But even without such symbolism the naturalistic playwright who managed to capture and fix his landscape or his statue in one intensely true, if momentary, aspect or gesture held the same secret of timelessness which the sculptor Praxiteles himself discovered.

For in naturalistic drama of the best kind no laugh is conclusive, no tears are the final expression of emotion. There is no finality about the dramatist's statement, although the statement may be complete. Chekhov's family groups end as they began, or nearly so, and have still to live out their lives. Pirandello's people stick themselves upon their own pins and remain wriggling, while we dare do no more than hold our breath lest we commit ourselves similarly. To imagine a continuation of the lives of Anouilh's characters is to ride further into the blind impasse of life where the optimist will only rub off more of his shine.

PORTENTS IN IBSEN

Ibsen, Strindberg and Chekhov are not equally dark nor evenly dark. While the dark tones are noticeably present in Chekhov, Ibsen is often more prepared to heighten his colours in the traditional way of Dumas and Augier to suit a more traditional purpose. Thus *Hedda Gabler* is a plausible attempt to shine a bright light broadly on a social and spiritual malaise, but Hedda's neurotic boredom is presented by methods deriving from Scribean melodrama. Even the emphatic death of innocent Hedvig, the pathetic residue of *The Wild Duck*, Ibsen's darkest and most modern comedy, is highly contrived in the manner of the 'well made' play.[1] When Ibsen uses the conventional frameworks of the period, one cannot be sure that the comic elements are not ultimately incidental. In comparison with

[1] It is apparent that Ibsen thinks out the details of his stage action in the blatant acting conventions of the nineteenth century, even toward the end of his career. Thus at the opening of *The Master Builder*, the initial sexual dominance of Solness is to be suggested by having Kaja speak '*passionately, clasping her hands and holding them out toward him*: Now there's only one person in the world I care about...!' and a moment later she '*sinks down at his feet*'. The end of this play, for all its accumulated symbolism, is a very competitive sample of melodramatic spectacle.

Chekhov's best comedy, the laughter at, say, Jörgen Tesman, Hedda's thick-skulled bridegroom, or at his pathetically silly Aunt Juliane, provides little of the true driving force behind our response to *Hedda Gabler* as a whole.

Nevertheless, different styles encourage different kinds of incongruity, and Ibsen's satirical edge introduces comedy at illuminating moments. Perhaps it is not too far-fetched to argue that in Ibsen, the most sober of modern dramatists in many ways, his earlier attempts at vaudeville comedy took a long time to die in him. They are turned to account in the unique *Peer Gynt*, a morality in which Peer is a figure standing for Norway and mankind itself, carefully mixed in temperament to be at once loved and despised. But in spite of moments of warm intimacy in the play, the methods of poetic fantasy somewhat smother our sense of being implicated. Emotional infection does not spread.

Even when Ibsen writes his so-called 'social' and satirical plays, the new element is not clearly present. In *The Pillars of Society*, *A Doll's House*, *Ghosts* and *An Enemy of the People*, the subjects are presented in terms of simple conflict between an individualist on the one hand and the community with its codes of behaviour on the other. Such a division must make for a degree of satire, but the essence of Ibsen is not found in this conflict. His deep interest in human motives and ultimately in the spiritual state of human beings gave the lie to such a thesis as Shaw's *The Quintessence of Ibsenism*. Ibsen's increasing attention to the accurate depiction of human psychology and suffering showed a grimmer side of the problems in question. Thus in *Ghosts*, the satirical conflict between human feeling and correct social behaviour is strongly present in the exchanges between Parson Manders and Mrs Alving. However, our real interest is soon drawn to Mrs Alving's depth of self-knowledge, and Parson Manders remains a rather easy caricature. He is the comic butt for the attack on bigoted views: his horror at finding Mrs Alving reading books of advanced ideas, or at Oswald's 'irregular union' in Paris, so conditions us that the actor today is hard put not to raise an unwanted laugh on his curtain line, 'It wasn't insured', when the fire at the orphanage is reported. This is hardly calculated to accentuate, rather to belittle, the vital and tragic slant of the play.

An Enemy of the People, while lacking the depth of feeling of *Ghosts*, manages, however, to strike a more even tone. The battle between the Doctor and his brother the Mayor over the contamination of the baths is fought out over a fairly even ground of lively satire. But even in this most social of social plays, the artist is exploring human personality, and Dr Stockmann lives and makes the play live. Natural man is personified in him by making him poor, yet lavish with food and drink and childlike in his pleasure at luxuries; by making him exuberant with high spirits at one minute, yet self-righteous the next; by making him Quixotic and idealistic, yet also untidy and immature and muddle-headed. A whole man emerges, and the man has a meaning in the pattern of the play: honesty is recognizably human in its opposition to hypocrisy and humbug. The play cannot rise to tragedy: in the end we think more than we feel. But neither is it comedy. It 'lies half-way between'. As a play it does not impose beliefs before it invites experience, and the naturalistic observation of Stockmann's character and the play's intensely personal interest lend warmth to cold satire.

Though it follows this play, *The Wild Duck* parodies all that Stockmann stood for. Hjalmar Ekdal is much less a 'hero' than he: Hjalmar is the cheerful, natural man who is this time *not* so honest, and our sense of personal feeling and kinship is warmer still. Many feel this play to be Ibsen's greatest achievement, and its exquisite balance of feeling may account for this reaction. Hjalmar is the inoffensive egoist who can only live by the white lies he feeds on. The subject of the play, the relativity of personal happiness, is as wide as anything Ibsen attempted before or after. More important, the enemy is not in a 'compact majority' this time, but in himself. The spirit of the play, therefore, is one of deep understanding and incisive and painful criticism. If it were not for this balance, the old attic in which Hjalmar and his father go 'shooting', and the comic parallelism of Old Ekdal with his son, like the parallelism of Fodal with Borkman in *John Gabriel Borkman*, would seem merely an intrusion from farce and destroy our sense of natural life in the play.

The attic in its conception daringly risks a breach in the play's structure in order to make us smile and then remember our own limitations.

The play could well have dropped into melodrama, and from the start Ibsen is working to avoid this. The idealistic busybody Gregers, Hjalmar's friend, has the knowledge and the wish wherewith to break up Hjalmar's and Gina's happy little home, but luckily Hjalmar is too real and too weak to decide for honour and leave his comfortable wife. He can never be the melodramatic sort, though he tries to be. When his father was put in prison, Hjalmar had considered suicide:

HJALMAR. ...I thought the whole creation should come to a stand, as in an eclipse.
GREGERS. I felt like that, too, when my mother died.
HJALMAR. It was in such an hour that Hjalmar Ekdal held the pistol to his own heart.
GREGERS. You, too, thought of —!
HJALMAR. Yes.
GREGERS. But you didn't shoot.
HJALMAR. No. In that moment of supreme trial I won the victory over myself. I went on living. But you can well believe it takes courage to choose life in those circumstances.[1]

Especially when the child Hedvig shoots herself, her naïve self-sacrifice could have been appalling and harrowing if Ibsen had not provided for this by the presence of the realist Dr Relling, who deftly pricks the melodramatic bubble in time. In the last sequence of the play we pass from Hjalmar's hysterical shriek, 'Ah, Thou above! If Thou *art* there! Why hast Thou done this thing to me!', to its undermining by the drunken theological student:

MOLVIK. Praised be the Lord. Earth to earth. Earth to earth.
RELLING. Shut up, you fool; your're drunk,

until our last illusion about Hjalmar is finally collapsed by the Doctor's dry comment, 'Before the year is out little Hedvig will be nothing more to him than a fine subject to declaim on.' Ibsen turns our eyes from Hedvig to Hjalmar, and reminds us of the strong

[1] Henrik Ibsen, *Three Plays*, trans. U. Ellis-Fermor (London, 1950).

67

element of self-sympathy we saw in him when he spoke to Gregers about Hedvig's approaching blindness, 'It's terribly hard for me, Gregers.' So we sit rebuked at the fall of the curtain.

Without quite breaking the naturalistic form, Ibsen sees us, like Hjalmar himself, slung between the attitudes of Gregers and Relling. The dialectic of the action, the farce taking its life from the pathos and the pathos from the farce, to use Eric Bentley's neat statement,[1] the tears and the laughter interpenetrating the discussion—this keeps the spectator wide awake. The delicious paradox is that Hjalmar is so like ourselves, but too like ourselves to be fully sympathetic.

With the achievement of *The Wild Duck* we may fairly leave Ibsen. Hedda Gabler's horror and disgust at Judge Brack's amused and sinister account of Lövborg's ugly death—'shot through the bowels',[2] when Hedda had so wanted him to die a noble and graceful death to satisfy her romantic perversions—is an echo of the ironic douching given by Relling to Gregers and Hjalmar. But an almost total lack of sympathy with the heroine, in spite of the singularly ill-matched marriage she has made, takes its toll of subtleties in *Hedda Gabler*. Brack's irony hits Hedda only, and cannot be turned upon the spectator. The somewhat kinder portrait of Solness in *The Master Builder* is wholly tragic, and in the plays of his last years Ibsen never repeats the technical complexity in manipulating the audience which he approached in his inimitable play *The Wild Duck*.

STRINDBERG'S NATURALISM

Nor need we stay too long in this chapter with August Strindberg, but for other reasons. This enigmatic, lunatic genius, obsessed for the most part (excluding the religiose dream plays) with the giant problem of sex, quickly found that naturalism was inadequate to communicate the convolutions of his mind, though he reverted to a quasi-naturalistic manner intermittently throughout a career in which he tried almost every theatrical style known to the modern theatre.

---

[1] E. R. Bentley, *In Search of Theater* (London, 1954), p. 45.

[2] Archer's translation, rather more pointed than 'in the stomach'. The original suggests more nearly our word 'belly'.

We shall return, therefore, to see him at work later in such surrealistic-expressionistic plays as *To Damascus* and *The Ghost Sonata*.

It is difficult, first, not to suggest that the theories of naturalism outlined in his fine preface to *Miss Julie* are mostly conceived 'cold', without direct relevance to the drama he was in fact writing. We should be unwise to turn to them for help in understanding his kind of realism. Looking back, we have, secondly, to accept that the better-known plays of intense realism, like *The Father*, *Miss Julie*, and the terrifying *Dance of Death*, are properly not naturalistic at all, and it may be impertinent to see them as naturalistic dark comedies. Their *manner* of presentation is in the last analysis independent of their matter; they depend very little on the detail of ordinary life for their expression. *The Father* asks as properties only a table-lamp for the enraged Captain to throw at Laura his wife, and a strait-jacket to be slipped over him at her moment of victory. To capture the play's demonic strength, it would be better played on a naked stage, as others have suggested—'his action is of the soul, not of the body'.[1] It is not surprising to learn that the issues in *Miss Julie* have been successfully abstracted to create a ballet, that most abstract of forms. Strindberg preferred *Creditors* to *Miss Julie* because it is simplified to 'three characters, a table and two chairs, and no sunrise',[2] a statement reminiscent of Alexandre Dumas's dramatic essentials, 'three planks, two actors and a passion'.

These plays suggest an incipient expressionism. They emerge as natural tragedies lacking the restraints of naturalism, domestic agonies lacking life's comic compensations. The thoughts and feelings of the characters scream aloud, their emotions flying 'like bullets at the enemy' and demanding what Eric Bentley considers to be 'Dionysiac' performance.[3] Strindberg displays realism in a cloak of personal melodrama: his tales are raw and macabre and his characters are fanatical and unbalanced. Surface manners are sometimes natural, but a symbolic war of sex is always raging just beneath, quickly to boil up and destroy the irony of appearances.

[1] A. Nicoll, *World Drama* (London, 1949), pp. 553–4.
[2] See M. Lamm, *Modern Drama*, trans. K. Elliott (Oxford, 1952), pp. 139–40.
[3] E. R. Bentley, *In Search of Theater* (London, 1954), p. 135.

It is strange that the battle of the sexes, a primary source of comedy in the past, should so little reveal its comic and social side to Strindberg. Profoundly concerned with spiritual issues, Strindberg's approach tends to suppress the treatment of genuine social problems in these plays. He seems time and again to argue against the emancipation of women, and in *Miss Julie* even seems to concern himself with the rise and fall of the classes. Yet the subject of 'the new woman', as it is for Shaw, is only a springboard into deeper waters, and Miss Julie is ostensibly mistress, and Jean is servant, only to reinforce the real theme of the drama, which demonstrates that Jean is 'sexually the aristocrat', as the author says in the preface, and that the loser in the war of sex shall be the spiritual slave. For Strindberg the question of sex is, then, a personal and not a social one, and in general the fierce drive of these plays prohibits any sense of the monotony which might have killed them. The crude, head-on conflict between man and woman is inexorable and capable of no solution; its expression can only be tragic. As in *Ghosts*, the rising of the sun at the end of *Miss Julie* casts long, fateful shadows.

Yet there is another Strindberg, who sees with an ironic eye at lucid moments: there appears also a kind of wan smile of grim self-relief which few would care to identify as comedy. We might recognize it in the country Pastor in *The Father*, with his ineffectual 'everyone has his burden', and the provincial Doctor, innocent tool of Laura, with his remarks on 'the sanctity of family life'. We might recognize it in Kristin the cook in *Miss Julie*, whose normality is there to set off the miseries and frustrations and the wretched guilt of Julie and Jean. She is the 'feminine slave' who is 'stuffed full of morality and religion, which she makes her cloaks and scapegoats. She goes to church as a simple and easy way of unloading on Jesus her household thefts, and of taking in a fresh cargo of guiltlessness.' The simplicity in her attitude to the nature of the sexual attraction, as shown in her mime of curling her hair with a hairpin, contrasts grotesquely with the aphrodisiac influence of the midsummer-eve dance and the insinuations of the others; the 'ballet' of the peasants

[1] Preface to *Lady Julie*, trans. C. D. Locock, in *International Modern Plays* (London, 1950), p. 11.

dancing drunkenly and singing bawdily while Jean and Julie are alone in Jean's room is a unique effect of ugly incongruity.

Strindberg insists upon calling *Comrades*, a play which precisely echoes the theme and spirit of *The Father*, a 'comedy'. The title at least is ironic: the wife who destroys her artist husband's talent and self-respect is no comrade. *Creditors* he calls a 'tragicomedy'. In it another female vulture first preys and feeds upon the strength of her two men, the first a teacher and the second an artist, each of them her husband in turn. The second dies in an epileptic fit. It is hard to see how Strindberg could declare this play to be 'human and amiable'. There is, however, a kind of implicit comic irony in the play, as when the first husband meets his former wife again for the first time after long separation. They commence their interview with the politenesses of convention which we know cannot survive the questioning of motives:

TEKLA. Sit down a moment. You don't offend me, for you possess that rare gift—which was always yours—of tact and politeness.
GUSTAV. It's very kind of you. But one could hardly expect—that your husband might regard my qualities in the same generous light as you.[1]

There is present first the attraction on all levels. Gustav talks of 'my secret longing to see her whom I used to love more than my own life', and when he pinches her ear he says, 'That tiny ear!—Think only if your husband could see us now!' 'Wouldn't he howl, though!' is her reply. But the masks are soon off:

TEKLA. Vindictive wretch—shame on you!
GUSTAV. Dissolute wretch—shame on you!
TEKLA. Oh! that's my character, is it?
GUSTAV. Oh, that's my character, is it?—You ought to learn something about human nature in others before you give your own nature free rein.

The ironic tone becomes more evident in such a play as *Debit and Credit*, which with grim humour tells the sorry story of a scholar and explorer who is now persecuted by those who helped him reach his present fame and position. His brother and his brother's wife,

[1] A. Strindberg, *Plays, Second Series*, trans. E. Björkman (London, 1913).

71

his old teacher, his mistresses Mariè and Cecilia, and Cecilia's former fiancé, all have their claim on the victim. These characters are presented with a slightly farcical touch, and luckily the hero for once is a bachelor. A point is made simply: 'What a peaceful, un-assailable position he holds who has nothing to lose!', but the theme of 'eat or be eaten' is the same as before. In all these plays, abnor-mality stifles potential comedy.

By far the most interesting is *There are Crimes and Crimes*, another 'comedy'. This introduces an ironic note more incisive than any that had gone before, and this play with its odd mixture of naturalistic detail and symbolic undercurrents is the link with the ironic dream plays to come.

Maurice is a struggling playwright in Paris. With his faithful mistress Jeanne and their little daughter Marion, he is hoping for some financial success with his latest venture in the theatre: we see them all meet first in a cemetery. When success comes he neglects Jeanne, and fame brings with it a predatory female, Henriette, who has a 'scent of blood' and whose father 'melted away like wax before a fire in the hatred of her mother and sisters'. She is the complete antithesis to the forsaken Jeanne, who is an irreproachable angel; but 'the victor's wreath seems worthless if you can't place it at the feet of some woman'.[1] This is a Paris which smells of sin, whose 'air is poisoned', and when Maurice learns that his child has died and that his love for Henriette was a destroyer, his sense of guilt grows to monstrous proportions, and the figure of the Commissaire of Police stands by like a symbol of death.

Maurice is cleared of the charge of murdering his child, who died naturally, but the terrors of nightmare begin: 'There are crimes not mentioned in the Criminal Code, and these are the worse ones, for they have to be punished by ourselves, and no judge could be more severe than we are against our own selves.'

In the Luxembourg Gardens, standing significantly beside the group of Adam and Eve, Maurice and Henriette prepare to take their own lives. 'The wind is shaking the trees and stirring up dead leaves, straws, and pieces of paper from the ground.' In accusing

[1] Trans. E. Björkman in August Strindberg, *Eight Famous Plays* (London, 1949).

each other thay are 'driving each other insane', 'torturing each other to death'. But the park is closed before their position can be resolved, and Maurice has second thoughts. Furthermore, now that his name is cleared, success returns to him. It is true he has apparently learned his lesson, since he declares that 'honour is a phantom; gold, nothing but dry leaves; women, mere intoxicants', and he will reckon with himself through the help of the Curé at the church. But before the curtain is down he decides not to forsake entirely the good things which a renewed material success offers him. From hell, Maurice ascends again to heaven, and finds it rather cosy.

Strindberg's ironic twist in this is less one of character and action and more an arbitrary and superimposed twist of mind and conscience: the audience is specifically invited to feel the pressure of guilt and then evaluate the incongruous outcome. The spectator is suddenly pushed to arm's length by a hero who should have renounced worldliness for the cloister or the grave, but who simply does not. The play suddenly shudders to *normality*, Maurice steps out of melodrama into a clear sane light, and judges us in return. 'Tonight I'll meet you at the church,' he tells the Abbé, 'but tomorrow evening I go to the theatre.' Strindberg is playing cat-and-mouse with us as only the comedian can do.

His attempts to express the inarticulate objectively on the stage led him further and further from naturalism into the symbolism of the last plays. Perhaps it is also true to say that the insoluble, destructive position in which he found himself by such probing into problems of the sexual struggle led him, too, into a dry, bloodless drama in which expression is only possible through a cadaverous grin. In *The Devil's Disciple*, Shaw's Minister Anderson tells his muddled wife Judith, 'After all, my dear, if you watch people carefully, you'll be surprised to find how like hate is to love.' John Osborne used this to initiate some of the momentum in his Jimmy Porter, but Strindberg's attempts to understand and express the ambiguities of the love–hate relationship between the sexes led him deeply into dramatic territory in which the irony is wholly individual and, one would think, inimitable in tone. If there is laughter in this, it is the most toothy and rasping laughter in modern drama.

CHEKHOV

We arrive at the achievement of Anton Chekhov, the most natural of the naturalists, and the first truly dark comedian. Chekhovian drama is nearer to the naturalism of the 'neo-realism' of the post-war Italian cinema, especially that of De Sica in *Bicycle Thieves*, *Miracle of Milan* and *Umberto D*, nearer to the English and American play of 'mood', to the television plays of Paddy Chayefsky, even to the realism of the 1950s in John Osborne and Arnold Wesker, than to the naturalism of Ibsen and Strindberg. It is a mistake to suppose that Chekhov's attempts to divide his audience against itself are really different from Osborne's to bring us to a state of awareness. Chekhov is able with an unruffled surface to reconcile all his contradictions, but beneath lies a ferment as troubled as anything Osborne is working for. In *The Seagull* and *The Cherry Orchard*, we are made to smile at both youth and age while we see ourselves as the young and the old; and we may not avoid resenting our laughter, since it is modified by pity. In some essentials the methods of these two authors are very similar: where they differ is in the stance the author takes, and the place where he stands. Osborne gesticulates at us from an unassailable point in the wings, which may account for the external contrivances of his plotting and the icy finger that touches his situations, while Chekhov sits with us in the stalls, accepts his own bruises and understands their pain for having suffered them himself.

The supreme difference is that Chekhov's fundamental concern is to give us the feel of life by showing us the balance of life. Every character and every attitude shall be seen from two sides or more; every posture of body or mind is its own critic, and this is to be demonstrated without distorting the truth. We are to understand this ambiguity as well in the tiny detail as in the structure of a play as a whole. So Medviedenko, the schoolmaster in *The Seagull*, declares his love to Masha: 'I love you. I can't stay at home because of my longing for you...'[1] To which Masha responds thus: 'I feel touched by your love, but I can't return it, that's all. (*Holds out the snuff box.*) Have some snuff.' Simply done, this gesture tells us all

[1] Anton Chekhov, *The Seagull and Other Plays*, trans. E. Fen (London, 1954).

we need to know of Masha's mood at this point, and Chekhov with a quick stroke effectively kills for the audience the pathos in the episode, though Medviedenko will whine on to the end.

So Natasha, the sister-in-law in *Three Sisters*, comes upon her husband reading a book: 'What are you doing, Andriusha? Reading? It's all right, I only wanted to know...'[1] Recognizably commonplace, this tiny episode is implicit with information and ironic feeling. Act I had just brought the curtain down on a 'shy' little Natasha busily capturing her man. Within a moment of the rise of the curtain on Act II, we know not only that they are married, but what sort of marriage it is, and will be. Andrey has lost his liberty and gained a domestic tyrant for a wife. Meanwhile, at another level, there lies implicit in Natasha's query the suggestion that touches off the next dramatic development: she is making the indirect approach of a woman who has something other on her mind and who means to speak of it. So our gorge rises slightly; we feel a sympathy with poor Andrey; and yet—the incongruity between what Natasha says and what she means is irresistibly funny on the stage. Our comic sense of human behaviour is tickled, and Chekhov has achieved his object of forcing upon us the gentle pangs of an ambivalent response.

'It is necessary', declared Chekhov, 'that on the stage everything should be as complex and as simple as in life. People are having dinner, and while they're having it, their future happiness may be decided or their lives may be about to be shattered.'[2] At about the same time, Maeterlinck was saying:

There is an everyday tragedy which is more real, deeper and more in keeping with our true existence than the tragedy of great adventures...I have come to think that an old man, seated in his armchair, simply waiting beside the lamp, listening, without knowing it, to all the eternal laws that reign about him, interpreting, without understanding it, what there is in the silence of the doors and windows and in the small voice of the light...I have come to think that this motionless old man was living in reality a deeper, more human and more general life than the lover who strangles his mistress, the captain who wins a victory or the husband who avenges his honour.[3]

[1] Anton Chekhov, *Three Plays*, trans. E. Fen (London, 1951).
[2] Quoted by D. Magarshack, *Chekhov the Dramatist* (London, 1952), p. 118.
[3] Maeterlinck, *Le Trésor des humbles*, quoted by M. Lamm, *Modern Drama*, trans. K. Elliott (Oxford, 1952), pp. 155–6.

These two writers approach the same goal from opposite sides, Chekhov as the comedian, Maeterlinck as the tragedian.

Neutralizing the pathetic with the comic and vice versa grows to be the sharpest weapon of the twentieth-century dramatist, incisive in effect, but all too easy to abuse. The swing of the pendulum within our minds sets up a fresh dramatic impulse over which the author has sole control. There seems to be a general principle to be observed here. The opposites must be so balanced as not to destroy, but to sustain, each other. We may be inclined to judge particular effects in Brecht and Tennessee Williams as both discordant and unbalanced when we feel the pendulum shudder.

Thus in Brecht's *Galileo*, we are, through our special knowledge, aware of the revolutionary implications of his telescope, and we sympathize with him as he tries to report on his vision of scientific development. But, for arbitrary reasons of uncertain satire, Galileo's genuine passion is echoed by the stupidity of the counsellors, who see only amusement or personal gain in the invention. The spectator can react only with irritation, not against the counsellors, who should offer the pleasure of derisory laughter, but against the ingenuous clumsiness of the balance in the scene.

The naïve concluding moments of Act II of Williams's *Cat on a Hot Tin Roof* follow these lines:

BRICK. How about these birthday congratulations, these many, many happy returns of the day, when ev'rybody but you knows there won't be any!

(*Whoever has answered the hall 'phone lets out a high, shrill laugh; the voice becomes audible saying:* 'No, no you got it all wrong! Upside down! Are you crazy?')

The evident intention here is for outside trivialities to grate sharply on the strung-up nerves of Big Daddy at precisely this moment of his disillusion. We are to resent the intrusion of the voice at the telephone to the same extent as we feel with Big Daddy the agony of his son's disclosure. But at this, the crisis of the scene, the horror of the father's self-deception has already made its mark: it offers an extreme of irony in itself. The irreverence of the family chorus at this point can only be gratuitous, and increasingly so:

BRICK. You told *me*! I told *you*!
(*A child rushes into the room and grabs a fistful of fire-crackers and runs out again.*)
CHILD (*screaming*). Bang, bang, bang, bang, bang, bang, bang, bang, bang!

Williams seems at present unable to judge when his play stands at the edge of the precipice—in *A Streetcar Named Desire*, too, he wrote one scene too many, unnecessarily sending Blanche to the madhouse as Kowalski shuffled the cards.

This effect of dramatic punctuation is not to be compared with the upstage laughter of Soliony and Tuzenbach, interpolated between the declarations of false optimism from Irena and Olga at the opening of another anniversary scene, Act I of Chekhov's *Three Sisters*:

OLGA. ...Oh, Heavens! When I woke up this morning and saw this flood of sunshine, all this spring sunshine, I felt so moved and so happy! I felt such a longing to get back home to Moscow!
CHEBUTYKIN (*to Tuzenbach*). The devil you have!
TUZENBACH. It's nonsense, I agree.

If the device is not delicate, at least the balance is precise, perhaps because at this early place in the play we do not resist the ironies as they are established, perhaps because they are created too subtly to disturb the naturalistic convention. Naturalism admits apparent irrelevancies. Who does not feel that Williams's presentation of Big Daddy's agony of mind is larger than life, and that the offstage interpolations tip the balance of credibility? *Cat on a Hot Tin Roof* drops too easily into melodrama.

Chekhov the dramatist learned his craft from two exacting masters, the short story and the one-act vaudeville sketch, the former being of especially great importance. He learned from Flaubert and Maupassant, Turgeniev and Tolstoy the detachment of the realist, and he taught himself to work from the minute observation of the raw material of everyday experience. He taught himself how to *see*. As J. Middleton Murry recognized, in the early days of Chekhov's introduction to the English literary world, 'immediate consciousness' was the criterion, and Chekhov strove to assemble 'those glimpses of reality which in themselves possess a peculiar vividness, and by virtue of this vividness appear to have a peculiar significance'.[1] The linking together of such glimpses in a particular and suggestive sequence accounts for the odd sense we carry away from both story and play of an implied, indirect statement; we know that 'nothing has happened', but we feel that a great deal has been 'said', and moreover said in a personal way and with a personal vision. For want of a better term, this manner of communication has been called 'impressionism'; at least the word rejects the idea that Chekhov, the supreme naturalist, was a mere photographer.

Through writing his stories, too, he learned to make his characters inseparable from their surroundings: people and places gently merge into each other. He learned to convey personality by what the person does not do as well as by what he does, and in the enforced economy of the short story the briefest touch must do this. He found this method invaluable for his drama, which accepts a similar physical economy. A multitude of quick, slight brush-strokes paint a complete portrait of the character as we see him, as he sees himself and as others see him. Chekhov perfected a kind of shorthand of communication. Through fine details he achieves a special precision, and apparent trivialities acquire a cumulative power of meaning we cannot resist because we have already swallowed so many so easily. He tells his story simply, without artificial devices, and we are left with recognizable experience, all of it essentially real and normal.

Chekhov insists, in a letter to a woman writer, 'You may weep and moan over your stories, you may suffer together with your heroes, but I consider one must do this so that the reader does not notice it. The more objective, the stronger will be the effect.'[2] Any such objectivity makes it almost impossible for us to find the author in his characters, and the technique tears down all barriers between ourselves and his subject. This is, of course, the way of Shakespeare and of all good dramatists. The author enters his narrative only to control the ironies which are to control us. Yet, as we shall see, these same ironies ensure that his vision of life is present and is felt. The

[1] J. Middleton Murry, *Discoveries* (London, 1924), pp. 142–3.
[2] Quoted in W. Gerhardi, *Anton Chehov, a Critical Study* (London, 1949), p. 110.

loneliness of man, the illusions he treasures, the mutability of his brief existence, are Chekhov's special province, and such methods as we have described make of such improbable material possible subjects for the artist.

This clipped account of his short-story writing has also indicated some of his qualities as a dramatist. In comparing play with story, we usually think of the differences: the physical limitations of the theatre as against the freedom with time and space possible to the story; the need to provide for the spoken word and bodily action of the actor, as against the power of the story-writer to make words think and tell. But the short story's call for unity and economy is that of the play; and the short story's answer in the use of impressionistic suggestion is the play's too. From both, we the audience deduce, we contribute and we create. As well as describe, naturalistic detail can hint and evoke, and the evocation can be that of poetry. The more we work, the less ground we cover, but the deeper we delve.

From pot-boilers and vaudevilles, like *The Proposal, The Bear* and *The Anniversary*, which seem simple but which Chekhov found fully demanding, he learned to create what he called 'a special kind of mood', admittedly 'a mood full of high spirits'.[1] These are plays entirely of situation, comic through a bald incongruity. *The Proposal* is an account of a gentleman who comes to make a proposal of marriage, but instead finds himself making an argument. *The Bear* is an account of another gentleman who comes to make a demand for payment of a bill, but instead finds himself making a proposal of marriage. And so on. There is great fun and mimicry and gusto here, and much apparently inconsequential dialogue and 'business'. But come to play one of these little plays, and one quickly finds that nothing is wasted, and that many minor incongruities are employed to enforce the major contradiction upon which the play turns.

When Chekhov found his dramatic 'conscience' and evolved a final convention within which to write, he was well prepared. *The Seagull* seems to be about a boy whose series of frustrations and failures in his writing and in his love for Nina eventually drive him to suicide. But the play is properly a comedy of time passing, of

---

[1] D. Magarshack, *Chekhov the Dramatist* (London, 1952), p. 54.

youth and idealism wryly countered by age and experience. For Treplev is weak and lacks faith in himself, and we cannot admire him; he is no hero and no one in the play gains by his loss. His mother, Mme Arkadina, is an ageing actress, and she simply grows older. Trigorin, the successful writer who steals Nina from him, is no villainous roué; he just makes himself unhappier. Old Sorin yearns for his youth as before. Masha, though still in love with Treplev, marries the dull old schoolmaster after all, but regrets it from the start. Her mother Paulina loves Dr Dorn, a man who virtually remains unaware of her. With this procession of negatives, the play cannot be a tragedy: it could well, however, have been a farce. Yet *because* the drama is enacted with delicate, springing touches for the most part, and not with brash and heavy jolts upon our sensibilities, the totality of the play is extraordinarily acceptable even today.

The naturalism of the play is not so restrictive that it does not allow room for a suggestive symbolism, and the imagination blossoms under its spell. The moonlight of Act I captures the dreamy, autumnal mood in which the characters are at first held; the thundery weather grows to a storm; the derelict stage of Act IV is a mark of thwarted ambition and a sad reminder of a gayer mood; the seagull itself is a symbol of a mother trampling over her son, of a young girl nearly ruined, of beauty disfigured. More organic than the symbols, the pattern of relationships works itself into our minds: the young turn to the old for understanding; the old, with the sole exception of Paulina and Dr Dorn, are concerned only for themselves.

All characters and all relationships play variations on the theme of 'I want', but every individual hunger, however trivial, offers a killing contrast to every other. Thus when Nina is speaking the earnest words of Treplev's play, Paulina is thinking of her beloved Doctor, Arkadina is in reality thinking of herself:

NINA. '[The Devil] is bored without Man...'
PAULINA (*to Dorn*). You've taken off your hat. Put it on before you catch cold.
ARKADINA. The doctor's taken his hat off to the Devil, the father of Eternal Matter.
TREPLEV (*flaring up, loudly*). The play's over! Enough of it! Curtain!

When Paulina speaks, Arkadina looks, and so we all look, and Treplev's reproach is addressed to actor and to audience too. Again, when the family group nonchalantly plays lotto towards the *dénouement* of the play, each character is engrossed in his or her own interests: Arkadina in her reception at Kharkov, the bailiff Shamrayev in money, Masha in her wounded feelings for Treplev, Paulina perhaps in the worries of her daughter, Trigorin in his position as a writer faced by younger competition; and Sorin snores in his chair. Meanwhile a tragedy is being enacted off-stage. Treplev, alone, is playing a melancholy waltz and considering the taking of his own life. This is an orchestration of discordant instruments which only harmonize within our own imagination.

Yet amongst all this there is no sentimentality. There are better people, Paulina, Dorn, Nina, and there are worse. Arkadina is a little vicious and egotistical, but we are compelled to laugh, for example, at her gift of one rouble to be shared between three servants. Masha is heart-broken at losing Treplev, but she can still play cards with zest. We love Medviedenko for his concern for his baby and his four-mile walk home, yet his teacher's tones and his obsession at all times with his salary are ludicrous. So we smile at all these people. Masha's initial appearance in black, and her statement 'I am in mourning for my life', funny and pathetic together, strike the note heard through the whole play. With *The Seagull*, Chekhov properly inaugurates the dark comedy of modern times.

This play did not satisfy Chekhov's demand for perfect balance: the final suicide of Treplev displayed the vestigial remains of another way of playwriting. *Uncle Vanya*, which followed, did not, however, take him much further forward. Vanya also wishes to kill, but this time the target is missed with a 'Damnation!' and a 'Devil take it!' His drama of hatred for his unfeeling brother-in-law the Professor, and of desire for the Professor's indifferent young wife Elena, thus ends in nothing. But the framework of the play is still conventional, the mood is more heavily handled than in any of the last great plays, and the balance of critical sympathy is not achieved without sentiment.

Three Sisters truly marks another departure. We meet another family, living a provincial life which torments them, and all yearning for Moscow as their means of escape. Like Beckett's tramps, they do not, of course, go. Irena, the youngest and weakest, declares irresponsibly, 'Oh, how good it must be to be a workman,' and does not turn a hand. She seeks marriage as the only way she knows to broaden her life, but her lover is killed meaninglessly. Olga is bored to exhaustion with teaching in school, but she finally accepts a permanent position and resigns herself to staying where she is. Masha has married another dull schoolmaster, and consequently has fallen in love with the idea of falling in love with Vershinin, colonel of the regiment lately garrisoned in the town. The regiment moves on; Masha stays behind. Their brother Andrey wanted to be a professor and so go to Moscow, but he makes the mistake of marrying a girl who saps his strength. She has a baby by another man and sells the house over their heads. But this recital of a 'plot' hardly suggests the spirit of the play. For the play is not about externals, but about a pattern of feeling which weaves itself in a felicitous design of delicate human entanglements.

To weave the strands together and adjust an equal emphasis on each of the four central characters draws attention to their meaning as a family group. 'Events' occur only to reorient the group as a whole, and a mood spreads through the whole company, modified and recast as it is touched by each of their idiosyncrasies in turn.

At the rise of the curtain, we learn that it is Irena's saint's day. Cheerful midday sunshine shines on to the stage. Olga is thinking of the past, and this makes her happy, if in a quaveringly nostalgic way: 'I remember so well how everything in Moscow was in blossom by now, everything was soaked in sunlight and warmth.' It is a bright, warm memory, and it is associated with beloved Moscow. Masha, absorbed in a book, has heard all this before and whistles a tune under her breath; she is not unhappy, but her whistling serves to underline the indirect comment on Olga's remarks made by the men laughing upstage. This touches off a more unpleasant sensation in poor Olga: 'Masha, do stop whistling! How can you? (*A pause*.) I suppose I must get this continual headache because I have to go to school every day and go on teaching right into the evening...' Her mention of

Moscow has meanwhile set in motion Irena's series of thoughts, pushing vaguely into the future: '...Sell the house, finish with our life here, and go back to Moscow.' A few minutes later the arrival of Vershinin starts a new train of feelings, and high spirits all round become irrepressible. Yet we are already made to feel the nostalgia and to judge the equivocal quality of their lives. There is a warm, dry humour in this detached view of simple human behaviour.

It is simple without being simplified: that is Chekhov's genius. As in life, we dare take nothing at face value. How far is Masha's love for Vershinin in reality a reproach to Kulyghin, her mild little husband? How far is Vershinin's love for Masha the sexual vanity of the male looking for pity? How far is Natasha's marriage with Andrey a social revenge for the ill manners of the sisters? Are Kulyghin's feelings for his wife, his attempts to amuse her by wearing a comic beard, for example, fit for our laughter or for our tears? Is Irena's resolution to marry Tuzenbach selfish or unselfish? How real is her grief when he is killed in the duel with Soliony? These and countless other questions that flash through our minds during performance are all of the intangible mysteries of human relationships, each complicated by two or more variable human factors, denying any complete solution.

There are countless small moments, like the following, when the feelings of the characters cannon off each other like so many balls on a billiard table. Tuzenbach has suggested that Masha should play in a public concert in aid of the victims of the fire which occurs in Act III. Kulyghin, so very proud that his own wife is being praised, agrees joyfully that she plays 'wonderfully well'. Irena provides a dry comment which shatters the atmosphere and reminds us of the forlorn creature under discussion: 'She's forgotten how to! She hasn't played for three years...or maybe it's four.' Then a comment from Kulyghin unwittingly hints at a reason for this: '...But would it be quite proper for her to play in a concert?' A devastating pause, carefully planned by the author, marks his narrow slavishness, and during the raw silence which follows, we and each of the characters feel the appalled reaction of everyone else. Even Kulyghin feels an irritation, and he flounders for an apology till we feel there can be no harm in him: 'I don't know anything about these matters, my friends. Perhaps it'll be perfectly all right. But you know, although our director is a good man, a very good man indeed, and most intelligent, I know that he does hold certain views...Of course, this doesn't really concern him, but I'll have a word with him about it all the same, if you like.' Our affectionate animosity thaws him into life.

The play ends as it began. But the sisters now stand huddled together as the military band fades into the distance, declaring with vehemence that 'life isn't finished' for them yet. And into this still, ironical microcosm of life the neutral indifference of every day flows as before. Kulyghin bustles in with Masha's hat and cape, happy to have her to himself again. Andrey, the would-be professor, pushes out the pram for the baby's constitutional. The useless old doctor sings quietly to himself:

CHEBUTYKIN. Tarara-boom-di-ay...I'm sitting on a tomb-di-ay...
(Reads the paper.) What does it matter? Nothing matters!
OLGA. If only we knew, if only we knew!...   *(Curtain)*

It is difficult to describe and explain the drama of Chekhov in terms other than those of the plays themselves, and this is especially true of his crowning achievement, the most complex and perhaps the greatest of all modern plays, *The Cherry Orchard*. For this reason, some extended analysis of the play's last act has been attempted in the next section.

ANALYSIS: 'THE CHERRY ORCHARD', ACT IV

The Cherry Orchard is a play which represents an attitude to life under stress and a way of life in transition. The orchard itself summarizes the hopes and regrets, the desires and ideals of this way of life. Just as the orchard with the town on the horizon epitomizes all Russia, so the play in its structure at once encompasses the range of social class from landowner to domestic serf, and brings the past hard against the future in its three or four generations. It achieves in its design as wide a statement as a naturalistic play could hope to do.

In the last act of the play, this structure of change and decay is welded into a firm whole, both because its parts are here drawn together and because the sympathies of the audience are under careful restraint and precise control. In this act the crescendo of finely chosen discords is heard and felt with inimitable impact. The following account is written, not to repeat what is well known, but to discover how the impact is caused.

The mood of the act is conjured immediately with the rise of the curtain. It is late autumn and the cherry trees stand bare outside the window. The nursery is in a pitiful state of nudity, with fade-marks on the walls where the pictures were, furniture stacked or covered with dust-sheets, luggage waiting for removal. 'There is an oppressive sense of emptiness.' It was a brilliant stroke to have this final scene played in the nursery of Act I rather than in the drawing-room of Act III, not only to balance the arrival of the family with their departure, but also because a setting of birth and childhood challenges the affections of *all* the generations, young and old.

Lopakhin isolated

In the desert spaces of this room stands waiting the new master of the cherry orchard, now an embarrassed and rather lonely man, Lopakhin. Embarrassed because the family has always been unable to forget his peasant origins; lonely because he now realizes how he has hurt those he loved by taking from them what they loved. He waves his arms a little in nervousness; beside him stands Yasha with a tray of champagne, Lopakhin's offering of farewell, according to Russian custom. He has done what is expected, but coming from him this same champagne needles them all, except Yasha.

We in the audience take in the situation at a glance: this is a situation we can recognize and know from experience. We can fully understand, and thus sympathize with, this man in this position, but if we see him only at the level of one who has to speed the parting guest, the irony of his situation keeps us from a complete identity. We now see him as the merchant away from his merchandise, the shopkeeper out of his shop, fish out of water, for all that, as Chekhov told Stanislavsky,[1] 'he must behave with the utmost courtesy and

---

[1] Quoted by D. Magarshack, *Chekhov the Dramatist* (London, 1952), p. 275.

decorum, without any vulgarity or silly jokes...it must be borne in mind that such a serious and religious girl as Varya was in love with Lopakhin; she would never have fallen in love with some cheap moneymaker.' We see him in his 'white waistcoat and brown shoes' (Chekhov writing to Nemirovich-Danchenko), taking long strides when he is lost in thought, stroking his beard back and forth. At this moment the comedy of his characterization half rises to the surface.

The irony of his situation is accentuated, too, because Chekhov so carefully contrasts this scene with the last. Act III bustled visually to an emotional climax; Act IV is toned so much lower as to be almost an anticlimax. It offers a pause in its first few minutes for us to soak up its bitterness. We left Lopakhin in a drunken hysteria, proclaiming half in joy, half in self-reproach, 'Here comes the new landowner, here comes the owner of the cherry orchard!' He is now involved in the complexities of sentiment which surround the departing family, unable fully to grasp what we in our Olympian seats assimilate in a flash.

His helplessness is enacted when Mme Ranevsky and her brother Gaev enter feverishly, cross the stage quickly, and go off, leaving him standing there perplexed, offering them the champagne they have ignored: 'Have some champagne, please do, please!' We balance this gesture against the depth of feeling in Mme Ranevsky; yet, in its own way, it too commands our sympathy.

The exchanges which follow with Yasha and Trofimov are all to explore the nature of Lopakhin's embarrassment with that clinical eye which is to keep us alert to the meaning of his suffering. The same Lopakhin is there displaying his classical comic obsession: business-like in his appreciation of the cash value of the wine— 'eight roubles a bottle', he tells Yasha; business-like in his time-keeping—'there are only forty-six minutes before the train's due to leave'. Though Chekhov uses him to supply one of his illuminating moments of the mood and atmosphere in the house with his 'it's devilishly cold in here', the practical man with his feet on the ground must add, 'Good building weather'.

Thus by suggestion we are told that Lopakhin is floundering, and the more he turns for reassurance to matters of money, of time and of business, measurable, accessible, firm and concrete things, the more we smile. Should we have wept to see him unable to cope with the huge and complex agony of a lost cause? So he puppets it back and forth across the bare stage, obeying the little laws of his own habits, while we weigh his inadequacy with mixed amusement against tender impressions sustained over three acts.

Trofimov and Lopakhin: twin clowns

The image grows denser when Trofimov, with an incongruous air of efficiency and youthful egotism, enters echoing Lopakhin: 'I think it's time to start. The horses are at the door.' We begin to notice now how Chekhov applies pressure to our sense of time in this last act, squeezing out our sympathy for the general distress on the stage, while at the same time neatly indicating how little the 'eternal student's' assumption of command for the operation of departure is justified. Against Lopakhin's 'We must start in twenty minutes. Hurry up' is set the dubious 'I think...' of Trofimov. Especially since he is chiefly bothered because he cannot find his goloshes; and in a personal flutter he calls to the one least likely at this time to be able to help him—Anya (it is Varya who throws a pair of goloshes at him a few minutes later). The humble detail derides the total appearance.

However, Lopakhin is grateful to have someone, even someone he in his soul despises, to talk to at the moment. Without being asked, he pours out his heart with an abrupt, 'And I must be off to Kharkov...' Then follows a long speech during which he is talking only to himself. Meanwhile Trofimov continues to hunt among the luggage and ignore him, until a breathless pause from Lopakhin brings Trofimov to a halt. With a bitter look and a curt reply, Trofimov puts him in his place: 'We'll soon be gone, then you can start your useful labour again.' Trofimov can be cruel in a way that the family itself would never dare to be.

Lopakhin now begins to draw on our sympathy more warmly, and it is Trofimov who comes more under scrutiny. Lopakhin in a sudden gesture of friendship, prompted perhaps by guilt, offers some of the champagne which Yasha is busily quaffing alone upstage. He is curtly refused. A little quarrel flashes out, and the sparks of their slight differences in social class and their greater differences in wealth catch fire, reminding us dramatically that behind the emotionality of the farewell unquenched antagonisms still burn:

LOPAKHIN. Well, well...I expect the professors are holding up their lectures, waiting for your arrival!
TROFIMOV. That's none of your business.
LOPAKHIN. How many years have you been studying at the university?
TROFIMOV. I wish you'd think up something new, that's old and stale. Incidentally, as we're not likely to meet again, I'd like to give you a bit of advice...

He goes on to criticize the 'wide, sweeping gestures' of Lopakhin's talk about building villas. We know that his criticism is really a criticism of himself, since he is the one who speaks in wide, sweeping gestures. We know, furthermore, that a Lopakhin who can buy the cherry orchard can also calculate precisely the profits from its summer residents. This is a farcical quarrel of tit-for-tat, but one with an ugly gist.

As if he suddenly realizes that he is dealing with a man of different calibre from himself, indeed that he may be saying things he will regret, Trofimov lets his anger die quickly. He sees that his comments on Lopakhin's personal behaviour have hurt far more than any criticism of his business methods: this attack on Lopakhin's social graces is of course a direct thrust at his class background. So Trofimov retracts and intuitively says the right thing, incidentally illuminating a little the mystery of the most complex character in the play: 'When all's said and done, I like you, despite everything. You've slender, delicate fingers, like an artist's, you've a fine, sensitive soul...' We are reminded of Lopakhin's dreams in Act II, that men should be 'giants' to live in consonance with a country of 'vast forests, immense fields, wide horizons'.

They would then have parted friends, and the moral would have suggested itself, we may suppose, that there is a basis for progress and co-operation between opposing classes on grounds of human tolerance, and so on, and so forth. Chekhov indeed hints at the need to link industry with culture and culture with industry, as he does less obliquely in the mouth of Vershinin in *Three Sisters*. But here Chekhov doesn't allow us any such immediate response. Lopakhin, in a final mistaken gesture of friendship, offers the younger man money for his journey—the sort of offer he might have valued himself in earlier days perhaps, an offer that makes sense to the practical man he is. Trofimov is of course touched on another raw spot. He sees Lopakin's generosity as a further sign of the vulgarity that distinguishes them, and the quarrel again flares up. He tells a lie about having had a translation accepted in order to refuse with dignity. They are, we recognize, two of a kind in matters of personal pride.

So Trofimov the idealist speaks. He is a free man, money can mean nothing to him, and, with the grand, abstract sweep of the arm of one who has nothing to lose and everything to gain, he drops into cliché:

> Humanity is advancing towards the highest truth, the greatest happiness that it is possible to achieve on earth, and I am in the van!
>
> LOPAKHIN. Will you get there?
>
> TROFIMOV. Yes. (*A pause.*) I'll get there myself, or show others the way to get there.

In that pause Chekhov allows just time enough to let the insidious irony seep back. During that moment of hesitation, Chekhov permits us to pin down all youthful revolutionary leaders with their own doubts: pathetic Trofimov becomes comic again, and Lopakhin makes his point. The vision of a glorious future clouds slightly, but it does not disappear, for we hear of it again with Anya. As if to mark the impression, the first sound of an axe cutting into a cherry tree is heard distantly off-stage. 'Life is slipping by,' says Lopakhin in a real gesture of shared sympathy, and irreverently identifies Trofimov's grand rhetoric, as we have already done, with infinite numbers of us, and not merely in Russia: 'How many people there are in Russia, my friend, who exist to no purpose whatever! Well, never mind, perhaps it's no matter.' He at least feels happier for working hard—he slips into the pragmatic view of the practical man again.

These two in their characteristic duologue embrace the conflict in our own minds. They offer not merely a restatement of a class difference in society, or of youthful idealism corrected by a maturer wisdom, though this symbolism is there. For it is a mark of the darkness of the comedy that both of these characters are specimens of broken-hearted clown: neither can therefore teach us a complete truth or give us a final answer. In the acumen of the one and the optimism of the other, Chekhov points to a rooted error of judgment. Behind them both lies the fading nostalgic beauty of all the cherry orchard stood for when circumstances were different. Chekhov is not indicting the Russian merchant or the Russian intellectual, any more than he is telling us what fools Lopakhin and Trofimov are: Chekhov is more subtle than this. There is some truth in Lopakhin's view and some in Trofimov's. We are to imagine a blend of Lopakhin and Trofimov, perhaps together with a little of Anya's lack of affectation and a good deal of Mme Ranevsky's heart. He is pressing us, in other words, to take a more balanced view. We are to discover that these two confused men are, like us, groping in a dark room while an unknown hand moves the furniture. Their differences of pragmatism and ideality are those that struggle within ourselves with each new experience that comes. If Chekhov leaves us in uneasy doubt about the righteousness of either, it is to encourage us towards impartiality; it is to induce a greater awareness of serious comic meaning in the extraordinary series of little episodes, particularities and attitudes that make up the *dénouement* of the play.

Infinitesimal tragedy: Yasha and the servants

As if suddenly to reduce the scale of our view, Chekhov now places the manservant Yasha centre-stage and completes the little story of the triangle Epihodov–Dunyasha–Yasha.

Yasha would be the one unsympathetic character in the play were he not also a little comic, and one must ask the reasons for this. As Lopakhin represents the new aristocracy of business-men, so Yasha represents a new breed of underlings, the smart servants who cheat their masters and lord it over their equals. They astutely take advantage of the social changes that only bewilder their superiors.

They grease their hair, Chekhov is saying, and, when they can, they smoke cigars and ape their betters. They can mesmerize silly girls like Dunyasha, and, for what they are worth, break their hearts. They despise the genuine affection towards the family of a domestic serf like old Firs. For Chekhov they sum up all that is *poshlost*, vulgar.

Somewhat indirectly, Yasha is to suggest what might happen to the minds of the other young people of the same generation, like Anya and Trofimov, had they too to fend for themselves in a commercial world. In this he is the complement of Lopakhin, illuminating a side of this character we would not otherwise see, the Smerdyakov facet of Dostoevsky's Ivan Karamazov, the Svidrigailev of his Raskolnikov. He is denied any of Lopakhin's sensitivity and generosity of spirit. Now a little drunk from champagne, he speaks with casual disrespect to Anya when she inquires whether Firs, his foil, has been taken to hospital: 'I told them to take him this morning. He's gone, I think.' But Anya knows Yasha too well, and calls to Epihodov, 'Semyon Panteleyevich, will you please find out whether Firs has been taken to hospital?' Yasha is not concerned. With the gentlest of touches, we are told incisively that the man is wholly egocentric and contemptuous of all about him.

This is confirmed when Varya calls that his mother has come to say goodbye to him before he returns to Paris. This reminder of his former life is unwelcome, and he shrugs off her old-fashioned sentiment with a superior air: 'She just makes me lose patience with her.' We may criticize this as altogether too strongly contradicting psychological truth: a rejection of a mother by her son shocks. It condemns him, and illuminates the impression that was dim before, that there is an amoral and destructive aspect of progress. Like Lopakhin's unwitting negation of what is personally delicate and living in the cherry orchard home, like the eliminating of the Mme Ranevskys who have their own contribution to make to the harmony of existence, subtle changes in the social order can tear up what is deep-rooted and valuable in human life.

Unlike some farcical intrusions into modern domestic comedy, Yasha's presence in the play is relevant to the whole. His part faintly echoes that of Lopakhin, for it shows us how silly ignorance may injure silly innocence. This is done lightly: the regrets and distress of Dunyasha, the pert maidservant, are her just deserts; there is no real suggestion that Epihodov's love for her has been mortally wounded—no melodrama here. In their miniature comedy, played very much in the remoter background, Epihodov is the sort who can say how much he envies Firs because he is 'beyond repair' and must soon 'join his ancestors', and this part, written for brittle comedy, written for the Russian comedian Moskvin,[1] must exclude bitterness. In the same way, Dunyasha is quite an accomplished actress: she shams 'delicacy', falls too easily in and out of love, powders her nose, faints at appropriate moments, and so on. Her story must exclude tragedy, although it allows for pathos.

Nevertheless, all that Yasha stands for is thereby effectively diminished. He drinks his champagne in spite of the fact that 'it isn't the real thing', dreams of the journey in the express train, and longs for Paris where something is always 'going on', where there is less 'ignorance'. In view of the character who purveys these ideas, they are received by us only with scepticism. This is given open expression in laughter when Gaev enters, fixes one look on Yasha's hair, and says, 'Who's smelling of herring here?'

Mothers and babies: Lyubov, Anya and Charlotta

The late owners of the cherry orchard, Lyubov (Mme Ranevsky) and Gaev, are two lovable fools, held in affection by all around them. They now re-enter. 'In ten minutes we ought to be getting into the carriage...,' and again we are reminded of time. Time was dogging us through the scene of the party in Act III, and now we realize that its pressure is not only of dramatic hours and minutes, but a poetic urgency fixing a paralysed attention on the treasure that is escaping. The loss of the orchard, prefigured from the outset, has grown in the imagery of the play to mean the loss of a whole way of life, with all the particularity of its hopes and frustrations, all the living experience of its memories and its expectations. There are ten minutes left for us, as it were, breathlessly to savour its sadness.

In the grip of a genuine nostalgia and a deep regret, Mme

[1] N. A. Toumanova, *Anton Chekhov* (London, 1937), p. 201.

Ranevsky takes a last look round her nursery: 'Goodbye, dear house, old grandfather house.' With the simplest of epithets, Chekhov paints a picture of generations, while directly expressing the character's emotions. It would seem we are to expect an emotive sequel, flushed with sentiment. Yet there is an ironic edge to every gesture and statement which are to follow. Our view of the play remains carefully under control.

Lyubov's ardent kissing of Anya, with all her desire for her future happiness, hardly conceals the dilemma of a woman caught between her uncertain regret for the past and her uncertain hope for the future. She is not happy, but perhaps her daughter is:

> MME RANEVSKY. Are you glad? Very glad?
> ANYA. Yes, very. Our new life is just beginning, Mama!
> GAEV (*brightly*). So it is indeed, everything's all right now.

Anya unaffectedly sees no past standing over her like a judgment as her mother does: she unknowingly clouds the nostalgic image of the dear past, and looks fearlessly forward to a bright future. But we sense that Anya is her mother as she was, and Lyubov is as her daughter will be.

Gaev's effort of gaiety confirms the ambiguities beneath the surface of their mood. Our impression of the inadequacy of Mme Ranevsky, for all her unselfishness, is here as elsewhere reinforced by the greater weakness of her brother. This man who has no money-sense at all, who let the orchard slip between his fingers also, is simulating happiness as obviously as she: we immediately recognize his instinct to console himself. He tells us that he is to become a bank clerk, of all things, 'a financier'.

Passionately embraced and passionately embracing, Anya, the innocent who has yet to face the world of hard experience, dreams of Mama's return, of passing examinations and working hard...'We'll read during the long autumn evenings, we'll read lots of books, and a new, wonderful world will open up before us...' For a perceptible moment seventeen-year-old Anya reverses their roles; she is the little mother comforting Lyubov, till she relaxes into golden fancies. Almost symbolically the child curls up on the dust-sheet over the sofa, seeing with the bright eyes of youth, reassured by the caresses of the mother who tells her she will come back. We have the authority of the play's cumulative ironies to doubt what we see and hear.

In case we too grow sentimental over this imaginary prospect, too reassured by the archetype of mother and child, Chekhov plays an ace. He had brought in Charlotta, the German-bred governess, and has had her downstage, looking with our eyes at the scene. Now, half to cheer the company, it would seem, half to express her and our scepticism, she plays one of her tricks:

> (*Picking up a bundle that looks like a baby in swaddling clothes.*) Bye-bye, little baby. (*A sound like a baby crying is heard.*) Be quiet, my sweet, be a good little boy. (*The 'crying' continues.*) My heart goes out to you, baby!

This must strike us as a naughty burlesque of the pathetic exchange we have just seen, belittling and colouring the impression the other three have created. The burlesque is offered with less of the gentle, shaded touch so familiar in Chekhov, and more with that callous juxtaposition to be found later in works like Anouilh's *Point of Departure*. Chekhov feels it necessary to give a more severe shock to dispel the more subversive sentiment. It is Chekhov's command to us to return to earth, and it is enacted when Charlotta almost viciously throws the bundle down and says, 'Are you going to find me another job, please? I can't do without one.' She is practical, for we remember what she told us on the garden seat in Act II, that she does not know who her mother was, that she has no past, that she is alone—as Anya may well be.

By the matter-of-fact tone of her last remark, a moment of farce is turned to wormwood. 'You should only sit down to write', Chekhov told Bunin, 'when you feel as cold as ice.'[1]

Enter Simeonov-Pishchik, fatalist

Pishchik, 'strong as a horse', eternally penniless, high with blood-pressure, puffing and sweating, is most part clown. He is an ineffectual landowner from another cherry orchard, and we are really unable to take his financial distresses seriously. His constant

---

[1] W. H. Bruford, *Chekhov* (London, 1957), p. 15.

borrowing of money is his comic 'gimmick', and Gaev by his scuttling exit reminds us of Pishchik's apparent role in the play. He will enter now to provide us with some crazy horseplay perhaps, a little knock-about relief, 'what a phenomenon!' But he too has a calculated place in the pattern.

He blusters in, out of breath as usual, greeting Mme Ranevsky and Lopakhin, pouring a glass of water, fumbling in his pocket, swallowing a mouthful. Between his gasps for air and comic business with the tiresome glass, he drags from his pocket—a handful of notes! Too late he repays money that might have paid the mortgage interest on the unhappy estate. For in bewilderment he has found that science and progress have overtaken him unawares, to his advantage and amazement. In joy and confusion he explains what has happened: 'Wait a moment...I'm so hot...A most extraordinary thing happened. Some English people came to see me and discovered a sort of white clay on my land...'

His perpetual simple astonishment at the phenomena of life around him is now given real cause for expression. Foreign capital was in fact being invested in Russia in the 1890s. Now indeed he can ridicule his naïve search for a philosophical justification for the forgery of banknotes—or taking one's own life. 'Just now a young fellow in the train was telling me that some great philosopher or other...advises people to jump off roofs. You just jump off, he says, and that settles the whole problem...Fancy that!' Thus subtly, farcically, does the author drop a thought among the audience, brushing it off as soon as it has settled. The sequence of the dialogue suggests that Pishchik had thought for a gossamer moment of a resort to suicide: now providence has relieved him of the need, just as it had left her token, ignored, with Mme Ranevsky. Could this same thought have occurred to her?—oh, but no—we dismiss the idea: Chekhov is teasing.

As if to strengthen our feelings, Pishchik has dashed about the room, sat down, stood up, drunk his water and gone—at such a pace that we have hardly had time to assimilate the impression he leaves us with. He has gone without noticing that the family is on the eve of departure. Lyubov calls after him, and the pace abruptly halts as he turns back and looks unhappily about him. He sees the bare room at last. Something did not 'turn up' for them this time. His tone changes: 'Well, never mind. (*Tearfully*.) Never mind...These Englishmen, you know, they're men of the greatest intelligence... Never mind...I wish you every happiness, God be with you. Never mind, everything comes to an end eventually.' Jumping off the roof was not so outrageous a notion after all—'everything comes to an end eventually'. What was stated in jest is now echoed with deep embarrassment; the puppet becomes a man.

Pishchik's little scene, brief and funny and pathetic as it is, fits into the design. The comedy misleads us momentarily, but the contrast in the tempo of playing between the time of Pishchik's entrance and that of his exit again reorients by a fine degree the play's whole meaning. Pishchik's primary function is to introduce that recognizable element of fatalism into the structure of the life being demonstrated, though we remain free to dismiss it. The chance purchase of Pishchik's clay by the astonishing Englishmen is the counterpart of the sale of the cherry orchard: the positive and the negative of the same picture. Are we equally subject to chance? Only death is inevitable. Comic Pishchik epitomizes mankind faced with insoluble problems: in bewilderment he blusters with joy, and in the same bewilderment he frets in misery. It is all very droll.

Characteristically, Chekhov allows his good-hearted Pishchik a tender moment before he takes his departure from the play. This is quoted in all its subtlety, and without comment:

And when you hear that my end has come, just think of—a horse, and say: 'There used to be a fellow like that once...Simeonov-Pishchik his name was —God be with him!' Wonderful weather we're having. Yes...(*Goes out, overcome with embarrassment, but returns at once and stands in the doorway.*) Dashenka sent greetings to you. (*Goes out.*)

A proposal does not come off: Lopakhin and Varya

The tiny tragedy of Charlotta was followed by the tiny comedy of Pishchik, and this in turn is followed by the tiny tragedy of Varya. But just as Charlotta could never of course have risen to any real stature, neither can Varya. Chekhov wrote to Nemirovich-Danchenko that she was to be 'a little nun-like creature, somewhat simple-minded, plaintive'.[1] Plaintive, but still a comedienne: 'She is a crybaby by nature and her tears ought not to arouse any feelings of gloom in the audience.'[2]

Yet the sequence[3] which follows that of Pishchik's exit moves into the friendly territory of common experience far enough to colour the action with a sufficient tincture of pathos.

First Mme Ranevsky gives us another reminder of time: there are but five minutes remaining. However, as she insists, there is still time enough to settle a final problem, that of Varya's future. It is firmly in the mother's mind, in spite of many protestations from the parties concerned, that Lopakhin must propose to her. 'We have another five minutes or so...' A moment later: 'You'll hardly need more than a minute, that's all.'

Much of the comedy, and much of the pathos, of this episode rests upon counterpointing two senses of time: on the one hand, that which presses from without, the waiting carriage and the approaching train; and, on the other, the inner reluctance of Lopakhin, whose emotional indigestion makes it so impossible to hasten the passing of this most embarrassing moment. His scene with Varya is to be played so slowly as to make an audience conscious of an intentional dramatic meaning through tempo. The contrast with the quicker pace of Pishchik's speech and movement is to make us feel Lopakhin's own confusion of mind about time. When he looks at his watch and when he finally leaves the room in unseemly haste, we must be made to ask ourselves, Were these actions the result of his anxiety for the family's prompt departure, or for his own? If this scene is to illuminate one more facet of the agony of the relentless advance of tomorrow, we must feel the state of Lopakhin's shuttlecock mind in wanting the moment to fly, and yet wanting it to stop. He asks only that human relationships may resolve themselves in natural harmony, for they will not obey the clock.

Chekhov's dialogue for this episode is masterly. With brevity, and

[1] *The Selected Letters of Anton Chekhov*, ed. L. Hellman, trans. Lederer (London, 1955), p. 316. [2] D. Magarshack, *Chekhov the Dramatist* (London, 1952), p. 274.
[3] This scene is discussed in more detail in the author's *The Elements of Drama* (Cambridge, 1960), pp. 73 ff.

yet with an adroit mustering of points in favour of a marriage, Mme
Ranevsky is made to use all her feminine wit to accomplish a
mother's last duty to a daughter. She excuses her for looking thin
and pale. But this is only because she has no work to do—an appeal
to a Lopakhin who would be expected to want an industrious wife.
She tells him that her Varya cries a lot—an appeal to his protective
sympathies. Finally she tells him that Varya loves him—an appeal
to his masculine pride. '...And I just don't know, I just don't know
why you seem to keep away from each other. I don't understand it.'
She implies a question: What reason can you give for your delay?

What reason *can* Lopakhin give? We guess: although Varya is
only adopted into the household to earn her keep as a housekeeper,
perhaps an illegitimate daughter of Lyubov's husband, nevertheless,
like Lopakhin's purchase of the cherry orchard, his marriage to
Varya would perhaps be a glancing blow against social tradition,
which he has always instinctively accepted. Lopakhin could never
aspire to the manners and graces Varya has acquired in her years
with Lyubov. A social barrier, however, is hardly used by Chekhov
as a dramatic crux: there is to be no melodramatic gesture of
defiance. The mother wants the marriage, as does the foster-daughter;
but how strong are the ties that bind Lopakhin to the older respect
for class? There is no defiance in his proposal, and Lopakhin remains
human, humble, and no puppet. But he is equally reluctant to make
a proposal of marriage because he is as shy as any man might be.
Thus, with sure control, Chekhov presents a socially symbolic
situation under a wholly naturalistic guise, as he had done with
Trofimov's poverty, Yasha's pertness, Pishchik's unexpected wealth.
Neither Mme Ranevsky nor Lopakhin is aware of the forces present
on the stage with them at this moment of decision.

MME RANEVSKY. ...I don't understand it.
LOPAKHIN. Neither do I myself, I must confess. It's all so strange
somehow...

We feel Lopakhin's emotional immaturity and awkwardness compared with Mme Ranevsky's experience and grace. But the practical
man will at last face the situation, and other members of the family

are ushered out of the room, and Varya is called, while Lopakhin waits alone on the stage.

We are prepared for comic relief by the interminable pause that holds us in suspense after the exit of the mother. It is a pause redolent of the agony of making an irrevocable personal decision. We are held until we are ourselves self-conscious and Lopakhin's discomfiture is ours. So we are ready to laugh when we hear the 'suppressed laughter and whispering' of the others behind the door, and when in even greater embarrassment Varya enters pretending to hunt among the luggage: 'It's strange, I just can't find...' It is with this new pause that the character of the scene begins to change, and a warmth of feeling begins to spread over it.

In a series of false starts, Lopakhin tepidly endeavours to make the bright opening gambit which might lead to the happy embrace of a potential bride and groom. But each time his leading questions only stress the misery of Varya's present position, and because she is the 'simple-minded, plaintive' little creature presented in the play, they lead her quickly to tears. He asks where she will go now that the family is leaving—she will go to the Rogulins to be a housekeeper. What is worse, her post will be seventy miles away—it might as well be in the antipodes. Husband and home will be left far behind, and for both Varya and Lopakhin a marriage must be contracted now or never. 'So this is the end of life in this house...' Upon Lopakhin's saying this, Varya, in the anguish of nostalgia and longing, buries her tears furiously among the luggage. She has not dared to look at him.

Lopakhin has said the wrong thing, and he must start again. But the same nostalgia grips him too. As he looks out of the window, he sees the cold sun of autumn and feels the frost descending. With another of his fine imaginative strokes, Chekhov invokes the weather to epitomize the mood of the scene and at the same time extend and make articulate the feelings that surround the characters. The irony of Lopakhin's estimating the degrees of frost with the accuracy of a farmer, and of Varya's exasperated retort that their thermometer is broken, echoes painfully through a further long pause. Time rushes onwards.

Suddenly a voice, perhaps Epihodov's, calls his name, and

99

Lopakhin is gone, his dilemma resolved for him. Varya is left to weep uninhibitedly with her face in a bundle of clothes. The precious moment is destroyed. How? By fickle accident, by the pressure of extraneous situation, certainly by a human inadequacy, perhaps by a deeper power of birth and blood, by all these things, by Chekhov's seeing life like this in such moments of time.

The idea of the mutation of things emerges through a succession of innumerable minute insights that are discovered to us. It will depend on what we contribute to the interpretation of this episode, however, and what these characters have grown to represent to us, if we are to see the scene as something more than an unhappy little fragment in two small lives that do not matter so very much; the rather pathetic surface of the action on this level will fail to affect us or the play. However, we are so well prepared for the anticlimax when it comes that we must pay another kind of attention to its meaning.

The false starts and proprieties of the man, the gentility and discretion of the woman, our sense of the limitations of a conventional behaviour in such a situation as this, must vividly illuminate human weakness. Varya and Lopakhin, if indeed the busy man ever really wanted marriage, cannot make a sufficient adjustment to the requirements of change. Two small people who cannot see their position except subjectively are shown buffeted by forces they cannot recognize, even less control. With an appalling irony, Varya, virtual mistress of the house, who had thrown her keys at Lopakhin's feet in Act III, must now go to the Rogulins 'to be their housekeeper, or something'. While she becomes a servant, he will be master. Against such a reversal, Lopakhin's well-meaning decorums are wholly misplaced, almost laughable. A pathetic loneliness, half-conscious maybe, is balanced by a comic awkwardness.

Chekhov is saying to us, in as positive a way as he can without breaking his naturalistic convention, that the smashing of one order need not necessarily comprehend the end of an existing harmony of relationships, certainly not of individual happiness. He is inviting us to see the position with an objectivity denied to his characters. He does it by enlarging and emphasizing their feelings, and presenting these in the white light of their comic littleness.

Ensemble

Chekhov now crowds his stage in order to empty it at the curtain. This is his last opportunity to bring together his small host of characters with the cumulative impact of all their petty, but overwhelming, little troubles. Before he finally dismisses the world of the cherry orchard, its fragmentary impressions are to be blended into a total image.

The room fills with people, as it did in Act I when it was a springtime, happier time of homecoming: Varya, Mme Ranevsky, Anya, Gaev, Charlotta with her dog, Yasha, Epihodov, Dunyasha, with other servants and coachmen. Trofimov and Lopakhin will enter in a moment. The house bustles with life and urgency once more, but it is the urgency of departure. The attitudes characteristic of this or that generation, each with a contrasting outlook fixed upon the future or the past, are by simple strokes compressed into a tone of voice, a gesture, a familiar form of words, which seem to echo and re-echo from the far walls of the play till they merge into its sombre reverberations.

The mother who resigned herself so quickly to the failure of her plan that we suspect that she had hardly anticipated its success, says flatly, 'Now we can start on our journey.' But her heart is in the past. Anya, representative of a younger generation, happy at new prospects and widening experience, echoes her joyfully: 'Yes, our journey!' Equally unrealistic, she is living in the future. Gaev, overwhelmed with personal memories, is least in command of his feelings, and after his habit slips from sentiment into rhetoric: 'My friends, my dear, kind friends! Now as I leave this house for ever...' Here it is dear old Gaev whom Chekhov permits to strike the seemingly false note of comedy, and it is emphasized by the girls, who implore him to stop.

Amid all the activity of preparation and dressing and gathering of personal luggage, Mme Ranevsky sits centre-stage, silent and alone in a pool of quietness. By her stillness she catches our eye: 'I'll just sit down for one little minute more. I feel as if I'd never seen the walls and ceilings of this house before, and now I look at them with such longing and affection...' She is sincere and articulate about her emotions, and suddenly this apparently feather-weight heroine becomes solid for us: Chekhov uses her as his spokesman for the suffering, conscious and unconscious, of all. But only for that moment: she will be once more fussing about the luggage as soon as she hears her brother's voice take on the oratorical tone again. She tears herself out of her mood: 'Have they taken out all the luggage?' For us, the serious mood remains and continues under the surface of trivialities.

Now with inspired cunning, forcing us to enter into his peculiar war of nerves, the author has the most obvious comedian in the play, Epihodov, register his one truly fetching moment of pathos. As a result of Lopakhin's 'See that everything's all right, Epihodov', we digest the following exchange:

EPIHODOV (*in a husky voice*). Don't worry, Yermolai Alexeyevich!
LOPAKHIN. What are you talking like that for?
EPIHODOV. I've just had a drink of water. I must have swallowed something.
YASHA (*with contempt*). What ignorance!

Like Pishchik, Epihodov is allowed his feelings, however limited, before the end. But precisely because he has never before done other than make us mock at his emotion, his present frog in the throat startles us, just as it surprises Lopakhin and challenges Yasha. Yasha asserts his difference from the peasant by a characteristic remark of derision. This mild friction between the two servants adds nearly the last of the pieces to the jigsaw of class rivalries, here well thrust home by pressure of exceptional circumstances.

The limelight shines on Lopakhin too, for a last time. Again Chekhov cleverly serves a double dramatic purpose by a single expedient.

MME RANEVSKY. When we leave here there won't be a soul in the place...
LOPAKHIN. Until the spring.

Hearing the despondency in Lyubov's voice, he tries to respond with a brightly engaging comment. Like the realist he is, he is concerned with the present. But again he has said the wrong thing. In his odd effort to make amends, he has intensified her distress. Spring is when strangers will live where they live; spring is when the orchard would have been in blossom; spring was when they came home, only to leave again.

At this moment, Varya pulls an umbrella from a bundle. It flies up, and she seems to be about to strike him. In a gesture that catches our eye immediately, an echo of the incident with the billiard cue in Act III, Lopakhin's reaction summarizes in a flash his place in the pattern: he raises his arm to ward off the blow, and we are reminded of his peasant relationship with the family. Yet it also reflects his essential lack of confidence and the guilt he feels surging up as soon as he has spoken, that of his outrageous presumption in buying the estate. With a laugh, he promptly turns his instinctive fear into a little pantomime that relaxes the tension between himself and Varya and makes them friends again. Like the whole play, it is a token of confused emotions.

As a gesture, it is also a signal for renewed activity by everyone. Trofimov takes charge and orders the party into the carriage. Varya finds his goloshes at last—Chekhov leaves no detail unfinished. Trofimov has to put them on while still giving his orders—Chekhov deflates even his last assumption of dignity. Lopakhin efficiently counts the heads. Anya and Trofimov, the younger ones, leave first, hailing the future:

> ANYA. Goodbye, old house! Goodbye, old life!
> TROFIMOV. Greetings to the new life!

The older ones leave their lives behind them; youth has the world before it. The rest follow, Varya unwillingly, Yasha willingly, Charlotta coldly, Lopakhin warmly. Lyubov and Gaev are left alone, two small figures clasping each other in grief in the centre of the bare, blank stage.

Vacuum

With unparalleled simplicity of effect, Chekhov has his two forlorn puppets stand motionless in the deserted nursery. The cherry orchard is already forsaken, and they are the life that used to be. The

lightness in Mme Ranevsky is now heavy, her feelings squeezed dry:
and she says what the orchard and the house mean to her in explicit
terms. They expresss the salt and bitter taste, the uneasy ache of the
experience of the whole play: 'Oh my darling, my precious, my
beautiful orchard! My life, my youth, my happiness...goodbye!...
Goodbye!' The orchard is the symbol for just those things: life,
youth, happiness, and their passing. The symbolism is not a loose
sentimentality: it is recognized in the astringency of our criticism.

They listen, as we do, to the excited cries from Anya and Trofimov
impatient outside the house in the carriage, impatient to plant
another cherry orchard. A world outside is calling, and another
beyond that. Inside, the sobs of regret are counterpointed with the
shrill calls outside, until Lyubov and her brother leave: 'We're
coming...(*Both go out*)'. The play is over; the point is made.

But is it? The curtain refuses to fall, and Chekhov tries his most
daring stroke. For an age we sit looking at empty, half-lit space,
while the master of pauses employs the longest pause of his career.
We are to assimilate the implications of the drama by the tempo he
ordains: 'The stage is empty. The sound of doors being locked is
heard, then of carriages driving off. It grows quiet. The stillness is
broken by the dull thuds of an axe on a tree....' The spirit of the
cherry orchard is allowed time to seep into us, and by sheer radio-
genic dramatics, we learn what it is to be left in a house when all
have departed; we learn what it is to *be* that house and to feel the axe
in our soul. There is no comedy here now: it is all twilight.

We wait again for the curtain to fall, but again it does not. We hear
instead the shuffle, the slow shuffle of old feet, and we dimly discern
Firs as he creeps in. The old servant has been left behind in the
general confusion. He moves with difficulty to the door that has just
been bolted, tries it unsuccessfully, and stumbles to the sofa covered
with its dust-sheet. He sits. 'They forgot about me. Never mind...'
He is content, for the world outside no longer has any call upon
him. Those of his generation cannot lose their cherry orchard now.
At his age, neither past, present nor future has much meaning.
With a final prick of comedy, almost a lifetime is compressed in his
speech: 'I don't suppose Leonid Andreyevich pu: on his fur coat,

I expect he's gone in his light one.... These youngsters!' He lies still, while once more we await the fall of the curtain.

Yet even now there is a last bold trump to play: 'A distant sound is heard, coming as if out of the sky, like the sound of a string snapping, slowly and sadly dying away.' Just as Chekhov had gathered together his players for their last *ensemble*, visually gathering together the joy and the sadness, hope for the future and regret for the past, so he attempts to epitomize the mixture of all our feelings in one unearthly and inexplicable sound, the sound we heard, unexplained, in Act II. To interpret it is to interpret the whole play. The curtain falls slowly with this in our ears, this and the sound of an axe striking a tree in the orchard far away.

The teasing structure of *The Cherry Orchard* easily accounts for its misinterpretation by producers from Konstantin Stanislavsky onwards. Where Chekhov's effect rests on a knife-edge balance of comedy and pathos in so many details, it is only too easy to tip the play towards one or the other. By inclination the sentimental majority of us lean towards the emotionality of the passing of an order. The substitution of one world for another is an excuse for melodramatics. Yet Chekhov was constantly making a plea to redress the balance: 'I am writing about life...this is a grey everyday life indeed...but not an eternal whimpering.'[1] He believed that a full, objective statement of what he saw of the behaviour of people would be sufficient to paint the unbiased picture he wanted. Although some may feel he should have made more direct statements, relying less on the vagaries of arbitrary mood of the audience, less on the caprices which abound in the theatre, to the end he preferred, as he said, to *show* us horse-thieves rather than condemn them.

Chekhov put on the stage a group of people. He made this the centre of attention; not events, unless they affected the characters; not characters, unless they were to disturb or cast a reflection on the group. His group lives by the commonplaces of life they display, and these carry the weight of the play. Thus he found a form for drama suited to the stage. He is accused of having no plot, but it is not the

[1] Quoted by N. A. Toumanova, *Anton Chekhov* (London, 1937), p. 201, from V. Feider, *A. P. Chekhov, Literaturny byt* (Leningrad, 1928), p. 450.

absence of plot, rather the presence of many little plots, suggestive phases of many little lives woven intricately together, that gives his play its careful, taut pattern in which every detail is intensely relevant. Every detail is relevant, that is, to the creation of that particular balance of sympathies which can recreate for an audience the fluid feel of life. It is not a gallows humour he offers, nor mere exuberance, but it embraces each of us in its restless appeal to truth.

THE 'MOOD' PLAY

Chekhov is the master and the measure of a large variety of lesser dramatists, and indeed of film and television scriptwriters, in the twentieth century. The English-speaking theatre alone provides a good sample. Some incline towards melodrama, like Elmer Rice (*Street Scene*), Eugene O'Neill (*The Iceman Cometh*), Terence Rattigan (*The Deep Blue Sea*), John Osborne (*Look Back in Anger*) and Robert Bolt (*Flowering Cherry*); some towards comedy, like John van Druten (*I Am a Camera*), N. C. Hunter (*A Day by the Sea*), and William Inge (*Picnic*). Some achieve a good balance in a narrow field, like Granville-Barker (*The Madras House*), though he would not have known of Chekhov at the time, Carson McCullers (*The Member of the Wedding*), Paddy Chayefsky (*The Bachelor Party*) and Ray Lawler (*Summer of the Seventeenth Doll*). Some, like Tennessee Williams, introduce a raw and forcing symbolism through the naturalistic surface, which suppresses the Chekhovian warmth and gentleness. Shaw in *Heartbreak House* makes an excursion into the Chekhovian world and emerges with a Shavian fantasy in which Chekhov is unrecognizable. The list could be extended indefinitely. All aim at a realism of statement which makes some use of a colouring of naturalistic presentation and a fair splash of human psychology in order to hold our interest. All stand or fall with the authenticity of their characterization and the conviction of their feeling. None is really concerned with 'telling a story'; all wish to show us a 'state of affairs', paint a 'mood'. It is an indicative mood.

From two opposite poles the word 'mood' has gained currency as a critical term in modern drama. It is used by Christopher Fry of his own comedies, *The Lady's Not For Burning* and *Venus Observed*, his April and October plays, plays of free poeticism.[1] And it is used by John van Druten in discussing plays with an underlay of Chekhovian naturalism.[2] Perhaps van Druten borrows the concept from Princess Toumanova, who first identified *The Seagull* as a 'drama of mood'.[3]

For Fry, a 'comedy of mood' is a play in which 'the scene, the season, and the characters, are bound together in one climate'—in other words, there is a quality which is directing all three elements and may be governing the whole play. Fry naturally uses his poetry to establish and maintain that mood throughout, and the playgoer has the strong sense that the play was conceived as a poem of quasi-lyrical feeling which is in fact developed and explored dramatically.

Van Druten wrote, 'If there is a new-born creature in the theatre of the past thirty years, I would say that it is the play of mood, the play whose main quality—far more important than its story or its plot—is the maintenance and communication of a certain mood, through which the entire action is presented.' It is likely to be a play of close, and occasionally witty, observation, which attempts by subtle overtones to evoke a specific atmosphere as precisely as possible. That atmosphere, rather than a sequence of events, provides the unity of the play. Usually the setting, the social environment, often the season, is strongly established in order to compel that atmosphere, like the Bronx and other New York locales (*Marty*, *The Iceman Cometh*), the Deep South (especially favoured by Tennessee Williams in plays and films like *The Rose Tattoo*, *Baby Doll*, *A Streetcar Named Desire*), the English country house (N. C. Hunter's *Waters of the Moon*, *A Day by the Sea*), high summer (*Picnic*, *Summer of the Seventeenth Doll*), and so on. *Street Scene* was a play about the interaction of an apparently motley collection of families living in a New York tenement, enacted on the doorstep. Elmer Rice said of it, 'I conceived the home as the real protagonist of the drama, a brooding presence, which not only dominated the scene, but which gave a kind of dramatic unity to the sprawling and

---

[1] C. Fry, in *Theatre Newsletter* (London, 11 March 1950).
[2] J. van Druten, *The Playwright at Work* (New York, 1953), pp. 36 ff.
[3] N. A. Toumanova, *Anton Chekhov* (London, 1937), p. 117.

unrelated lives of the multitudinous characters and lent the whole whatever "meaning" it may have.'[1]

Van Druten and Fry can be brought together in this context because it seems clear that the play of mood is at its best a poetic structure, that at its best it is prompted and bound by an impulse from within, an attitude, a state of mind in the author which is in a sound tradition of drama. It follows that our critical approach to these plays must be to estimate the efficient value of that state of mind, and to judge where and when the dramatist has slipped into broad generalities of character or of sentiment which are untrue, when the confidence of the author in his own purpose has failed, where a public convention of feeling has settled on the play to blur its precision. We may recognize the superiority of Tennessee Williams's *The Glass Menagerie* over his *Summer and Smoke*; of the first version of Act III of his *Cat on a Hot Tin Roof* over the second; of *The Bachelor Party*, with the exception of the declaration of love at the tail, over *Marty*, also by Paddy Chayefsky, which glamorizes what it sets out to de-glamorize, the likelihood of a Marty ever finding his partner; of *The Member of the Wedding* over *A Day by the Sea*; of Terence Rattigan's *The Deep Blue Sea* over his *The Browning Version*.

It is not so much the form of these plays as the subjects that demand that form which tends to make them somewhat unpopular with the public. It is not a question whether these assertions of mood and atmosphere could not be 'better dealt with in the novel than in the theatre', which is quite an irrelevant hypothesis: the nature of our experience of the novel is of course different from that of a play in the theatre. Delicate subjects like those of the maladjusted, of the solitary adolescent, of sexual awakening; the frustration and loneliness of old age; the decadence of a way of life; the claustrophobia of a home or village; the need for love or self-respect; all demand that a hot light shall be shone on the soul of the playgoer. To evoke a state of nerves on the stage, it is necessary to play upon the nerves of the spectator, and without an easy line of development to follow, without a comforting 'right' or 'wrong' to recognize, any subject tends to be unpleasant.

[1] Quoted from *Radio Times* (London, 13 November 1959).

The scale of the play of mood is necessarily small, and its action cramped. Details must be uncommonly accentuated, like these of Archie Lee's room so carefully collected, each to underline one aspect of the husband's sterile life, in *Baby Doll*: 'On the bed table behind him is a half-empty bottle of liquor, an old alarm clock, ticking away, a magazine called "Spicy Fiction", and a tube of ointment.' Environment and character in the drama of mood will be unmistakably intertwined.

This is true of those plays of Eugene O'Neill in which a romanticized naturalism is the dominant mode, plays in which the author uses a careful excess of 'local colour', insists upon almost a rhetoric of tough dialect, and stresses his characters' psychopathology at the expense of their psychology. *The Iceman Cometh* is, for example, a play about a large and mixed bunch of men each hugging his personal illusion to his breast in appalling futility. O'Neill characteristically gives them a detailed and sordid setting in which to get drunk, sober up and get drunk again:

> The back room and a section of the bar of Harry Hope's saloon...In the left corner, built out into the room, is the toilet with a sign 'This is it' on the door. Against the middle of the left wall is a nickel-in-the-slot phonograph...The walls and ceilings once were white, but it was a long time ago, and they are now so splotched, peeled, stained and dusty that their colour can best be described as dirty.

To steal Michel Saint-Denis's phrase from its context, this is indeed the mud of naturalism.

Not only has Chekhov's method of shading together effects of the pathetic and the comic by their ironic implications killed the instinct to write the formal comedy for which we remember the drama of Ben Jonson, Molière and the Restoration in England, but the new play of mood is notoriously difficult to write well. Failures and part-failures abound, on two counts: because the sensibility of the writer must to a high degree be tuned to the subtle discordances of every day; and because the art of presenting them to an audience so that the fine balance is struck between laughter and tears cannot be achieved by following a set of rules, but can be forged only from the materials of the specific subject chosen, and with a suggestion of the rhythms the subject imposes. The element of life the author has selected for treatment must determine the form the play will take. Chekhov is a hard master.

Television may contribute to the growth of this kind of writing, just as the film encouraged the growth of melodrama. The intimacy of the television medium, the unavoidable visual tightness of the scene and its detail which encourages the domestic subject, the dominance of the actor in close-up, the necessity for his sustained performance and the slow motion of television action and editing, with its general sense of actuality—all these elements will make for the dark and shaded grey comedy of small contemporary life. At its worst the medium could produce hour upon hour of thin kitchen-sink drama; at its best, an immediate and exciting reflection of ordinary life under the pressures of our society. Already American television has produced one fine writer in Paddy Chayefsky, whose plays *Marty* and *The Bachelor Party* are almost documentary with detail of American home life.

Chayefsky has been helpfully articulate about his intentions, and in his notes on *Marty* and *The Mother* he says, 'I tried to write the dialogue as if it had been wire-tapped, I tried to envisage the scenes as if a camera had been focused upon the unsuspecting characters and had caught them in an untouched moment of life.'[1] The implied use of the hidden tape-recorder and the candid camera indicates precisely the new techniques of spontaneous naturalism. A sense of immediacy is to be one of the objects of the new television comedy, an extension of the dramatized documentary programme in which principles of strict 'impartiality' are to be pursued. These are the new techniques; what are the new directions? Assuming that actuality has been caught, the dramatizer is still faced with the need to make actuality *creative*.

Chayefsky suggests that a particular interest in psychological subjects is likely to follow. 'Television drama', he says in his notes to *The Big Deal*, 'cannot expand in breadth, so it must expand in depth. In the last year or so, television writers have learned that they can write intimate dramas—"intimate" meaning minutely detailed

[1] P. Chayefsky, *Television Plays* (New York, 1955), p. 173.

studies of small moments of life...the digging under the surface of life for the more profound truths of human relationships.'[1] The dramatic action will be vertical and not horizontal. Later, he goes on,

In television, you can dig into the most humble, ordinary relationships: the relationships of bourgeois children to their mother, or middle-class husband to wife, of white-collar father to his secretary—in short, the relationships of the people....We relate to each other in an incredibly complicated manner. Every fiber of relationship is worth a dramatic study. There is far more exciting drama in the reasons why a man gets married than in why he murders someone...[2]

The thought of a larger and larger number of psychoanalytical case-studies of no relevance to general life, or of no interest beyond the satisfaction of a morbid curiosity, is not encouraging. But one thing is certain. The excerpt from the tape-recording, the shots cut from the camera's film, the actual or assumed blur of fragmentary details, must still be selected and arranged for dramatic meaning. In this we shall doubtless defer to Chekhov once again.

In Britain, Alun Owen's plays of Liverpool life, particularly *No Trams to Lime Street* and *Lena, Oh My Lena*, display a lyrical impressionism which he achieves by a microscopic scrutiny of his material: 'Little incidents and moments for me were full of poetry, the poetry of everyday speech, caught and isolated...But for television I was going to have to shape these moments and give them a continuity that would illuminate people's behaviour.' He goes on, 'The things I wanted to say were about the way people behave to each other, and I have tried to strike chords in the mind of the viewer. I am constantly trying to say, "It was like this when it happened. Not factually like this, but this was the climate, the feel of the situation. Surely you remember something like it?"'[3] Intense authenticity of place and individuality of character have been the result, and Owen checks the sentimentality implicit in the art of chord-striking by the kind of comic undercutting present in Chekhov's dialogue.

[1] *Ibid.* p. 132.   [2] *Ibid.* p. 178.
[3] Introduction to *Three Television Plays* (London, 1961).

However, it has been evident that Chekhov's own plays do not televise well, principally because his family groups are larger than the narrow lens of television can include. In *Uncle Vanya*, the camera eye, concerned to pick up individual reactions to the Professor's announcement that he intended to sell the estate, gave us nothing of what his speech meant to the group as a whole, nor of its dramatic shape, which could only be communicated by our seeing the emotional response of all the family.

A final judgment on plays of mood must turn on the use or abuse of their peculiar nervous vitality. Should the playwright impress his atmosphere upon the spectator by a steady intensification of feeling, to ensure that his audience is at one with the mood? Or dare he keep his audience sober enough to have the ability to assess the values of the world he is painting? Too many of these plays, in their anxiety to capture the sympathies of the spectator, stamp their way into melodrama and sensationalism or try to win us with sentiment (Terence Rattigan's *The Deep Blue Sea*, William Inge's *Come Back Little Sheba*, Tennessee Williams's *A Streetcar Named Desire*, Robert Bolt's *Flowering Cherry*). The best retain a splendid compassion by an equally strong evocation of detail and mood, while yet with delicate wit modifying our sympathies: certain moments in Ray Lawler's *Summer of the Seventeenth Doll*, Chayefsky's *The Bachelor Party* and Williams's *The Glass Menagerie* for this reason suggest at least that they are in the tradition of *The Cherry Orchard*.

Nevertheless, with the play of mood we are today merely drifting along one stream in the history of the twentieth-century theatre. Elsewhere the wit was soon to oust the compassion, and in the 'twenties we were jerked into the territory of Pirandello and Anouilh; in the 'thirties and 'forties, of Bertolt Brecht; in the 'fifties, of Beckett and Ionesco and Genêt.

3

TOWARDS TRAGIC INVERSION

Yes, my dear fellow, you wear a cook's hat! And you beat eggs!
And do you think that, having these eggs to beat, you then have
nothing more on your hands? Oh, no, not a bit of it...You have
to represent the shell of the eggs that you're beating!

PIRANDELLO, *Six Characters in Search of an Author*

A NEW FREEDOM OF FORM

The twentieth-century theatre has offered the dramatist a dizzy
variety of forms and conventions within which to work, with
infinite opportunities to break the continuity of one mode to startle
us with another. The historian of modern drama will remark on the
one hand the movement towards overt theatrical symbolism at the
end of the last century, with its concomitant adventures into surrealism and the 'dream' play, into expressionism, 'epic' drama and
verse fantasy; and, on the other, surviving elements of the high
comedy of manners, melodrama and grotesque farce. Woven through
all these is an irrepressible interest in the naturalistic experiment, as
we have seen. Moreover, the playwright has had at his disposal all
manner of media through which to speak, from the expert sorcery
of the theatre of illusions, whether behind a proscenium arch or on a
cinema screen, to the theatre of free imagination, the bare stage, the
open stage, theatre-in-the-round or theatre on the air. It is small
wonder that today's serious audience at times seems to be a tormented creature with masochistic tendencies.

Thus the dramatist has had an unprecedented freedom to mix his
effects and discover new responses in us. Where, before, the laughter
and the tears had been so shaded together that they were effectively
indistinguishable, now they have been thrust upon us in deliberately
incongruous, jarring arrangements. If once we could be made to
accept some realm of fantasy, then the dramatist could juxtapose his

113

impressions in innumerable combinations and in innumerable varieties of proportion. He hoped that the general act of synthesizing which had taken place more on the stage might now take place inside the mind of the spectator. The success of the new comedy would rest upon our exceptional 'suspension of disbelief' if the fusion was to occur, just as in neo-impressionistic art the pointillist anticipated that small splashes of pure unmixed colour would blend behind the eye to create a consistent effect of extraordinary vividness and luminosity, if the spectator stood far enough away.

Outrageous effects were to free the imagination of an audience trained by tradition to judge plays by their likeness to life. A new stylization in drama was to permit the contrasts necessary to project those monstrous ironies of life which are the great subject and the world theme of the modern stage. An exaggerated chiaroscuro was the intention—but each writer had an immediate problem to select a form to match his own statement and to manhandle effectively a reluctant audience.

Shifts of style and tone could be gentle or violent. Thus Dylan Thomas, with a wicked ear, takes full advantage of the loose form of his radio play *Under Milk Wood* and embraces an astonishing range of tickles and shocks, from the purely theatrical trick to a subtle impregnation of the mind. With ease he can sway us to sleep with the musical sounds and rhythms of his narrator's voice crooning, 'The sunny slow lulling afternoon yawns and moons through the dozy town...', and then jerk us awake as the knife-edged voice of Mrs Pugh jerks her husband:

> MRS PUGH. Persons with manners,
> VOICE. snaps Mrs cold Pugh,
> MRS PUGH. do not nod at table.

Equally effectively he can paint a conventional backcloth of spring and then slyly pursue a development of feeling through a rapid series of differentiated attitudes. Spring in Llaregyb becomes vital to us as it is felt vividly in Evans the Death, Gossamer Beynon, Jack Black, Captain Cat and Mary Ann Sailors, each in his or her own way; it grows the more alive as impressions are gently played off one against another. Undertaker, schoolmistress, cobbler and ship's captain in contrasting ways feel the dignity of winter slipping from them 'in the young sun', solemnly, childishly, puritanically, bawdily, until Mary Ann Sailors can declare with a natural reverence for life, 'It is Spring in Llaregyb in the sun in my old age, and this is the Chosen Land.'

Some variations of tone and complexion have their place in most drama. On the other hand, jumps in convention, leaps from one 'plane of reality' to another, are readily accomplished where an author has boldly adopted an artificial convention for playing. His motive for doing this may be as different as Eliot's in *Murder in the Cathedral* and Brecht's in *The Caucasian Chalk Circle*.

In the former, the reasons have often been discussed for the surprise of switching from the stylized heightening in verse and gesture of the murder of Thomas, stressed by the near-hysterical, terror-stricken language of the Women of Canterbury, to the colloquial clichés of the Knights as they turn on the audience in direct address. Breaking the convention of playing and of language serves a number of purposes, but above them all is the extraordinary spur felt among the audience. We are made abruptly aware how contemporary and relevant in an age of political murders is this apparently remote martyrdom.

No different in kind, perhaps, is Brecht's method of telling his tale; only with Brecht the little thumps and raps persist through the play until we take a general concussion, and feel only that chill in the air that we associate with his 'realism'. Thus, in *The Caucasian Chalk Circle*, after Grusha has melodramatically moved us in her heroic, if fairy-tale, crossing of the rotten bridge in the storm with the child, and after the Story Teller has soothed us with the bland and measured, if somewhat cynical, lines,

> 'When I enter my brother's house', she thought,
> 'He will rise and embrace me.'
> 'Is that you, sister?' he will say,
> 'I have been expecting you so long.
> This is my dear wife...',[1]

[1] Trans. E. R. and M. Bentley (London, 1956).

we are suddenly and ironically introduced to 'a fat peasant couple', the characters of farce. The sister is a garrulous hypocrite and the brother a weak, self-centred hypochondriac, and they offer her neither rest nor food, though she is barely able to stand. A few minutes later, after Grusha has decided to give the child a name and a roof, sacrificing herself in becoming a wife (albeit to a man nearly dead), her pathos is sharply eclipsed by uproarious farce once more. The guests hope to celebrate simultaneously both a wedding and a funeral. A tipsy monk must conduct the twin services. The dying man abruptly recovers when he hears it said that the war is over. This odd structure of mixed slapstick and melodrama is cumulative in its effect. It allegedly stimulates us to a state of un-sentimental alertness while proposing a naïve and simple Sunday-school sermon. How far Brecht's much discussed effect of 'alienation' results in superficial sensation, how far it *does* leave us unemo-tionally free to think our way through his play, and how far it falls within a strong tradition of the comic-pathetic, must be scrutinized.

Very different in intention is the drama of Anouilh, who mixes the tragedy of *La Sauvage* Thérèse with the buffoonery of old Tarde her father, the tragedy of Orpheus and Eurydice with the farce of their Father and Mother, the tragedy of Ardèle and her hunchback lover with the mannered comedy of the Count and the Countess, the tragedy of the marriage of Julien and his Colombe with the cartoon characters who surround them, the tragedy of General St Pé with the vaudeville of Emily his wife and Ghislaine his one-time mistress. It is different because in these instances a volatile element of tragedy is distilled from a comic situation. The author practises a cruel deceit, and condemns us for our laughter after we have laughed to order: he is using the freedom of convention that comedy grants him. Francis Fergusson has recently diagnosed a comic success and a comic failure: 'When Scaramouche gets a beating, we do not feel the blows, but the idea of beating, at that moment, strikes us as funny. If the beating is too realistic, if it breaks the light rhythms of thought, the fun is gone, and the comedy destroyed.'[1] Anouilh beats his 'Scara-

[1] F. Fergusson, *The Idea of a Theater* (New York, 1954), p. 191.

mouche' realistically hard, wrenches and rends the light rhythms of thought; and yet brings off a success. Comedy is certainly destroyed—if we must call it comedy—and the dramatic impact of the fission is tremendous. It may be beyond articulate analysis to say how this happens; only an examination of the intangible impressions an audience receives in performance could do it, and this is attempted below.

What happens when the writer takes an element of the ridiculous and thrusts it into tragedy? When the tragic heroine bursts her stays, when the tragic hero trips over the carpet? A laugh will kill a tear, we may say, but does it then remain a laugh? If hot steel is plunged into cold water, there is a tempering; if yellow is poured over blue, there is a new colour, the brighter for the brightness of the originals.

In dark comedy there are moments when, in counterpointing his effects, the author takes his play to the very edge of disintegration. So in our minds the image grows perilously brittle, and we the audience are on the point of making a destructive analysis. But a synthesis and reconciliation of the parts will follow if their dramatic chemistry has been perfectly calculated.

Counterpointing the pathetic and the comic within the same experience by demonstrating their object from more than one angle must have the effect of sharpening the awareness of the onlooker. Shaw had us mock his Eliza Doolittle by the high comic trickery of the tea-party scene; he reduced her natural dignity to the level of a shabby music-hall turn, in order that the shock of the fourth act, where the insensitive soul of Professor Higgins is revealed by his treating her as if she were still at the tea-party, should be felt by us as a personal recrimination. Nearly fifty years later, with the experience of Anouilh's black comedy, of Brecht's violent juxtapositions of styles and effects, and of Beckett's grim-gay nihilism behind him, John Osborne leaps wider and crazier gaps to have us denounce ourselves. The music-hall turn presented by Archie Rice in *The Entertainer* flashes upon us intermittently with the false abandon of coarse songs like 'Why should I care?', 'We're all out for the good old number one' and 'Thank God we're normal', and then the author drops us callously back to the sordid subnormality of domestic life or else to the whimsical nostalgia for the Edwardian days of Billy Rice: 'They were graceful, they had mystery and dignity. Why when a woman got out of a cab, she descended. Descended...'

The swinging of the pendulum within our minds, the dialectic of laughter and tears with its energizing effect on the spectator, is to be observed through much of the drama of our time. In the sections that follow, a sample has been selected of those playwrights whose influence has been or is likely to be strongest, and whose forms and modifications of dark comedy are most striking, namely, Strindberg in his expressionistic manner, the Irishmen Shaw, Synge and O'Casey, Pirandello pre-eminently, and then Eliot, Brecht, Anouilh and Tennessee Williams, with Beckett, Ionesco and Genêt from the Parisian theatre of the 'fifties.

STRINDBERG'S DREAM PLAYS

Strindberg was very quick to break the rules of naturalism, as we saw briefly in *There Are Crimes and Crimes*. His increasing need to strip the soul naked, uncover its illusions and at the same time make his meaning as transparent as possible led him more and more to adopt the methods of symbolism and expressionism. Neither of these terms is really adequate to describe the processes of stage representation that are found in the apparently slack structures of *To Damascus*, *The Dream Play* and *The Ghost Sonata*. In each the symbols are virtually so private and the order of the action so subjectively ordained that commentators may be forgiven for passing over them quickly and missing in them the sardonic logic of feeling which binds them.

As Strindberg declared in his programme note to *The Dream Play*, 'anything may happen; everything is possible and probable. Time and space do not exist. On an insignificant background of reality, imagination designs and embroiders novel patterns, free fancies, absurdities and improvisations.'[1] But the fragmentation of character and all the other eccentricities of his method should take our attention less than the ends in view. Strindberg hastens to add that the

[1] Quoted from A. Nicoll, *World Drama* (London, 1949), p. 562.

118

dreamer of the dream remains the 'one consciousness' for whom the kaleidoscopic impressions make sense, and we should fasten on this. For the one consciousness must not be the author's alone: it must be no less than the spectator's in the theatre.

Yet none of these plays obeys the rules of comedy or of tragedy: they make their own laws, directed and unified, if at all, by a total feeling to be traced through the details of the action. Any complexity that follows is to be seen as the intrinsic complexity of personality, of life and reality, not merely the complexity of a wild dream or a nightmare. The inarticulateness of an individual mood and attitude must be made articulate, and the darker mysteries of human personality illuminated.

In his religious morality play *To Damascus*, comic methods of intensification and exaggeration of character are replaced by those of character distortion. These distortions are chiefly of facets of the Stranger's own personality as he wanders through the play in search of himself. For this reason, standards of judgment familiarly applied to either farcical or naturalistic characterization are useless for the estimation of the audience's response. The numerous ghosts whom the Stranger encounters in his travels are all fragmented aspects of his own soul, and thus suffer from being almost depersonalized. While they indeed assume nightmarish qualities in this way, they yet remain cold and rather unmanageable phantoms.

Equally embarrassing is the shaping of the action in the long series of rich expressionistic scenes. Strong, bold and simple in their manner of presenting several stages in the condition of the mind on its road to redemption, nevertheless they risk losing much of the usual willing compliance of the spectator with the action, because he is largely asked to inspect it without the usual guides to feeling. He is granted little with which to identify the experiences on the stage as normal experience, and Strindberg makes little effort to draw the spectator into the play. These, of course, are faults endemic in any expressionistic drama.

Symbolism of character and situation such as is used in *To Damascus* is there to make articulate what is thought and felt; it can add a depth and complexity to a thought and feeling which might otherwise reveal itself rather nakedly in a new framework, but only if the symbolism is linked with traditional concepts common to the playgoer; it can be intensely illuminating if a narrow and seemingly personal sensation can in this way be connected with universal human experience. Thus the dramatist who uses symbolism takes upon himself an added responsibility: if the symbols are not sufficient in their own right, he owes it to his audience to teach it, within the context of the play, how to understand them. The play must build its meaning, else it sinks into private language. Strindberg scarcely establishes his symbols in this play, but continues relentlessly to take us through territory well known to himself, but for us uncharted. Precision of communication at times is therefore very much at a premium, while at others we move in vaguely recognizable regions on the fringe of our consciousness. When this happens, the effect is overwhelming.

One short episode must suffice to suggest the play's style, and also bring into focus the uneasy ironies to which the enforced link between present reality and the chimerical shapes of the past give rise.

The first banquet scene of Part II of the play (Act III, scene i) enacts the slow destruction of a particular self-delusion, but here in the fantasy of the theatre and the telescoped sensation of nightmare it is accelerated to a pace where horror turns to hysteria, and the pattern of disillusionment is seen in crude outline by an effect of glaring myopia. The Stranger, an Everyman, finds himself at a sumptuous repast. Tables are set with golden goblets, and weighed down by dishes of peacocks, pheasants in full plumage, boars' heads, entire lobsters, oysters, salmon, bundles of asparagus, melons and grapes. By degrees this luxury is to vanish. There are four tables set, and the Stranger sits resplendent at the highest among frock-coated civic dignitaries; but he sits where he cannot see a crowd of beggars sitting at the fourth table. Among them are people from his former life, at once his victims and aspects of his own identity. To the solemn accompaniment of chords from Mendelssohn's 'Dead March', a Professor acclaims the Stranger as 'the greatest man of a great century',[1] places a laurel crown upon his head and hangs a

---

[1] *The Road to Damascus*, trans. G. Rawson (London, 1939).

shining order round his neck. For the Stranger has seemingly manufactured gold, symbol of the material achievement and earthly success which he desired in order to restore his self-confidence and kill his doubts.

Against the fine rhetoric of the Professor's speech and the Stranger's reply, the mutterings of subversion and disruption are already to be heard from the beggars' table. The banquet is slyly removed, the rich tables become trestles with bare boards, and the beggars take the places of the frock-coated gentlemen. As the Stranger's soul is stripped, poverty, ugliness and bareness surround him. Gradually his creative achievement is belittled, questioned and finally destroyed by the figures from his past: 'Is it true he's made gold?' 'So it's said. But it's certain he left his wife while she was in childbed.'...'I don't know whether he's succeeded in making gold. I don't worry about that, and I hardly believe it.'...'Did you ever hear anything so impudent? That we should honour a mystery man, an arch-swindler, a charlatan, in good faith.' Further, the Stranger is told that the civic reception was a mockery, in fact organized by the Drunkards' Society. A slut accuses him of having indirectly corrupted her mind as a young girl. The bill for the whole banquet is thrust upon him. And upon his being unable to pay, he is dragged off to prison as a thief and an impostor amid the hurrahs of the beggars.

The complete transformation takes place in less than ten minutes, a transformation of social status, of self-confidence, of health of mind. As all the external signs of riches are turned to those of poverty, a poverty of spirit strikes the agonized consciousness of the hero while he protests with the pathetic dignity of a tramp. With the half-amused shudder of one just woken from a bad dream to the safety of cool daylight, we observe all this from without. We sit omniscient with the gods and see and coldly criticize the mortal pretensions and sufferings of our representative. The speed of the change and the startling deflation of the man in his blank dismay border on the ludicrous. Yet we cannot laugh. 'To think I've been so duped,' he utters in black despair. Scene after scene of this tormented play presents a view of human experience refracted and

contorted because it lies just below the uneasy surface of consciousness. Popular audiences will never thank Strindberg or his successors
for trouncing them with a fierce and often private surrealism.

An interest today in the dream plays, and especially in *The Ghost
Sonata*, could be justified by the successful virtuosity of Samuel
Beckett's fantasies of the 'fifties. *The Ghost Sonata* of 1907 curiously
anticipates elements in *Endgame* of 1957. Both have the disconnected
form of dream in which 'everything is possible and probable' and
in which 'time and space do not exist'. Both draw characters which
are intended to be facets of a single consciousness, suited to an
'intimate' theatre. Both deal in deliberately half-explained symbolism. Both appear bizarre before their real horror is assimilated.
They echo elements found in Maeterlinck's *The Interior* and *The
Intruder*, in which the momentous terror of destiny and of Sweden-
borg's unseen universe surrounds those who live either in innocence
or in ignorance. They reproduce the stripping action with which
Pirandello habitually attacks his characters. Their drama is of
waiting and of self-discovery, a drama of silences and immobility
without quiet or repose.

The action of *The Ghost Sonata* is bound together by the one view
of the young Student, an idealist who has selflessly saved human life
and who has bright visions of the future. It is his misfortune to meet
old Jacob Hummel, a man whose inherent evil is not apparent at
first, though hints of his power to poison the lives of others are
dropped early in the play:

STUDENT. Do you speculate in houses? [*sc.* homes]
HUMMEL. Mmm-yah! But not in the way you mean.[1]

A little later the Student speaks to Hummel's servants:

STUDENT. Is this man to be trusted?
JOHANSSON. You may trust him—to do anything!
STUDENT. What is he doing around the corner now?
JOHANSSON. Watching the poor...dropping a word here and a word
    there...loosening a stone at a time...until the whole house comes
    tumbling down, metaphorically speaking.

[1] Trans. E. Björkman in August Strindberg, *Eight Famous Plays* (London, 1949).

In the first scene Hummel squats in his wheelchair before the façade of a two-storey house; in the second, the scene of the 'ghost supper', the façade is literally and figuratively removed, and the reality of his power to corrupt is revealed.

It is a house of pollution and degeneration: 'A house gets mouldy when it gets old, and when people are too much together, tormenting each other all the time, they lose their reason.' The house symbolizes life itself, in all its monotony and recrimination and pathos. Its ghosts, day in and day out, say nothing to each other for fear of facing the truth, but each is tied to the other by his sins against the other's humanity:

> (*The company is seated in a circle, no one saying a word for a while.*)
> COLONEL. Shall we order the tea now?
> HUMMEL. What's the use? No one cares for tea, and I can't see the need for pretending.
> (*Pause.*)
> COLONEL. Shall we make conversation?
> HUMMEL (*speaking slowly and with frequent pauses*). Talk of the weather, which we know all about? Ask one another's state of health, which we know just as well? I prefer silence. Then thoughts become audible, and we can see the past. Silence can hide nothing—but words can...
>
> (*Long pause during which everybody is subject to silent scrutiny by all the rest.*)

Hummel, who is so willing 'to tear up the weeds' and unmask the horrors of their sins, is then terrifyingly unmasked himself: the insane wife of the Colonel reduces his speech to that of a grotesque parrot, in the way she herself had spoken before, and the 'death screen' is placed in front of the closet into which Hummel has been ordered. Even the voice of the vampire who 'sucked the house of all nourishment' must become outlandishly lifeless; the vampire must suffer annihilation himself.

For the very reason that *The Ghost Sonata* is a play of indirect communication, to say the least, it can infect us and leave us aghast with the fear of the half-apprehended. The eternal oppositions of illusion and reality, innocence and experience, youth and age, are seen in the shuddering light of monstrous delirium. The final words of the Student to the Young Lady, illegitimate daughter of Hummel and the Colonel's wife, and a girl who is dying from exposure to the truth, are partly addressed to the troubled spectator: 'You poor little child—you child of a world of illusion, guilt, suffering, and death—a world of eternal change, disappointment, and pain—may the Lord of Heaven deal mercifully with you on your journey!' These are sentiments that echo through the serious drama of the years that follow this strangely premonitory play.

THE SHAVIAN TOUCH

The Shavian touch can at times leave a distinctly dark stain. It was Shaw's avowed intention to disturb us. In his preface to *Man and Superman* he declared, 'It annoys me to see people comfortable when they ought to be uncomfortable; and I insist on making them think in order to bring them to conviction of sin.' This very proper attitude to his complacent *fin de siècle* audiences led him into extravagances of theatre which justify his place in the pattern we are tracing. Desmond MacCarthy observed in Shaw what he called his 'high-spirited agility in modulating out of serious and even poetic comedy into intellectual farce'.[1] If we look into Shaw again we will find him modulating freely from intellectual farce into serious comedy too. Shaw behaves instinctively, guided by what adjustment of mood he feels his play demands, aiming at a dominant tone of audience recrimination. He will allow us no romance and no tragedy: the 'alienation' of the stage from the auditorium by some surprise in the tone of the play is his favourite device for controlling the processes of our thoughts and responses. The resulting image we conceive of the plays has generally been called 'satirical', a loose term revealing a need for closer and theatrical analysis.

The most glaring example of Shavian alienation is the 'Dialogue in Hell', Act III of *Man and Superman*. In this the change of convention from drawing-room comedy to that of a 'cosmic theatre' permits a philosophical restatement of the meaning of the action. The change is not integrated in the structure of the play, but

[1] D. MacCarthy, *Shaw* (London, 1951), p. 150; reprint of a review written in 1943.

provokes a sharp effect of distancing; in order to press upon us explicit ideas on the function of the sexes and to force us to view the last act more allegorically, Shaw risks stopping the show. But the dialogue of this act is more than a quartet of voices: its dialectic of attitudes is constructed in an operatic pattern by which the impulse behind one speech generates the heat in another. Before we can claim to know how Shaw's drama works, we need to establish the link between this dialectic of speech-building and the dialectic of the play's meaning, and then examine the tensions thereby set up for an audience.

The Shavian play is still an unexplored field, and this is not the place to explore it. But certain issues have to be recognized. Shaw the politician and Shaw the philosopher, now mostly dead, have bothered us for too long. Shaw the dramatist has hardly been noticed: we persist in looking for the ideas-monger and do not see the artist. Yet the plays remain very much alive because they display the sure touch of the theatre-wise dramatist. Eric Bentley a few years ago called the Shavian play 'dialectical', a play not *of* argument, but *about* argument, a particular and individual approach possible to any theme under the sun, an approach which has rightly become associated with Shaw's name. All good plays are 'plays of ideas', but few are dialectical in structure. In the nature of drama, all good plays are 'problem plays' too, but some are plays insisting upon a thesis, putting an ultimately comforting case like Wilde in his 'serious' moments, or like Galsworthy most of the time. Whereas Shaw does not recognize an easy distinction between good and bad, with Wilde and Galsworthy and their kind we can sit back and relax, knowing that the play will satisfy our consciences. With Shaw, the audience may have no rest. Critics tend to look in the wrong direction, towards the characters who remain for them 'ventriloquist's dolls' and towards the plots which are merely the 'manipulation' of ideas. They would do better to look out into the house, at the unique activity in the auditorium during performance. For something new happens in the Shavian theatre, and the play will seem to have stopped on the stage when it is most alive in the audience, static in its physical action while intensely disturbing in the mind.

We forget that the comic artist must in the first instance understand his audience, how its mind works, how to flog it on when it is lazy. 'Nobody will trouble themselves about anything that does not trouble them,' reiterated Shaw, and the indispensable basis of his comedy is a knowledge of the attitudes and prejudices, the beliefs and illusions of the average spectator. However, the average spectator will shut his ears if he suffers a frontal assault, and methods must be devised to woo him to laugh at himself and think again, and yet applaud the author who makes him do it.

Shaw's effort to keep his audience alert and its mind itching determines again and again the particular inflection of a line of his dialogue, the shaping of a scene and the form of a whole play. Each is constructed in its particular way as an indirect guide to us. Thus Robert de Baudricourt in the first scene of *Saint Joan* sits 'magisterially' in his place, scowling hard while he waits for Joan to enter: Shaw has built him up punctiliously by setting him baldly against the 'trodden worm' of his Steward. Joan breezes in, bobs a curtsy and all in a rush says, 'Good morning, captain squire. Captain: you are to give me a horse and armour and some soldiers, and send me to the Dauphin. Those are your orders from my Lord.' If Robert is taken aback, so are we. The whole of the scene is a steady deflation of poor Robert, its purpose to give us the first of many insights into the kind of power Joan exercises over her contemporaries, and to prepare us to see her face bigger game. The scene is also to set an initial tone for the play as a whole, a tone which is to be subtly turned against us. It is also to give us to believe we are dealing with a real girl, naturally flushed with the excitement of quick success, the better to have us accept the heroic and symbolic Joan who is to resist the religious and social order of the times.

This is not a medieval play, but a play with a strictly modern reference, one which is not fully explicit until the much-criticized Epilogue arrives. 'We are lifted on waves of emotion,' said Mac-Carthy, 'and dashed on thought,' much as in the earlier *Major Barbara*. We are deceived into the pleasure of suffering 'tragic' feelings, only in order to be shown our self-indulgence by the sudden return to farcical fantasy. After our sympathetic identification with Joan in her trial, abruptly we are given Charles, the most obviously comic character in the play. He is sitting up in bed in his nightcap, leaping in fear, hiding under the bedclothes, a pure figure of fun; yet it is he who becomes our new and mocking representative. With cool comic calculation all the attitudes of the players assembled in Charles's bedroom are seen again in the light of our passionate feelings about the burning. The play risks cracking its backbone, but the best art takes such risks.

Pygmalion, to select another well-known play from the canon, is a fine example of a switching of styles in a reverse order from that of *Saint Joan*. The exquisite tea-party is generally felt to be the crux of the play—it is certainly the crux of the laughter. We cannot fail to notice in retrospect that our laughter is here directed equally against the astonishment of the Eynsford Hills and against the simplicity and incongruity of Eliza in her new social role. To laugh at the earnestness of her account of 'the shallow depression in the west of these islands', at the incongruity of the story of her aunt who was 'done in' for the sake of her new straw hat, is irresistible. But we have been trapped. We have quite forgotten the now lifeless humanity of the Covent Garden Eliza of Act I, and we are liable to forget what Mrs Pearce in Act II had advised: 'She should think of the future'; and what Mrs Higgins in Act III calls 'the problem of what is to be done with her afterwards'; and the dilemma Eliza in Act IV finally recognizes when she cries, 'What am I fit for?' The live woman has been turned into Pygmalion's cold, dead marble: transplanting this natural flower into strange soil has withered it with the dry laughter of farce.

Act IV is to show us the results of Higgins's thoughtlessness and our blindness. In fully theatrical terms we see Eliza revived. This is no paradox, no trick of illusion, but a simple expedient to revive the audience too. Eliza returns from the ball a successful duchess, but in an agony of mind. As she sits apart from Higgins and Colonel Pickering in silence, she listens to the selfish insults of their yawns: 'Thank God it's over.'...'The whole thing has been a bore.'...'No more artificial duchesses. The whole thing has been simple purgatory.' When Higgins at last leaves her to go to bed, the storm in Eliza's brain breaks, and when he is heard looking for his slippers outside the door, she throws them at him viciously and with intent to kill. Then watch: the tempo of the scene changes, comedy is submerged, and the true climax approaches. We stand accused of ignorant romancing, and, to crown our guilt, Eliza marries Freddie the fool in outright preference to Higgins himself.

Shaw takes an Irish delight in refusing us comfort. Eliza ought to be thrilled at the new opportunities open to her, but she is not. Caesar will have none of Cleopatra, because he is 'too busy'. Louis Dubedat dies to the comic chorus of the doctors, and Mrs Dubedat's grief is marked by the persistent Newspaper Man who wants 'a few words on How It Feels to be a Widow'. Candida chooses to mother her apparently solid clergyman husband rather than the sickly poet Marchbanks. Dick Dudgeon emerges as a natural hero, but will not love the pretty heroine Judith Anderson. Delicious heroines in their masses of Edwardian frills and flounces talk hard about hard cash and have hard heads screwed firmly on. Ann Whitfield in her mourning costume of black and violet silk, and softly framed within her feather boa, has all the hidden strength of tempered steel; the brash idealist Jack Tanner crumples before her. Violet, the married version of Ann in the same play, openly defies the rules of propriety from her position of marital infallibility.

Such characters are unashamed puppets speaking the restricted language of artificial comedy. Shaw's scenes are built up as contrasts and contests of attitudes to life in which neither side is necessarily in the right: Ann and Tanner, Undershaft and Barbara, Joan and Bishop Cauchon, Doyle and Broadbent in *John Bull's Other Island*. The list is almost inexhaustible, for frequently the duellists are re-deployed within the same scene, as, in the first act of *Man and Superman*, Ramsden is matched with Tavy, Tavy with Jack, Jack with Ramsden. Somewhere in the struggle we shall find our own fine champion and our own precious notions taking a beating.

That ragbag of a play which so many admire as Shaw's most timeless work, *Heartbreak House*, suggests his powers of audience control as well as any. It is written to show us a portrait of society, sweet like 'rotten fruit', and drifting towards a rugged catastrophe. We are to see it through the eyes of an innocent, Ellie Dunn. But our view is not allowed to be a simple one. Heartbreak House is for Ellie and for us 'this silly house, this strangely happy house, this agonizing house'. The mixture of her nostalgia and her hope is universal. The disorder of the drunken ship offers a disastrous gaiety.

Ellie is given an eccentric education in the play. She is brought from ignorance to apparent wisdom, and then retreats to irresponsibility. She is told the truth about her romantic Hector; so she turns to the practical man Mangan until she is told the truth about him too. She learns finally that Captain Shotover, on whom she rested her faith, is a rum-soaked dreamer, no different from herself, only happy when 'stripped of everything, even of hope'. The last scene is a shock treatment of crazy behaviour and painful humour. The family sits in the blazing lights of the house in an air raid. 'A dull distant explosion is heard': Hector dashes to turn on more lights and tear down all the curtains at the windows, crying, 'It shall be seen for a hundred miles.' 'Another and louder explosion is heard': Hesione Hushabye and Ellie 'throw themselves into one another's arms in wild excitement'.

MRS HUSHABYE. Did you hear the explosions? And the sound in the sky: it's splendid: it's like an orchestra: it's like Beethoven.
ELLIE. By thunder, Hesione: it is Beethoven.

Lady Utterword refuses to go down to the cellars, but tells Randall to play 'Keep the home fires burning' on his flute, and we note the ironies in the choice of melody, and indeed in the choice of instrument. 'A terrific explosion shakes the earth. They reel back into their seats, or clutch the nearest support. They hear the falling of the shattered glass from the windows.' Then slowly the danger passes. Shotover calls, 'Turn in, all hands. The ship is safe,' and promptly falls asleep. Ellie cries out in disappointment, 'Safe!' But the war is not yet over:

MRS HUSHABYE. But what a glorious experience! I hope they'll come again tomorrow night.
ELLIE (*radiant at the prospect*). Oh, I hope so.

A few years ago, John Fernald said of his production of the play,

In *Heartbreak House* Shaw has done something . . . which the limitations of 'real' characters would have prevented him from doing. He has made a synthesis of human attributes and has examined them in conflict with the whole gamut of problems which face civilization. Hector, Hesione, Shotover and the rest, each presents a particular aspect of humanity: regarded separately they are not 'human beings', but looked at together they express the complete comical-tragical paradox of Man, the animal who can think but who has yet solved few of the problems that really matter.

The symbolism of this muddled group of lovable people is not far to seek. Shotover is a poet of wisdom, and at the same time a clown and a fraud. Ellie is a wide-eyed Desdemona who discovers that 'there seems to be nothing real in the world except my father and Shakespeare'. All of them are summed up by Hector as 'heartbroken imbeciles'. The modulations of tone within characters are echoed by the farcical modulations of the style, concluded by this leap into the perverse and lunatic scene which ends the play. This was a deliberate distortion to point his moral: 'Heartbreak House, in short,' we read in the preface, 'did not know how to live, at which point all that was left to it was the boast that at least it knew how to die: a melancholy accomplishment which the outbreak of war presently gave it practically unlimited opportunities of displaying.' In this play Shaw offers us a new dialectic, a dialectic of feeling, and it places him squarely in the twentieth century.

SYNGE AND O'CASEY

Within a tradition more or less their own, the Irishmen J. M. Synge and Sean O'Casey were among those who were quick to strike the fantastic note and through our willing imagination try to undermine our self-satisfaction. The riots over Synge's plays are readily explained by the political and religious feelings running strongly in a country enamoured of nationalism; but we should not forget that his kind of comedy was written with the same intention of disturbing his audiences as was Shaw's in a different social context. The shock of Synge's first play, *The Shadow of the Glen*, lies in the curious mixture of cynical kitchen comedy and seductive lyrical feeling, and the author is being logically merciless to us when he rejects the anticipated punishment of Dan's erring wife for an imaginatively just ending. Nora, the wife who lives on another level of feeling, shall escape from her spiritually dead husband.

Synge brought with him from Paris a sophisticated approach to life and a comic and ironic eye which mingled oddly with the peasant Ireland he wished to rediscover. It is his French wit which introduces into his plays what Yeats called 'a new kind of sarcasm' and which did so much to invigorate the Irish Dramatic Movement after Yeats's own romantic start. Nora of *The Shadow of the Glen* shares the romantic and the materialistic qualities of us all, and her cynical story hangs between tragedy and farce, like the styles within the play. Synge was refusing to be a propagandist for the Movement: 'The drama, like the symphony,' he says in his preface to *The Tinker's Wedding*, 'does not teach or prove anything.' But there was more to it than this.

His idiom in *The Well of the Saints* beautifully splices with wit the pathetic story of the old blind beggar and his old blind wife. In blindness they think each other lovely; granted their sight, they see only ugliness and part in anger. In Act III their blindness has returned, and they can begin again to be happy in each other's company: 'Well,' says Martin, 'we're a great pair, surely.' So, when the 'Saint' who cured their eyes before is heard approaching, Mary cries, 'The Lord protect us from the Saints of God!' When the Saint raises his can of holy water, Martin sends it rocketing across the stage with our full consent. Though their vindictive neighbours lack understanding, we acknowledge that human illusion is a sacred treasure which Martin and Mary will not easily part with. Synge has his own way of reading his lesson.

The superbly simple piece which marks the maturity of Synge's gaunt mood is, of course, *The Playboy of the Western World*. From the beginning we are carefully put in two minds about the blasphemy of its subject: that Synge should make his parricide such a figure of admiration to his audience in the shebeen, and hence such a charmer to his audience in the theatre, was a naughty sarcasm indeed. As Yeats said, the outcry against the play was an outcry against its way of seeing. The last sequence in the play was more than a way of seeing; it was a spit in the eye, or, to be more precise, three or four spits. When Mahon, Christy's father, arrives very much alive to drag his son back home, Christy turns on him with real viciousness, another loy in hand. He has so enjoyed the praises of the girls that he will earn them again, and in earnest this time. We observe that the first response of the crowd is now 'half-frightened, half-amused'. Then, convinced that the actuality of parricide is less admirable in hard practice, and led by his beloved Pegeen, they rope him fast: 'There's a great gap between a gallous story and a dirty deed.' Synge brings sharply home to us the ugly reality of the situation by having Pegeen herself burn Christy's leg with a lighted sod. Yet we are shocked in another way when the father returns once more, proud to claim a son who has such gristle in him. And Pegeen's own famous last words, cried out alone under her shawl and in the despair of one seeing her illusions shattered, echo back over the comedy of the play, a lament for a girl's lost love and a lament for the lost vision of a whole community. We may admit that Pegeen, and all she stands for, deserves to lose Christy, and all he stands for, and yet dare we place blame when we know the human mind to be so fallible? In this masterpiece, the pattern of ironic feeling at least is unequivocal.

That Synge's drama reflects the spirit of the age in some degree is suggested by the way in which Sean O'Casey takes up the challenge where he left off. Whatever we may think of O'Casey's uneven work, with its frequent lapses into blatant unsubtlety of tone and its un-governed spells of affected rhetoric, with its final reliance on the melodramatic situation to justify itself to us, his plays continually fascinate as experiments. As we might expect of any good, developing dramatist, each new play he wrote was an experiment, not by any winning achievement in the expressionism he attempted, but in exploring his peculiar territories of feeling. The special irony found in *Juno and the Paycock* and *The Plough and the Stars* must seem to us now entirely appropriate to the unrest of his time and place, and indeed relatively simple in conception. But not uninspired. The decision to present to a still impassioned Irish audience of 1926 the events immediately preceding the hallowed Easter Rebellion of 1916 through the talk in a squalid public-house was a deliberate act of comic provocation. O'Casey splits his stage in Act II to show the great events through the window of the pub, like a play-within-a-play, an arch within the arch, and thereby distances and splits his audience. When the listeners hear the language of the Leader outside the window parodying the Eucharist, 'Bloodshed is a cleansing and sanctifying thing', they hear his words as an echo of the disgruntled sentiments of Rosie the street-walker. For her, the Rebellion merely hurts her business: 'They're all in a holy mood. . . You'd think they were th' glorious company of th' saints, an' th' noble army of martyrs thrampin' through th' sthreets of paradise.' O'Casey's early drama provides an extension of the Chekhovian shading in his use of the everyday scene, and echoes Synge's alternating farce and poetry; but he adds a fair larding of sarcastic melodrama of his own.

The violent contradictions of the pathetic and the comic in *Juno and the Paycock* are not preposterous, but they are too flagrantly juxtaposed at the level of naturalism their author has chosen, and the mechanism creaks. The resulting effect is sometimes merely hysterical. In its violent context of civil war the comedy of Fluther, Peter and the Covey in *The Plough and the Stars* mingles more naturally with the near-tragic feelings of Nora and Jack Clitheroe, Mrs Gogan's daughter and Bessie. Its setting and mood encourage us to accept a caricatured and categorical ordering of life's incongruities. The play's overcharged sentiment and its sensationalism are saved only by the injection of laughter. The interwoven tragicomedy he arrived at in this play guided O'Casey towards the arresting form he devised for *The Silver Tassie*.

The daring in the structure of this play is unmistakable. But our interest in it today does not rest on its method of sliding between the naturalistic and expressionistic manners from Act I to Act II, and then doggedly back to naturalism for the last two acts. Nor does it rest on its curious attempt to show the particular ugliness of war in the general and impersonal terms of an unidentified bunch of common soldiers. It chiefly impresses in its attempt to enlarge the audience's vision by effects of calculated irony. These grow as the play proceeds: the expressionism gives them an anti-naturalistic licence for grotesquerie.

The battlefield scene of Act II introduces the first bold stroke which marks O'Casey as a writer of real originality. Into the ugly picture of 'jagged and lacerated ruin', with its heaps of rubbish and spiky stumps of trees and its barbed wire, dominated by the sinister outline of a squat howitzer in giant form, into the exhausted and bitter soldiery who themselves serve to decorate this setting, he pitches two figures of pure caricature. One is the Visitor, 'a portly man with a rubicund face', 'dressed in semi-civilian, semi-military manner', who can utter only Blimpish clichés of the parade-ground fighting spirit: 'Penetrate a little deeper into danger. Foolish, yes, but then it's an experience; by God, it's an experience. The military authorities are damned strict—won't let a...man...plunge!' The other is a Staff Officer, 'prim, pert, and polished', who moves with a clownish springing hop. He enters only to wake the sleeping men and to order them to attend a lecture on the 'Habits of those living between Frigid Zone and Arctic Circle'.

The audacity smacks of the sensational and its effect is somewhat unsure. But the introduction of raw farce into a scene of desolation and human misery is an expedient designed to unsettle an audience with a vengeance. It may well induce that cynicism of mind which is to be a prelude to a series of 'false notes' and a preparation for the dramatic argument to follow.

As the stretcher-bearers carry off the wounded, the 'Corporal' hands the '3rd Soldier' a parcel from home. It is a prayer-book. The '2nd Soldier' meanwhile is also opening a parcel from home. It is a red and yellow coloured rubber ball with a note attached: 'To play your way to the enemies' trenches when you all go over the top. Mollie.' By juxtaposing these two gifts and showing them in this setting, the author reduces them both to a level of callous stupidity and suggests a gruesome irony. The scene closes with the soldiers singing a litany to their gun, with the Corporal as priest—an effect repulsive in the extreme.

Act III is set in a hospital. The stylization of Act II does not in this act wholly slip back to the naturalism of Act I, but remains half in evidence. The clowns of Act I, Simon and Sylvester, semi-choric at first, are easily identified again. The shadowy figures of the exhausted soldiers become human, though they remain the 'numbers' of a military hospital ward. The nurse is not the Susie we knew, but a cold, mechanical creature, like the Surgeon in charge. This is a most remarkable device within the play to make us recognize the particular individual in the general symbol. Further, this act is successful for having boldly juxtaposed the farcical discussions of Simon and Sylvester on having a bath or an operation, with the sobering entrance of once athletic, now legless, Harry in a wheelchair, the cold cruelty of Jessie his former lover, and the unfeeling atmosphere in the hospital.

In the last act, O'Casey mixes his contradictory ingredients with a vicious piquancy. The war is over, and the stage is exuberantly gay with decorations of coloured lanterns and streamers. Off-stage, a dance-band plays a fox-trot. The scene bristles with people dancing and passing, wearing 'fantastically shaped paper hats'. We see the reverse side of the battlefield scene. Naturalistic drama would have thought it enough to present the football club dance simply: the weight of feeling from the rest of the play would itself have suggested the irony of the image, as it does with the ball in Act III of *The Cherry Orchard*. But O'Casey makes his point unequivocally: lost in this bright festivity is a blind Teddy Foran who cannot see its brightness, and a legless Harry who must watch his girl dancing with other men.

There is no question of action to further the story in this last act. The incongruities make the dry statement:

HARRY (*singing softly*). Swing low, sweet chariot, comin' for to carry me home...
VOICE. Balloons will be given out now! Given out now—the balloons!
MRS FORAN (*excitedly*). They're going' to send up the balloons! They're goin' to let the balloons fly now!
HARRY (*singing*). Swing low, sweet chariot, comin' for to carry me home...

Even to cap the blatancy of this trick, Surgeon Maxwell closes the scene with a song as he waltzes Susie in his arms:

> Swing into the dance,
> Take joy when it comes, ere it go;
> For the full flavour of life
> Is either a kiss or a blow.
> He to whom joy is a foe,
> Let him wrap himself up in his woe;
> For he is a life on the ebb,
> We a full life on the flow!

It does not need to be more than the doggerel it is; the dance tune gives the author licence to speak in almost direct address to us. Unsubtle though this is, yet it is strong in its dramatic effect, a stageworthy comment on the callousness of war. Perhaps O'Casey's satirical eye was never so jaundiced as when he wrote *The Silver Tassie*.

O'Casey since the 'twenties has signally failed to find a form to make his moralizing dramatically objective. The bald, balletic expressionism in *Within the Gates*, with caricatures for its characters and a naïve story of a bishop's lost daughter who for consolation turns from prostitution to the 'Dreamer' in preference to the Church, is instinct with ironic but ill-articulated ideas. *Red Roses for Me* also assumes an expressionistic freedom, but for all its vivid splendours of speech and feeling, its humour and its pathos, the strict discipline of form that expressionism demands is lacking.

Cock-a-Doodle Dandy will serve to illustrate the sad demise of the later O'Casey. The play has the same passionate vitality that he retained throughout his long apprenticeship of a career. It presents the worlds of the spiritually dead and the physically alive, the worlds of those who hate and those who love the Cock, symbolic of young vigour, which appears from time to time through the play. Michael and Mahan are crabby little Irish capitalists eaten up with lechery while their distemper is cloaked in the dogma of religion deriving from the parish priest, Father Domineer. With a pious vindictiveness and brutality, the priest, 'a green glow enveloping him', halts the happy sensual dancing of the girls with the villagers. Shame replaces their abandon. With a blow he murders the man 'living in sin'; he tells Michael to pack his daughter Loreleen off to America and hounds her out of the village in rags with Michael's consent; he sends the crippled girl Julia ceremoniously to Lourdes only to return in pitiful despair 'without even a gloamin' thought of hope'. Here is indeed a crude portrait of all the 'base-born' 'life-unbelievers', if we may use D. H. Lawrence's terms. The presentation of this sombre subject is intermittently counterpointed with the mad antics of pantomime which almost manage to relieve the starkness of the pulpit from which O'Casey is preaching. Yet we may guess that no stage tricks could make much difference to a play so black and white in its conception.

PIRANDELLO

The finest plays of Luigi Pirandello are those in which a gentle, naturalistic introduction is the prelude to a violent wrench as the rational world of the audience is questioned. So it is in *Each in His Own Way* (*Ciascuno a suo modo*) which begins with a quiet and respectable tea-party. The guests discuss whether one's opinions are true if one can change them according to circumstances. In particular they discuss the tragic conduct of the beautiful courtesan Delia Morello and the feelings of others towards her. But in two interludes we are staggered to find that Delia is given an existence apart from her character in the play. After Act I a 'real' Delia is under discussion apparently by members of our own audience, so that, as Pirandello has put it, the first act now assumes the shape of a fiction. Later the opinions of the 'spectators' themselves are thrust back a remove into fiction when the 'real' Delia leaps on to the stage from the stalls where we sit and flies at the actress who is playing her part. In the confusion, the 'third' act is not played at all, and we wonder whether we are not in fact players ourselves, subject to the observation of another and more omniscient audience. At each step the spectator's image in the mirror of the play is distorted until he is forced to adjust his own position. When the balance is restored, the image is distorted again.

In *Six Characters in Search of an Author* the curtain of the magic world of the play has no need to rise, for a rehearsal is in progress. In other words the actors and actresses in the theatre are as real as we are. This world of conventional reality is paraded long enough to relax us comfortably. Then six creatures of a half-composed fiction come upon the stage, creatures apparently as far from reality as Pirandello is able to devise. But in the course of the play they grow to such proportions of conviction that their make-believe becomes a reality and the reality of the original actors becomes make-believe, until we dare not try to distinguish the two. *Henry IV* encourages us tamely to accept the statement of Henry's insanity, only to discover that his madness is too cruelly sane. In *Right You Are If You Think So*, one statement is taken for truth, until it is flatly contradicted by another. We attempt each time to solve the problem by rational conjecture, only to find that another contradiction is proposed. We either press our reasoning to its limits, or admit a temporary insanity to gain relief from the satanic taunts of the author. These devices are designed to call up with a vengeance Pirandello's *sentimento del contrario*, the sense of the opposite.[1]

Pirandello's drama is a contest with the feelings of an audience as to whether these are to be preserved or destroyed. A play of his is often in the first place given its peculiar form to make us think, feel and comment, and then revise our feelings and comment on our commentary. We are to see from a new viewpoint, just at the moment when we thought we had established with some certainty the vantage point we had gained. Like each section of Browning's *The Ring and the Book* or each episode in the Japanese tale of *Rashomon*, each thrust in the action of Pirandello's comedy undermines our respect for what has gone before and for the decisions we made. We analyse and re-analyse the logic of our thought and feeling until we can neither think nor feel, nor even laugh. If we sit and gape perplexed, this is our tragedy, since we are the anti-heroes of the drama.

Pirandello's output has been very large, and somewhat mixed in quality. At his best he achieves the dark effect, not so much by the naughty arrangement of incongruous parts, but rather within the frame of the play set up as a whole. His theme does not suffer contradictions in its elaboration; it is contradictory in its conception. He conceives a tragedy and writes it as comedy. Domenico Vittorini tells us that Pirandello declared *Man, Beast and Virtue*, an early play, to be a tragedy stifled by comedy.[2] In this play a lady married to a sea-captain finds herself pregnant by her lover, and an aphrodisiac has to be devised to induce her husband, who usually locks himself away from his wife, to spend a night with her. Here is a subject of traditional farce. In Pirandello's hands it becomes a bitter play in which the sin of the beast in man can only be covered by his own beastliness, and morality is used to hide his immorality.

[1] Pirandello, *L'Umorismo*, 2nd ed. (Florence, 1920), p. 178.
[2] D. Vittorini, *The Drama of Luigi Pirandello* (New York, 1935), p. 369.

Pirandello shows us human suffering and turns its tragic note of exultation from triumph to humility and from dignity to indignity. We are shocked. Legislating from himself, he has explained his work in these terms: 'Ordinarily in the conception of a work of art, reflection is like a form of feeling, almost a mirror in which the feeling is watching itself. Pursuing this idea, one might argue that, in the conception of humour, reflection is, yes, like a mirror, but of icy water in which the flame of the feeling is not only watching itself, but plunges and extinguishes itself.'[1] Emotion is to be douched by the cold scrutiny of the reason.

Pirandello's intention is to show man the contradictions within life and within himself, but especially to transmit to the spectator his own obsessed interest in man's erratic and impermanent mind, with its capricious motives and behaviour. In a state of near-hysteria, man will break into painful laughter, and the twin impulses of ridicule and pathos will come together in a completely felt, but pessimistic, image of the human condition. We know that what is funny to us is often misery to others; Pirandello will have us live in two or more minds together, objectively and subjectively at once. Laughter as well as tears is an expression of grief, and, as a character in *Each in His Own Way* says, 'That's my way of laughing and my laughter hurts me more than anyone else.' Pirandello's 'humourism' suggests an attitude limited in breadth but profound in insight. It recognizes that man may hold within himself at the same time the power to mock and the power to sympathize. Humour for Pirandello is the exquisite coition of laughter and grief.

Aspect after aspect of commonplace human behaviour offered Pirandello his subject-matter: our instinct to preserve youth and to hold on to the youthful image we have of ourselves, to fix in immutable shapes the essentially fluid thing we know as life; our tendency to apply to others the attitudes we cherish ourselves, and

---

[1] Pirandello, *L'Umorismo*, 2nd ed. (Florence, 1920), p. 186. The original reads, 'Ordinariamente, nella concezione d'un'opera d'arte, la riflessione è quasi una forma del sentimento, quasi uno specchio in cui il sentimento si rimira. Volendo seguitar quest'imagine, si potrebbe dire che, nella concezione umoristica, la riflessione è, sì, come uno specchio, ma d'acqua diaccia, in cui la fiamma del sentimento non si rimira soltanto, ma si tuffa e si smorza.'

to live in a world of dreams reinforced with all the logic in our power; our need to 'build ourselves up' and to create the 'reality' of ourselves from our own imagination; our intuitive way of presenting one appearance to one person and another to another, with our horror when we realize that we have grown so accustomed to using multiple masks that we may never know the face beneath; and our inevitable terror when we realize that we do not know where actuality ends and fantasy begins, and that at the end we are enshrined among our carefully hoarded illusions, naked and utterly alone. This is Pirandello's limitless mine of dramatic material.

Naked (*Vestire gli ignudi*) is the story of a girl, Ersilia Drei, who attempts to poison herself partly out of remorse for the death of her charge, a child who fell from a terrace, and partly out of despair at the emptiness of her life. Sentimentally, but humanly, she had desired only a modest enough success in life, and had fallen in love with a young naval officer who had jilted her. She thus wishes it to be known that she died for love. In hospital she recovers, however, and tells a reporter a lurid version of her story; in the sensation that follows she is befriended by a novelist. While seeming to help her out of pity, in fact he wishes only to use her for 'copy'. The officer returns to her apparently out of compassion, but in fact he too had been jilted by a second fiancée, and is coming to her on the rebound. Then we learn that her former employer was in fact her lover, and that it was through their joint neglect that the child had fallen to her death. No one is as he seems, and poor Ersilia recognizes this at last. She tells them that she had not lied in order to live, but in order to die, to cover herself 'with a decent dress'. Now in earnest she takes poison a second time because she truly feels herself to be stark naked.

When all that Pirandello has to say to us about art and life, the individual soul and the world outside it, has been turned over in discussion, his central problem of communication in the theatre remains one of the most interesting sides of his work. He attempts communication at once by presenting character on the stage in all its instability and by compelling his audience to undergo a corresponding sense of instability. Leone Gala in *The Rules of the Game* (*Il gioco delle parti*) is both the protagonist of the action and its chorus. Through him we too are encouraged to play a dual role, understanding his mind with compassion while simultaneously commenting on the triangular action: his relation to his pretty wife Silia and her lover Guido. As in *Henry IV*, the theatrical task is to marry the external action of the play precisely with our direct response to the suffering of Leone's soul in order to bring us to a fully realized emotional and intellectual sense of the play's meaning. When the character on the stage is stripped of its mask simultaneously with the stripping of the spectator, Pirandello achieves a first objective of great drama. If in this way Pirandello, like Kafka, can lower our defences, the nightmare can run its course.

Leone is meticulous in his habits and scrupulous in his morality. He now lives apart from his wife, devoted to cookery on the one hand and books on the other, all he needs for physical and spiritual nourishment. He visits his wife for precisely one half-hour each evening. It is evident that Silia is haunted by this man, drawn to him, yet she cannot abide him: his eyes are 'sharp as needles and vacant at the same time'. Significantly the comedy of his character is established in this way well before he enters: we are prepared for some kind of ludicrous monster. In fact he is seen to be quiet and unassuming, and within a few minutes we are playing our dual role.

For we quickly discover the tragedy of his life. His apparent non-chalance is a most careful pose: he has consciously drained himself of feeling and lives the life of a rational automaton in the face of the cruel and uncertain world of other people, and particularly of his wife, who is all perverse irrational instinct. The pessimist Leone treats life merely as a 'game', the only way he knows to survive its vicissitudes. Silia for her part finds this intolerable and determines to seek a way to have him killed. She invites an insult from four drunken young men, one of them a noted duellist, and then demands that her honour be avenged. Leone accordingly arranges for the fiercest of duels to the death, knowing that he has no experience whatever with sword or pistol. When all is prepared, he calmly informs the lover Guido at the last moment that it is for him to defend his wife. In a melodramatic *dénouement* Guido is killed. His death is but one more move in the game: it is an ugly joke, one which in its terrible outcome shocks us into understanding the tragedy in the comedy of life.

This account hardly suggests the skilled counterpoint of the macabre and the farcical in Act III of the play, and the calculated modulations of the tempo which sound the ticking of the clock to the end. With thoughts of the ugly duel planted strongly in our minds, Pirandello opens the act with the slow, ponderous servant Philip, comically only half awake at the early hour set for the event, reluctantly opening the door to the doctor who is to be in attendance. Philip lays out the breakfast table as Dr Spiga lays out his instruments: 'Scalpels...bone saw...forceps..dissectors...compressors...' Now the pace accelerates as the agitated seconds Guido and Barelli enter and make a stiff and formal greeting, only to find that Leone is, astonishingly, still asleep. He finally enters and stands sleepily in his pyjamas and slippers. At this point comes a complete change of tone and tempo, from that of near-farce to the terrible tension of Leone's revelation that he will not fight, but that the strictly honourable Guido must replace him. At the end, the fatal result of the duel is communicated to the distraught Silia, and to us, in a frightening mixture of acute sensations by the dishevelled Dr Spiga, who 'dashes in with grotesque discomposure: flings himself at his surgical instruments laid out on the table: rolls them up in the cloth, and rushes out without saying a word'.

Like his successor Anouilh, Pirandello is often at a loss to know what more there is to be done once his audience is naked, and, like Anouilh, he must repeat himself somewhat negatively from play to play. Often at such points of no return he will weaken his effect by argument, telling us what we have already felt through the agency of his play; at other times he will wisely drop the curtain with the spit and the laugh we conceded to Shakespeare's Pandarus. At the curtain, the announcement of Leone's breakfast, the laughter of Laudisi of *Right You Are*, or of the Stepdaughter of *Six Characters*, packs us off with a flea in the ear, as do Undershaft in Shaw's *Major Barbara*, Jacques in Anouilh's *Dinner with the Family* and M. Henri in his *Point of Departure*, Barbette in Giraudoux's *Duel of Angels*, and Irma in Jean Genêt's *The Balcony*.

Although Pirandello calls *Henry IV* 'a tragedy', lets it run to the limits of its sardonic conclusion, and takes the laughter to the point of vomit, it seems to me no different in kind from the 'comedy' of his other plays. Since nowhere has Pirandello more successfully employed his 'humourism' than in this play, it is used in the next few pages to demonstrate briefly his exquisite sense of theatre.

ANALYSIS: 'HENRY IV', ACT III

Preparation for torture

The story of *Henry IV* is ingeniously worked out, though only the barest framework is supplied to hold the play together and to tease the audience. We gather that, at the age of twenty-six, Henry had played the part of the eleventh-century German emperor Henry IV in a pageant. A fall from his horse had rendered him insane, and his insanity had taken paranoiac form: he continued to think himself the Emperor. For twenty years he has kept his household as counterfeit as himself: his servants dress in eleventh-century costume, and pay court to him as if he were a despotic monarch. But for about the last eight years it is 'suggested' that he has in fact been sane, though he now so hates his fellows that he prefers to remain playing the part he has grown used to, somewhat like Gaston, the soldier suffering from loss of memory in Anouilh's *Traveller without Luggage*, a man who so hates himself that he prefers his anonymity. Henry is 'a poor devil already out of the world, out of time, out of life'.[1] Now his friends—Matilda, his former lover, and Belcredi, his former rival— have brought a doctor to try to cure him. With them are Matilda's daughter, Frida, and her fiancé, Charles di Nolli. The Doctor has devised a dangerous cure: Frida is to dress as her mother was twenty years before, and so shake into life 'the stopped watch' of Henry's brain.

The structure of the play is devilishly planned to give the audience two split focal points for their sympathies and interest, and these are dramatically in opposition. First, Henry's own mental suffering must invite our compassion, and his pain is in the end to be our pain.

---

[1] Trans. by E. Storer from *Three Plays by Luigi Pirandello* (London, 1923).

Second, our other, perhaps better, selves are represented by all those who pay court to him, the apparently sane; in effect, the second centre of interest is in the auditorium, and our sympathy is to be checked by our sense of the cowardice of a sick man trying to stop the movement of time and make the transitory permanent. Yet, for all that the horror of this inhibits intimacy, some intimate and subjective feeling for Henry's plight is to war with our objective understanding of his insanity, for the more we enter into his mind and make his standards our standards, the more we make his insanity temporarily our sanity, and the more we make the other characters' sanity our insanity. Here is a revolving see-saw of a play devised to send us home dizzy and startled, for an audience must lose its free will in any tussle with Pirandello's stage.

The first two acts of the play set a tone not far removed from farcical, and it is important to notice this attempt to put us off our guard. The servants mix their modern speech and behaviour, their cigarettes and their modern nicknames most incongruously with the medieval costume and décor. The hero and his problem are introduced to us only through the uncommitted eyes of such servants and with their kind of levity. The visitors in their modern dress again strike the ludicrous note when they enter the medieval scene. Henry himself, with his badly dyed hair, the 'two small doll-like dabs of colour' on his pallid cheeks, there to mark fantastically the grotesque tragedy of a man trying to defy the onset of age, in fact looks both clown and puppet at the same time. When Matilda, Belcredi and the Doctor are received by the Emperor, Henry's diatribe tests their powers of masquerade and reveals their embarrassment, and this is the funnier since we are not at this point sympathetically attached to either party.

This tone continues to colour our impressions well into Act II. The Doctor's plan is proposed and prepared with not a little mockery; and the Doctor himself is painted as a figure of fun, with the pomposity of his 'analogical elasticity', his 'symptomatized delirium', his 'considerable cerebral activity' and so on. Unexpectedly Henry seems to let his mask of madness slip for a moment, suggesting that he knows the truth. We, like the servants and the visitors who thought him mad, begin to wonder too late whether we have been trapped.

Productions of the play have sometimes destroyed its important central irony by demonstrating to the spectator that Henry *is* sane, but Pirandello is very careful not to have him confess in so many words that he has been merely playing the madman. He speaks in an ingenious series of ambiguities which suit equally the enraged Emperor and the fiendish impostor: 'Don't you see, idiot, how I treat them, how I play the fool with them, make them appear before me just as I wish?...' Then he seems to tell us the truth—by the astonished reactions of the servants we are encouraged to believe him—until we begin to ask ourselves desperate questions. If a sane man says he's mad, he may well be sane. If a madman says he's mad, he too may well be sane. But if a madman says he's sane, must he be sane? We arrive at the centre of the puzzle of 'All statements in this square are false'. So we return to his behaviour for guidance, only to hear him giving his imperious orders in a terrible voice once more, bringing them all to their knees. Yet further teasing is to follow. In a flash his thunder turns to crazy laughter as he mocks them—and us:

HENRY. ...Let's have a jolly good laugh!...
   (*Laughs*): Ah!...Ah!...Ah!...
LANDOLPH–HAROLD–ORDULPH (*looking at each other half happy and half dismayed*). Then he's cured!...he's all right!...
HENRY. Silence! Silence!

Pirandello has his hero voice a thought as it chases across our mind: 'It's a terrible thing if you don't hold on to that which seems true to you today.' We look at this man as we look at ourselves.

The moonlit darkness gathers in the room, and in our ripe imagination. We are as uncertain of the truth as ever, but the scene has been set for the horror of Act III, the shaking of the watch.

The biter bit

On either side of the throne, the two life-size portraits of a young man and woman dressed in the carnival costumes of the Emperor Henry and the Marchioness Matilda of Tuscany have, since the start of the play, dominated the room. They have been the reminder of present misery accentuated by the knowledge of a happy past and careless youth, though we have by now taken their presence for granted. At the rise of the curtain they have imperceptibly changed, and they stand on a darkened stage. Within the frames, dressed for their new parts, Charles di Nolli and Frida have become the portraits. We had not been told directly what the Doctor's trick was to be: it was hinted that this exchange would take place, but the details were whispered only to Charles and Frida. We are ourselves to be sufficiently startled by the discovery of the impersonations, that we may begin emotionally to understand something of the shock Henry will suffer. This is essentially an effect of theatre, and is not to be reproduced on the printed page. We must sense Henry's horror from within, and, when Henry enters with his lamp, what he sees shall be what we see.

Now a tired man, he walks slowly across the stage—until he is stopped by one word, the first of Frida's prepared speech: 'Henry...' It is enough. Immediately the play leaps alive again. We see him stop, we see his terror-stricken face, grotesque with the red spots on its cheeks, we see his arm raised in fear. We do not halt the careering of the image to ask why he is afraid, for we have caught his fear. One word has destroyed his composure and ours. We must ask again whether he is sane; for him, his command of the game he was playing is challenged. Terrible doubt lingers through the act. As the biter is bit, so the comedy is transformed in tone: it is a hint of what is to come. Henry has been so long confident of his acting, secure in his knowledge of his part, that one jolt to his control, one detail of performance which goes awry, must make him doubt his free agency. It flashes across his mind that there is a control outside himself that he is defying: this is the hint of the essence of the tragic conflict. Perhaps he is the puppet and not the puppet-master? We feel his deflation of spirits, just as we are amused by marionettes until make-believe becomes reality.

We are not into tragedy yet. Frida's fear remains an object of curious interest. Upon Henry's 'dreadful cry', she continues to scream his name 'like a mad woman'. She fulfils a double dramatic function as innocent victim, hysterical-mad herself, and as chorus cognizant of madness in others. She passes on her fear to us as the stillness of the stage is broken by her movement from the picture-frame and by the rapid entrance of the rest to comfort her, all talking together. They crowd in the upper part of the stage, which is now lit: they remain the reasonably clear world of sanity. They look towards us and towards Henry, who stands stock still, a silhouette in the darkness downstage, symbolizing the uncomfortable recesses of our mind.

Like each new revelation of 'the truth' in *Right You Are*, which sharpens the point of the play but serves only to confuse us more, the problem here has been accentuated by this moment of terror, but neither character nor audience knows any the better whether Henry is mad or sane: if mad, we should weep; if sane, we should laugh. We do neither. We sit transfixed.

The tables turned again

We sit transfixed, and Pirandello takes his pleasure in confounding our brains. He uses the formula of the age-old riddle of the man who looked at his son's portrait and declared, 'Brothers and sisters have I none, but this man's father is my father's son.' In a revenge of sheer dialectical brilliancy, the madman is to make each doubt his own sanity.

Agnes, the mother of di Nolli and the sister of Henry, had died a month before, firmly convinced that her brother would regain his sanity; but for all her care of him, Henry had refused to comfort her on her death-bed by disclosing his recovery to her—if he had any such recovery to disclose. Now di Nolli accuses him of deceiving her 'right up to the time of her death', and Henry retorts, 'It isn't *your* sister only that is dead!' Pirandello's italics make it clear that Henry must be looking upon his new rival, di Nolli, as someone pretending to be his twentieth-century self, since di Nolli has no sister. The two emperors stand facing each other dressed exactly alike, and, venomously, Henry sees the younger man both as a character playing the part of the Emperor and as the actor behind the character, that is, as Henry's double. Or, of course, perhaps Henry too is pretending.

The confusion increases when di Nolli asks in bewilderment, 'My

147

sister? Yours, I say, whom you compelled up to the last moment to present herself here as your mother Agnes!' Agnes was also the name of the mother of the eleventh-century Emperor, and Agnes, Henry's sister, had been play-acting for the sake of flattering Henry's delusion: for twenty years of 'insanity' the sister had been accepted as the mother. We are to assume, therefore, that Henry sees her as di Nolli's mother in his part as Henry the Emperor; thus he can say, 'And was she not *your* mother?' Agnes was di Nolli's mother in real life, and di Nolli quickly assumes that this is what Henry means: 'My mother? Certainly my mother!' But it is evident that Henry does not mean it so, since he retorts, 'But your mother is dead for me, *old and far away*!' Here 'your mother' can only mean the mother of the Emperor who died in the eleventh century, and his statement suggests that he now has a twentieth-century sanity upon him, seeing di Nolli as his old self, the insane play-actor.

Henry has contrived to spin the wheel full circle. For di Nolli, a flesh-and-blood mother has become a figment of another man's imagination remote in the past, and to prove Henry sane, di Nolli must almost prove himself insane. Or so perhaps Pirandello would have us see it, since the dramatizing of the argument has to a degree failed in the realization. Nevertheless, the author kept his effect even incomplete as it is, and he was quite justified in retaining it. The spectator is confused and left gasping at the vicious brilliance of the man supposedly mad. It is no wonder that Matilda looks with dismay at the others.

This is Henry taking his revenge indeed. Do you wish to guess whether I am mad or sane? he seems to be asking. What impertinence for you fools to imagine that one can recognize sanity, identify mask or face, in others! First tease your brains and decide, if you can, whether you are sane yourselves, whether it is not you who are wearing the mask.

Henry pursues his victims, Belcredi and the others, and, through their agency, us. He turns on Frida and addresses her as if she really is the Marchioness of Tuscany, asking her whether Agnes was not the Emperor's mother, prepared to cross-examine her savagely as he did di Nolli. Frida, the Doctor and Belcredi respond in the three separate ways in which we are at that instant responding ourselves, with fear, with belief, with doubt:

FRIDA (*still frightened, draws closer to di Nolli*). No, no, I don't know. Not I!
DOCTOR. It's the madness returning...Quiet now, everybody!
BELCREDI (*indignant*). Madness indeed, Doctor! He's acting again!...

Henry has his friends in an impasse; and thus Pirandello has us. Yet can we avoid sharing some of the joy of his triumph over those who tried to test him so cruelly? We trust and mistrust our judgments, and love and hate ourselves.

The touch of a flower on the neck

There follows an extraordinary sequence of confusions, both the characters' and ours. This sequence is in fact a clever equivalent of the dramatic pause which permits an audience to weigh a new impression and adjust the shifting pattern of the play's meaning to a point of temporary equilibrium. The pause that is traditional allows us to review the situation, as when Robert de Baudricourt is left winded by his encounter with the Maid: we sum up the situation and estimate her power, anticipate the opposition to her and guess at the probable extent of her success. When the Steward runs in and cries that the hens are laying, our judgment is confirmed.

The crux in *Henry IV* differs from the traditional pause in that the author knows we are unlikely to reach a point of equilibrium, although he also knows we must try for it. He has so devised it that with one utterance we pronounce Henry sane, and with the next condemn him to insanity. We do this in order to maintain the rational order of things; we must try to the end to measure Henry from the standpoint of what we take to be normality. The truth is, we are undergoing, and we are to feel, the self-delusion of every man who attempts to pass judgment on his fellow.

Thus, in this 'pause' the action is in no way furthered, but in it Pirandello leaves us rope enough to hang ourselves. On the stage we hear only a futile contest of words: from Belcredi and Donna Matilda, who think him cured; from the Doctor and the servant

Landolph, who thought him cured, but who are now none too sure; while Henry himself passionately declares that he is cured, though his every remark casts further doubt on the truth of this. He talks of his recovery, yet because of his burning anger, his sudden turns, his trembling, his sharp changes of mind in the full course of passionate speech, we remain unconvinced. Is he still deluded? He speaks of the triumph of the Marchioness at the carnival, addressing his remark to Donna Matilda, yet pointing to Frida, who is of course still dressed as Matilda was then. He alludes to the servants' betrayal of his 'recovery' as if they had denounced him merely to make fun of him; but since the visitors now laugh 'shamefacedly' at this, perhaps they are still in doubt whether the servants did not tell them a lie to have a further joke at their expense.

This sequence might well be tinged with farce, were it not for two comments from Henry, directed, as it were, straight at us. These relate the contorted action going forward on the stage to conventional life as we know it. They provide sheet-anchors for the play, extending and deepening its image.

Our consciousness of time and of its power, which will not let us rest, which gives us no comfort, which defeats our efforts to control ourselves and our environment, which at the last sets at nought the emotions and impulses of human nature, as at the last it does with Henry, this sense of time has been one of the strongest threads running through the first two acts. Now the keynote of this theme is sounded when Henry refers to his lost years:

HENRY. Look at my hair!
BELCREDI. But mine is grey too!
HENRY. Yes, with this difference: that mine went grey here, as Henry IV, do you understand? And I never knew it! I perceived it all of a sudden, one day, when I opened my eyes...

Pirandello first provides the link with everyday experience: we recognize those appalling moments of realization when we sense the speeding passage of the years. Such an experience is one to savour gently, and to grow used to slowly, that ageing may be gracious. Here the way that Henry discovers his age is sudden and terrifying; we hear the horror in his voice. Thus Pirandello presses on us the full statement he wants to make, the sense of irretrievable loss, the worse because youth did not exist: '...and I was terrified because I understood at once that not only had my hair gone grey, but that I was all grey, inside; that everything had fallen to pieces, that everything was finished; and I was going to arrive, hungry as a wolf, at a banquet which had already been cleared away...' The meaning of this fearful statement Pirandello has still to recreate in us. His malicious effort to disrupt our moral security is to become explicit at the crisis.

· Our false trust that we have the knowledge and power to lift or replace our mask at will is the second thread woven into the play, one that is indeed tightly interwoven with the theme of our powerlessness against time and its mysteries. The force that controls our dying also holds the tyrannous mirror which will not allow us to know whether we see our real selves or not.

Henry declares that we are the involuntary puppets of a continuous, everlasting masquerade, just as madness had caricatured the life of the Emperor Henry. For who, other than the astute artist, can tell what is true and what is caricature in our behaviour? Certainly not ourselves. Henry gesticulates in the tragic manner: 'You know, it is quite easy to get accustomed to it. One walks about as a tragic character, just as if it were nothing...' To stress the point, he tells the story of an Irish priest, asleep and dreaming in the sun in a public garden:

One may be sure that in that moment he did not know any more that he was a priest, or even where he was. He was dreaming...A little boy passed with a flower in his hand. He touched the priest with it here on the neck. I saw him open his laughing eyes, while all his mouth smiled with the beauty of his dream. He was forgetful of everything...But all at once, he pulled himself together, and stretched out his priest's cassock; and there came back to his eyes the same seriousness which you have seen in mine...

That touch of innocence is something we may never re-experience. We may continue forever to play our part, be it that of priest or emperor or humble man, and never know the repose of reality and integrity. If we did awake, it might be only to realize the terror of our loss, not in lowering and losing a mask, which in itself matters nothing at all compared with finding alien the genuine life we might have led: we should be 'all grey inside'.

Henry felt the touch of the flower on his neck when Frida called to him, and his horror was absolute. Pirandello has set himself to make us feel that touch as well. Is the task proving greater than his playwright's art? Else why should he stop to tell the stories of his grey hair and the Irish priest? They re-emphasize Henry's realization of his central problem, but will they persuade us to the realization of it too?

Fiction becomes fact

The play's argument on the relativity of madness has risked being too conceptual, each event providing only for the further development of the argument. We have reached, in this manner, a final paradox. Henry is sane because he knows he is mad; he is cured because, as he says, he can act the madman to perfection. The author cannot resist a fling at us, pursuing the natural corollary: 'I do it very quietly, I'm only sorry for you that have to live your madness so agitatedly, without knowing it or seeing it.' Pirandello has used the others on the stage to demonstrate our immediate state of mind, as he has used the play to demonstrate our general state of ignorance. In this pursuit of truth, Henry has remained the omnipotent figure, the author-figure, the puppet-master using his puppets for a cynical revenge. Now with a masochistic joy, Pirandello twists his comedy to a tragic *dénouement* and turns cerebral excogitation to vividly realized sensation in the auditorium. He has Henry take his triumph one step further, and one step too far. It is *hubris* indeed, for in allowing Henry to believe he has removed his last mask, and that the sanity he had discovered in himself is the absolute one, the author, as it were, acknowledges his limitations in writing the play at all.

Henry's gross error, and the annihilating stroke, is his attempt to mix fiction with fact. He returns to his role of emperor, and tries with make-believe to govern events that lie outside the make-believe world, as is our frequent habit in ordinary life. Of course, as he declares, di Nolli is not the Emperor, because Henry wishes to be; but Matilda is not the Marchioness, because after twenty years she has become a woman he can no longer recognize. The Marchioness he *can* recognize is the young girl dressed in the carnival costume— Frida! Frida, young, pretty, innocent of the world, stands there in fear as the masquerade makes its claims on reality: 'The dream alive in you! More than alive in you! It was an image that wavered there and they've made you come to life! Oh, mine! You're mine, mine, mine, in my own right!' As he holds her in his arms, 'laughing like a madman', we suddenly sense a reality above the masquerade: we see an ageing lunatic claiming a terrified girl twenty years his junior, the mad and the sane intermingled preposterously. Pirandello has dramatized his paradox; we are revolted, and the true cutting edge of this kind of comedy makes its incision felt.

When Henry lays claim to Frida, innocence is trapped by experience and polluted by life. Frida has played her part unknowingly and fallen victim to society's jest. In life, suggests the author, we unwittingly enter a masquerade which is devitalizing, which will kill our souls. Frida must now play the mad game of society in earnest.

On the other hand, Belcredi was never innocent. He has seen Henry's tragedy growing to its crisis and he has laughed. He was Henry's rival and his mind's assassin. Fortune now decrees that it shall be Belcredi who moves to stop Henry's assault on the girl: 'Leave her alone! Leave her alone! You're no madman!' In a flash Henry takes a maniacal and physical revenge on his enemy: he draws a sword and drives it into Belcredi. The line that marks the climax is superb in its complex simplicity: 'I'm not mad, eh! Take that, you!...' It is a line which brings together the several strands of the play's paradox in one astonishing contradiction, and even if we have by now guessed that Henry could not consciously control reality with the same success as his attempt to live in history, this single gesture in a waste of words, like the shot fired in *Uncle Vanya*, like that in *Six Characters in Search of an Author* and that in Anouilh's *Ardèle*, like the vicious slap on his Colombe's face after Julien's laughter, is calculated to leave us dazed and wholly unsure of ourselves.

In the confusion that follows—again our horror echoes the actors'—Pirandello stresses the absolute and inseparable mixture of appearance and reality we have been faced with since Frida assumed her character as the Marchioness. Still Henry refuses to say directly whether he is mad or sane, and still we are left to deduce what we can for ourselves. If Henry is taking a just revenge on his rival, it is the action of a sane man perhaps momentarily crazed by his fury, but nevertheless that of a man with his mask removed, not acting a part. On the other hand, the strange assassination by sword thrust strongly suggests that Henry is more than using the licence of his 'authority' as Emperor, more than acting a part, but may be so obsessed by his role that he has followed his absolute prerogative as despot. Any man may in part assume a mask, but at any time a less conscious part of him may erupt to shatter it. The excitement of the debate within our minds is thus completely dramatized, and Henry's anger against the limitation of life is translated into an energy at once keenly critical and highly emotional.

Belcredi is carried off crying with his last breath that Henry is not mad—which might mean that Belcredi feels his enemy was justified in striking him and that he had been responsible for the accident twenty years before, or that in spite Belcredi wishes to ensure that Henry will pay the penalty even though he is mad. We remain desperately uncertain. Nor even can we be sure that the thrust of the sword, an action incongruous amid so much logistic argument, was not itself another symptom of make-believe.

Then follows the ace the playwright has been waiting to play. The stage is at last suddenly silent. Henry, standing between the stupefied servants, enacts a gigantic pause, which is broken by a piercing cry from Donna Matilda—Belcredi is dead! Henry has committed murder...as a man, not as an emperor.

HENRY (...*with his eyes almost starting out of his head, terrified by the life of his own masquerade which has driven him to crime*). Ah now...yes now...inevitably (*calls his valets around him as if to protect him*) here together...here together...for ever...for ever.   (*Curtain*)

Henry for his *hubris* is caught in the toils that bind us all. The man who thought to rise above his human limitations by disentangling fact from fiction has so intermingled them that he has unwittingly condemned himself to continue, like the rest of mankind, in the life of masquerade he was so anxious to discredit. His parable is tragic in the extent to which his struggle towards the superhuman has brought him down hard to the lowest level...'inevitably'. A power greater than he has condemned him to his madness.

Comic and tragic

But this is no tragedy, although Pirandello calls it one. The world against which the hero has been struggling is that of petty humanity as well as his own. It is a comic world, depicted in strong critical colours. For us to realize that our man has been pushed down among those we despise, for us to realize that Henry is another Belcredi, holds no exultation, only bitter debasement. The social comedy which had provided the excuse in its fantasy and had given weight to Henry's struggles of evasion must leave us in that characteristic discomfort of dark comedy. The play grew away from its author's hands.

If this discomfort is Pirandello's 'tragic' note, it echoes that shrill familiar Pirandellian laugh which torments the theatre at the end of *Six Characters*. Nobody, neither villain nor hero, audience nor author, leaves the play with peace or honour. Whatever efforts Henry made to be master of himself, whatever efforts the author made towards an analysis of personality, life reasserted itself. In defeating Henry, life defeats his creator, and Pirandello in the magnificent gesture of his curtain lines is acknowledging his own limitations: we withdraw a mask only to discover another beneath it, and life will compel us to act another part to the end, whether we know we are acting or not. Again, our puny impotence is ludicrous—and to do anything else but laugh at this 'tragedy' is to court a terrible humiliation.

Yet it is a play, like many of Pirandello's, which takes its greatest effect after the final curtain. The play's technique is geared to the task of outwitting its audience, shaking our faith in order that we may look twice at ourselves and the world around us. In the issue, drama and life perform a mutual service. It is because of this that the tragic impulse of the play, although presented within a comic framework, has its unusual repercussions.

6-2

The play's special note of terror is intensified because of a re-markable dramatization of a sense of time and its tyranny. Its examination of the mind and its powerlessness to govern itself would have less meaning were it not for what the Doctor in a lucid moment calls 'the sensation of the distance of time'. The Doctor's intention, of course, is to have Henry realize that he is living in the twentieth century and not in the eleventh, a very limited objective after all. It is Pirandello's intention to have us realize how relative time is: to the individual, those eight hundred years of history matter far less than the precious twenty of personal experience. For the Doctor, the 'stopped watch' is a very general problem of mental delusion. For Pirandello, Henry, and us, it is the immediate horror of being 'out of the world, out of time, out of life'. Henry had comforted himself with the knowledge that he was 'already in history', with 'every-thing determined, everything settled'; he was not like the men of the twentieth century 'torturing themselves in ceaseless anxiety to know how their fates and fortunes will work out'. But Henry also tasted the misery of living an existence in which every event took place 'precisely and coherently in each minute particular', while life passed him by. Our sympathy for Henry is in his intensely personal experience.

Thus, from this position, *Henry IV* is certainly not only a play of social criticism, no mere comedy of manners, but a deep exploration of mind and soul, of a psychological and spiritual problem. It offers a statement about the way we live in terms of comedy, and proves it in an experience of tragedy. A deep acquaintance with time, and the knowledge that we have no control over its passage, is the driving power in the play. Its determinism gives it the complexion of classical tragedy, but its ultimately hysterical, even farcical, pessimism is characteristic of Pirandello's touch and another sign of the spirit of the age. As the mind is a maze, in which to seem to find an exit is only to re-enter the maze, so *Henry IV* offers us, in the end, spiritual anarchy.

Pirandello's definition of his theatre, which Professor Tilgher has called *teatro dello specchio*, 'the mirror theatre', is particularly ap-propriate to this play:

When a man lives, he lives and does not see himself. Well, put a mirror before him and make him see himself in the act of living, under the sway of his passions: either he remains astonished and dumbfounded at his own appearance, or else he turns away his eyes so as not to see himself, or else in disgust he spits at his image, or again clenches his fist to break it; and if he had been weeping, he can weep no more; if he had been laughing, he can laugh no more, and so on. In a word, there arises a crisis and that crisis is my theatre.[1]

He is here helping to define dark comedy.

Pirandello's influence on modern drama is ambiguous and difficult to assess. His tone is pervasive through the century, but it is possible to see explicit correspondences in the particular treatment of plot and character especially in plays by Anouilh (from *Traveller without Luggage* to *Colombe*) and Tennessee Williams (from the illusions of the mother in *The Glass Menagerie* to the self-deceivers of *Camino Real*). Yet the approach also seems to be applicable to subjects and content as diverse as those of Priestley's *They Came to a City* and Robert Bolt's *Flowering Cherry*. It seems that the Pirandellian stance, once caught, is firmly held. It is sometimes melodramatic and sometimes paradoxical in a forced and narrow way, but the achievement for which he is unlikely to be forgotten is his astonishing ability, at his best, to play the disturbing dramatic game of cat-and-mouse with the spectator. He wrote a new Socratic drama whose only parallel is that of Bernard Shaw.

[1] Quoted by W. Starkie, *Luigi Pirandello* (London, 1926), from A. Tilgher, *Voci del Tempo* (Rome, 1923).

4

COUNTERPOINT AND HYSTERIA

> NELL. One mustn't laugh at these things, Nagg.
> Why must you always laugh at them?
> NAGG. Not so loud!
> NELL. Nothing is funnier than unhappiness, I
> grant you that. But— SAMUEL BECKETT, *Endgame*

ELIOT'S 'DOUBLENESS'

In spite of his early censures in his essay on 'Four Elizabethan Dramatists' against mixing realistic and abstract conventions, T. S. Eliot made the following arresting statement at the conclusion of his book *The Use of Poetry and the Use of Criticism*:

I once designed, and drafted a couple of scenes of, a verse play. My intention was to have one character whose sensibility and intelligence should be on the plane of the most sensitive and intelligent members of the audience; his speeches should be addressed to them as much as to the other personages in the play—or rather, should be addressed to the latter, who were to be material, literal-minded and visionless, with the consciousness of being overheard by the former. There was to be an understanding between this protagonist and a small number of the audience, while the rest of the audience would share the responses of the other characters in the play.[1]

This implied division of characters and spectators into the two groups of the sensitive and the insensitive has run through much of Eliot's drama, and has often lent an ironic and satirical force to his

[1] T. S. Eliot, *The Use of Poetry and the Use of Criticism* (London, 1933), p. 153. An interesting and relevant discussion of 'pure and impure drama' is to be found in chapter 2 of D. Krause, *Sean O'Casey, the Man and his Work* (London, 1960). Krause anticipates our theme when he writes, 'Playwrights like Shakespeare, Chekhov, Shaw, Synge, O'Casey, Pirandello, Giraudoux, Anouilh, Sartre, Wilder, Beckett and Ionesco have freely used "music-hall devices in the service of the highest dramatic aims" (a phrase from S. L. Bethell, *Shakespeare and the Popular Dramatic Tradition*, London, 1944, p. 29). All of these playwrights, and many others in our time, write what is essentially impure drama. One might even say that the bastard *genre* of tragicomedy has been one of the dominant forms of twentieth century drama' (pp. 51–2).

playwriting which is characteristic of the modern theatre. Leaving aside the obvious point that a divided audience of the kind he envisages can never ensure an embracing artistic success for such drama, since only a presumed minority of the spectators could receive the ironies central to its structure, we should nevertheless look briefly at some of the creative results of this policy.

The statement in *The Use of Poetry* has, of course, direct application to his experiment in *Sweeney Agonistes*, two fragments of a verse play demonstrating a life of dull parties and empty living in which the girls Dusty and Doris entertain a variety of men in their flat. Two or three times a menacing note is introduced, through the sinister background figure of Pereira who 'pays the rent' but who is never seen, through hints of dark evil in an interlude of fortune-telling, and through the melancholy Sweeney, who eclipses the gaiety of the second scene by suggesting that existence for these girls is bound by the repetitive facts of life:

> SWEENEY. Birth, and copulation, and death.
>   That's all, that's all, that's all, that's all,
>   Birth, and copulation, and death.
> DORIS. I'd be bored.
> SWEENEY.   You'd be bored.

Sweeney then embarks on a smoke-room story of a horror hidden behind the vacuous normality of daily living:

> I knew a man once did a girl in
> Any man might do a girl in
> Any man has to, needs to, wants to
> Once in a lifetime, do a girl in.
> Well he kept her there in a bath
> With a gallon of lysol in a bath.

Behind this flat toneless voice is the grim tinsel life of *The Waste Land*, of Madame Sosostris, of the neurotic sophisticate who sits in Cleopatra's chair, creatures who are foils for the makeshift existence of Lil in the pub and the typist seduced in her bed-sitter, peopling the limbo of the half-alive. Voices and attitudes set one against another and the underlying threat of the unknown introduces a sly dramatic element in these early non-theatrical attempts at communication.

Perhaps the most successful of such semi-dramatic gambits is the earlier and lesser poem *Portrait of a Lady*, in which the predicament of society, its disillusion and its nightmare of inarticulate feeling, is given expression through the silent young man caught in the web of an over-civilized but ultimately insensitive lady whose boredom with life feeds upon his vulnerability.

In his essay on John Marston, which appeared just before *Murder in the Cathedral*, Eliot wrote, 'It is possible that what distinguishes poetic drama from prosaic drama is a kind of doubleness in the action, as if it took place on two planes at once.'[1] This 'doubleness', or, as he calls it later in the essay, this 'sense of something behind', this 'pattern behind the pattern', Eliot attempted to exploit as a method in his own plays. The ironic address of the Knights in *Murder in the Cathedral* springs immediately to mind. Naturally, most of the characters in this play are apprehending their situation on a plane lower than that of the hero Thomas à Becket, whether the Tempters, the Priests or the Women of Canterbury. The Knights not only think and feel with all the limitations of their calling, but offer the only instance in the play where the difference of levels is *realized* for the audience in the theatre or the congregation in the church. When after the killing of Thomas they step out of the play with all the force of an aside in Molière and a *Verfremdungseffekt* of Bertolt Brecht rolled into one, they cease suddenly to be symbolic figures in an abstract design, and become recognizably representative men from modern political life. This abrupt shaking of the audience's confidence in the image they have been creating is sufficient to jolt it into reassessing the play's meaning in modern terms. The untrammelled direct address to the audience has become more and more familiar in the contemporary theatre, and even in television and the cinema.[2] It is proving a refreshing means of shattering the image of an audience largely lulled into anticipating a

[1] T. S. Eliot, *Selected Essays* (London, 1932), p. 229.
[2] Cf. the effect of Olivier's first soliloquy in his film of *Richard III*, seemingly the first time that a soliloquy in a film of Shakespeare has been used as originally intended.

complete naturalism. This device of the Knights is a fully legitimate shock tactic.

For instances of Eliot's comprehensive exploiting of the theatre for his own ends we must return to *The Family Reunion*. In this play the experiments with verse forms and the adroit sliding between prosaic conversation and the more 'poetic' inner thoughts of the characters are most happily married to the two or three levels of sensibility in the characters and the two or three levels of action on the stage. The Ibsen-like story of Harry and his family and the attempt to link the Greek curse of an ancient house with a Freudian domestic trouble at Wishwood are neither of them so successful as the moments of fully theatrical irony when Harry's theme of self-discovery and the audience's image of a dead society are given stage life.

Lord Monchensey, in love with his wife's sister Agatha, had many years before planned the murder of his wife Amy, who was at that time pregnant with the unborn Harry. Because Agatha felt that the child was in part her own, she prevented the crime; but the sin of the wish to kill was not so readily suppressed. When the father died, Harry grew up in the care of the sisters. When Harry chose to marry, his mother had other plans and her possessiveness compelled Harry and his wife to leave the house. They led an itinerant life abroad until, one 'cloudless night in the mid-Atlantic', the girl was drowned. Whether Harry drowned her or only desired to drown her, we never know; but the sin of the father had been visited upon the son. In the course of the play, Harry learns finally from Agatha that the cause of his suffering is hereditary and not personal. His mind is so illuminated and so relieved that, although he knows his action will kill his mother with grief, he leaves Wishwood and the play happily able to expiate the family's curse.

The play is a construction of contrasting attitudes, of Harry living a life of fierce intensity set against the four uncles and aunts of the Chorus who 'do not understand'; of Amy, slave to a dead and helplessly chronological past, set against Agatha, who wisely recognizes the 'loop in time' and understands that the 'curse is like a child'. Very soon after the rise of the curtain we begin to place the characters by the way they think and speak and respond to Harry's predicament. We place them on a scale which corresponds to the intensity of the verse, and as soon as this scale is meaningfully established, the larger jumps between its two extremes become immediately noticeable. As the drama proceeds, we become more sensitive to slighter jumps. We respond more and more in the way in which we respond to thoughtful comedy with its calculated contrasts of values.

To select a short instance of this effect in operation we need turn only to the opening scene of the play in which most of the family have gathered to celebrate Amy's birthday and Harry's homecoming. Ivy is a type of impoverished snob who freezes in Bayswater 'by a gas-fire counting shillings'; Violet is a snob of a more inverted species, harder and more malicious, but equally a 'type'; Charles is a soft country-bred clubman who enjoys 'a glass of dry sherry or two before dinner'; Gerald is a vapid Indian Army soldier who misses his native servants. It is these ludicrous, cardboard people who prepare us for Harry's entrance by irritating us with generalities about the younger generation and their lack of stamina and responsibility. Amy, only slightly less hollow a person than these, because she is now an old woman afraid of death, speaks of the past as something to be firmly reclaimed for her son's future, and she is angered by Agatha's suggestion that 'everything is irrevocable' and 'the past is irremediable'. For Agatha too has affectionate thoughts of Harry's future, although she knows that 'he will find a new Wishwood' to which he will not easily be able to adapt himself. In this way the family plans to make Harry 'feel at home', most senseless of clichés, and Amy with finality issues these words of advice:

> Do not discuss his absence. Please behave only
> As if nothing had happened in the past eight years.

Although we had in some degree been forewarned of what now happens, by Agatha's stronger verse, by her position on the stage apart from the family group, by the innuendoes of her tones, nevertheless the verbal tautness of her next speech so destroys the illusion of naturalism that the action of the play stops in its tracks and our image flutters madly till we readjust it:

> Thus with most careful devotion
> Thus with precise attention
> To detail, interfering preparation
> Of that which is already prepared
> Men tighten the knot of confusion
> Into perfect misunderstanding...

This is another alienation-effect. The faint hint of rhyme, the
formality of the rhythms and the incantatory weight of the Latinisms
after the looser, lighter colloquial manner of what preceded, take us
out of this play into another. It is as if the 'exposition' is complete
and the actors are fixed in time, and Agatha speaking in soliloquy—
for she is addressing none other than the audience—gives us direct
instructions for the interpretation of the narrow views we have heard.
To the rhythm of the lines we see her move for the first time from
her place apart, walking like a visitation round the statuesque group
of the Chorus, gently and sadly accusing them on our behalf.

Then Agatha halts to address us with the emotive imagery by
which the Women of Canterbury guided our feeling in *Murder in the
Cathedral*. She accuses us of

> Neglecting all the admonitions
> From the world around the corner
> The wind's talk in the dry holly-tree
> The inclination of the moon
> The attraction of the dark passage
> The paw under the door.

Suddenly the flat abstractions have sprung alive to suggest sen-
suously the mysteries and the terror of living in time. Speaking
together with expressionless faces and expressionless tones, the
Chorus now voice the nightmare of their failure to understand:

Why do we feel embarrassed, impatient, fretful, ill at ease,
Assembled like amateur actors who have not been assigned their parts?...

This is a daring attempt by the author, risking indeed the 'titter in
the dress circle', to mark out firmly the plane of the lesser mortals
of the play, to make articulate their inarticulateness. It is designed to
promote the irony of the contrast between those whose 'ordinary

day isn't much more than breathing', like brother John's, and those who are 'living on several planes at once', like Harry. The Chorus have the traditional task of speaking the unspoken, saying what we might wish to say ourselves; they do not explain the past or anticipate the future or excite us emotionally at all; and they are different from most choruses in that they remain actors in the play who negatively enhance our sense of Harry's solitude and suffering, offer a social context for his martyrdom, and identify Wishwood as a place without a soul. As much as Harry, the family group of Ivy, Violet, Charles and Gerald are the subject of the play, since with every step towards illumination that Harry takes, the Chorus are cast into greater darkness. To the end their presence contributes to the play's meaning, and such tricks as this switch in the play's angle of vision intermittently reinforce the doubleness of the action throughout.

Eliot in his post-war plays is less anxious to break the continuity of his drama for the sake of securing the positive awareness of his audience; he encourages a more even and sometimes more convincing, certainly more naturalistic, performance. *The Family Reunion* suffered from a theatricalism which often distracted the spectator from the issues of the play; and Eliot could not in any case have repeated this play's kind of chorus. Yet his vision of a split between two worlds of sensibility continued to exercise his mind, and he continued in spite of himself to introduce ironies of interpretation. Unhappily, he could never make his prosaic people strong enough to withstand the imaginative assault of his more spiritual heroes and heroines; he seemed unable to grant them a philosophically justifiable and theatrically demonstrable value in their own right. In *The Cocktail Party*, a play which traces the translation of sinners into saints of greater or lesser degree, Celia Coplestone, Peter Quilpe and Edward and Lavinia Chamberlayne all begin the race together, each contributing equally to the inanity of the social whirl. Before long Celia has outstripped the rest of the field, and even in the last scene when she is dead, her unseen presence dwarfs the merely banal plodders. Like the action of *The Family Reunion*, that of *The Cocktail Party* 'ceases' with striking effect as Alex and Julia perform their ritual before Reilly their priest, suddenly showing us the roles of guardian they are playing, suggesting with a sudden, if not quite convincing, clarity that such people are moving among us as potential directors of our fate. But the play in its unbalance loses the ironies present in *The Family Reunion* since the Chamberlaynes are not granted the unnatural power of a chorus to accentuate their part.

The Confidential Clerk has the form of a superficial farce of recognitions in which a number of foundlings discover both their parentage and their true vocations, their past and their future. The farce provides a good deal of the repartee which might well belong to such drama. However, the play manages to evoke some serious overtones: most of the characters have two parts to play, one at the surface and one more thematically significant. Thus Lady Elizabeth, trivial follower of society cults, suggests also that she has a prophetic insight; her husband Sir Claude, the successful financier, when not making money seeks the inner satisfaction of making pottery; kind old Eggerton, the confidential clerk, when not on duty has also the ways of a guardian, showing Colby his spiritual vocation; Lucasta is the spoilt child, but she is also disillusioned with her empty world. Colby wanders among these people trying to find his destiny. But while in this play there is now almost no gap between the levels at which the characters play, since each embraces his doubleness within one personality, the quick tempo and improbable pattern of farce sort ill with the sober themes of freedom and destiny, faith and understanding, and as a whole the play hardly avoids fragmentation. The two levels fail to govern the spectator's fleeting centrifugal impressions.

Like Coleridge's, Eliot's range of work is notably of a kind. Therefore it may be appropriate to call upon evidence of his thinking from a different context. In his seminal book *Notes Towards a Definition of Culture* we may read this: 'Neither a classless society, nor a society of strict and impenetrable social barriers is good; each class should have constant additions and defections; the classes, while remaining distinct, should be able to mix freely; and they should all have a community of culture with each other which will give them something in common.'[1] The people of Eliot's drama have in a sense

[1] T. S. Eliot, *op. cit.* (London, 1948), p. 50.

been moving towards another community of culture, one which seems to have thrown over the very additions and defections which he declared were essential to a vital society. Acknowledged distinctions between tones and attitudes were a source of real dramatic vigour in his earlier writing, which was then dramatically capable of bringing both tragic and comic life to his stage. Now the ironic pincer of contrasting planes of sensibility has relaxed its grip, and his tragicomic interest has finally slipped away. As we watch his latest play, *The Elder Statesman*, we are distinctly not involved. We sit like a smug audience of psychiatrists listening as their patient, Lord Claverton, strips himself of his illusions for purely clinical purposes.

BRECHT'S 'ALIENATION'

Modern morality plays from Brieux to Brecht must inevitably suffer from some of the pains of propaganda. Whether by devices of emotional persuasion on the one hand or of disguise by exaggeration or other comic method on the other, we are given a necessarily limited view which, however sane, can be unpalatable. When the preacher moves into the theatre, his play risks the gripes of sentimental over-persuasion, or the cynical over-exaggeration of the subject. An attack of moral righteousness brings out the characters in rashes of naked black or white, and otherwise healthy people are thrust into procrustean sick-beds. However, it must be said that most good dramatists are preachers at heart, reinforcing their work by some preconceived moral pattern, though only the best know how to sink themselves and their lessons in living characters in a living play.

The play by which to date we shall remember the naturalistic but moralistic Arnold Wesker is one which survives the death-kiss of theatrical lecturing by an astonishingly virtuoso piece of dramatic trickery. *Roots* is a play in which the audience is alienated by villain and victims alike. It presents a raw, real and therefore largely unsympathetic family of simple country people whom Beatie, a daughter down from the metropolis, tries to educate into more liberal ways of thought. Through Beatie, of course, Wesker is intent upon educating the audience too. But, delightfully, it is made clear that all she has to say is really the second-hand, even ill-digested, tub-thumping of an unseen boy friend Ronnie, who indeed deserts her before the lesson is done. Thus in pitying our teacher Beatie, despising the family who might otherwise have stood as pupils alongside us, the author has us drop all our defences.[1]

Bertolt Brecht's indefatigable pursuit, in both his playwriting and his directing, of an effect of estrangement or 'alienation' could be argued as a cover for his teaching, a lifelong attempt to avoid the responsibility of the greatest drama, which uses the theatrical medium to explore reality in communion with its audience. As a playwright he has no doubt been overrated, because his impulse to treat the sentimentality of his subjects with the comic eye of the estranger produced a series of plays having the rough edge which appealed to a cynical generation. Brecht started writing in the atmosphere of a theatre purveying the abstract expressionism of Georg Kaiser and Ernst Toller in the chaotic Germany of the 'twenties, an enthusiastic, revolutionary and committed drama now almost forgotten. Drama had to be relevant to the times; the artist could only achieve something with 'some wind in his sails'; and this wind had to be 'the wind prevailing in his own period, and not some future wind'.[2] Brecht would write dramatic parables: 'Once I've found out what modes of behaviour are most useful to the human race, I show them to people and underline them.'[3] The confidence of youth was in such hasty, categorical terms.

As for the actor, he too must adopt a socially critical attitude. He must see his task as being the leader of a discussion group: 'His

---

[1] J. Mander has published an interesting essay on *Roots* in *The Writer and Commitment* (London, 1961), in which he draws attention to this alienation-effect in the dialectic of the play. 'The play is swarming with ideas; but they are Ronnie's ideas, and the spectator is meant to take them with a large pinch of salt...By the end of the play we know for certain what we had suspected all along: Ronnie is a phoney. No playwright could do more to revitalize his own ideas, and to alienate the autobiographical element by the use of critical irony...What is more, he can afford to let his audience laugh into the bargain, as Mr Osborne in *Look Back in Anger* cannot' (pp. 198–200).

[2] From *Berliner Börsen-Courier*, 6 February 1926, eight days before the production of *Baal*, his first play. Quoted in J. Willett, *Brecht on Theatre* (London, 1964), p. 7.

[3] From *Exstrabladet*, Copenhagen, 20 March 1934, soon after he had left Hitler's Germany. Quoted in J. Willett, *ibid.* p. 67.

performance becomes a discussion (about social conditions) with the audience he is addressing. He prompts the spectator to justify or abolish these conditions according to what class he belongs to.'[1] This was written at the time when Brecht was working on his finest plays, and his acceptance of more than one point of view for the sake of a dramatic dialectic suggests a new generosity. At this time, we increasingly find Brecht modifying his theory of alienation to embrace its actual practice. Sentiment was valid, given certain critical controls; he found himself understanding the later characters with some feeling for them; conviction of belief, if not illusion itself, is used to engage the audience's attention, and this in the best of naturalistic traditions; and he emphasized that educational theatre must operate like any other, by delighting its audience: 'In so far as it is good theatre it will amuse.'[2] Brecht ended his dramatic career by seeking every means to shake off the naïve sermonizing of early expressionism while still holding fast to its moral purpose.

The advance of the 'epic' theatre over the romantic and expressionistic theatre appeared first in its particularity. Brecht put on the stage characters with recognizably firm physical and sometimes psychological individuality. He tried to give his subjects the concrete reality of ordinary life, in the rough justice of the underworld in *The Threepenny Opera*, the suffering of the oppressed in *The Private Life of the Master Race*, the detailed business of keeping body and soul together in *Mother Courage and her Children*, the broad hypocrisy of people in *The Good Woman of Setzuan*, the simple compassion of a woman for a child in *The Caucasian Chalk Circle*. Enough drama, one might say, for any playwright. But in spite of their subjects' naturalistic elements, all these plays display in the strongest terms the symbolic fight of the individual in an alien society, sometimes protesting, sometimes acquiescing, but always dramatically purposeful. Brecht remained to the end a didactic dramatist.

What must chiefly interest us here are the forms his dialectics took. They were not the give-and-take of contrasting attitudes with

---

[1] From 'Short Description of a New Technique of Acting which Produces an Alienation Effect', written in 1940, *Versuche* 11, trans. J. Willett, *ibid.* p. 139.
[2] From *Schriften zum Theater*, 1957, although the composition is of uncertain date. Trans. J. Willett, *ibid.* p. 73.

which Shaw efficiently cloaked his preaching. Nevertheless, as Brecht, like Shaw, repeated at length, his drama was designed to unsettle the composure of an audience.

His theoretical starting point was an attack on the 'Aristotelian' theatre, the 'cathartic' theatre, the theatre of 'trance'. These woolly terms need not embarrass us; his point was simply that it was a waste of time mounting a play of ideas in a form which, by its conventionality, dulls the mind. We should gloss this kind of drama merely as bad theatre to save ourselves sterile arguments about the viability of great plays of the past (is one uncritical of Othello, Antony, Coriolanus, or any other Shakespearian tragic hero?). For there *is* a case for a theatre of reason, a theatre of sober objectivity, when the bulk of popular modern drama purveys easy sentiment without truly engaging the mind at all.

Brecht's notion of epic theatre, therefore, is far from being that of the heroic tradition which the word may suggest; rather, it describes a pantomime which only incidentally narrates a story, while all the apparatus of chorus and narrator, song and music, placards and titles, guides us to the cool, reflective kind of attention we should pay to its meaning. While enacting a moment in history, the actors must speak their lines as if conscious that they are moving in the contemporary world of the audience; while the view of history is to be sharply unfamiliar, the business of Grusha's scrubbing her husband's back in *The Caucasian Chalk Circle*, or of Mother Courage's plucking a capon, is to be done with meticulously real detail, making the world on the stage human, recognizable and familiar. On occasion a mask, like the masks of cruelty devised for the Governor and his Wife in *The Chalk Circle*, fixes a character in a role which is wholly direct and unmistakable in its statement, creating a morality-figure from whom the possibilities of growth have been drained; or a character will be typed by costume or song, like Yvette Pottier, the prostitute in *Mother Courage*, with her coloured hat, her striking red boots, her 'swaying gait' and her Fraternization Song. But such '*gestus*', the designed attitudes of the role, are supplied only in order that one statement about people can be boldly set against another. Every detail of the *persona* is to be functional, in order to force a judgment from the spectator. Galileo has a passion for science and at the same time a passion for food and good living, and when these are put together, we find that science too can be a 'self-indulgence';[1] in the process, the glamour of scientific invention is made visibly unromantic.

Along with this work of the actor, all the apparatus of theatre was in due course brought to bear upon the defenceless audience. Not now the extravagances of proscenium-arch illusion: where a Chekhov concentrated all his effects of setting, lighting and characterization to make the spectator a member of his family group, Brecht wishes to alienate us from the start, and to continue to do so repeatedly during the performance. It is as if his actors are to break out of the arch in breaking the illusion of theatre. The sets are to be unreal, and if there is to be some form of scenic representation, it is to be simple and seen to be false. When the actors pull Mother Courage's wagon, they pull it on a revolve, so that we see real human effort. Simultaneously, we also see that, although the wagon seems to be lugged all over Europe, it scarcely moves; indeed, if the revolve turns faster than the actors can pull, and they seem to move backwards, so much the better for the meaning of the play.

At the Deutsches Theater in Berlin, Brecht eventually abandoned the normal use of the front curtain to divide his scenes, and ran a very obvious wire from wing to wing, from which a rough curtain was visibly drawn back. And in contrast to the naturalistic theatre, the *sources* of light were to be shown, just as in a sports arena. The light

---

[1] *Galileo* 'begins with the man of forty-six having his morning wash, broken by occasional browsing in books and by a lesson on the solar system for Andrea Sarti, a small boy. To play this, surely you have got to know that we shall be ending with the man of seventy-eight having his supper, just after he has said good-bye for ever to the same pupil? He is then more terribly altered than this passage of time could possibly have brought about. He wolfs his food with unrestrained greed, no other idea in his head; he has rid himself of his educational mission in shameful circumstances, as though it were a burden: he, who once drank his morning milk without a care, greedy to teach the boy. But does he really drink it without care? Isn't the pleasure of drinking and washing one with the pleasure which he takes in the new ideas? Don't forget: he thinks out of self-indulgence. . . ' This is Brecht in 'A Short Organum for the Theatre' in *Sinn und Form* Sonderheft Bertolt Brecht (Potsdam, 1949), trans. J. Willett, *ibid.* pp. 198–9.

itself was to be harshly white, in order to dispel false atmosphere and externally imposed moods:

> Give us some light on the stage, electrician. How can we
> Playwrights and actors put forward
> Our view of the world in half-darkness?[1]

As for music, this is no longer to support and emphasize the dialogue, issuing from some subtle source unseen to the audience; the musicians are to be observed playing in a box, their instruments seeming to join in the argument and their music seeming to have a cynical voice of its own. Music is to be played *against* the voice of the actor, while the actor should speak or sing *against* the music. Brecht even had Paul Dessau put tacks in the hammers of his piano, so that in its lack of resonance the instrument should compete with the voice of the actor.

These lively innovations left their mark. Many dramatists have been happy to find a leader who might take them back to the kind of 'complex seeing'[2] associated with the Elizabethan theatre. Often this has resulted in a superficial larding of Brechtian stage mannerisms on an essentially melodramatic form. In spite of his use of the grotesque, the menacing and macabre tragicomedies of Friedrich Dürrenmatt, particularly those of his later style, *The Marriage of Mr Mississippi*, *The Visit* and *The Physicists*, are crazily alienated parables of political power and personal crisis. *The Fire-Raisers* of Max Frisch, with its chorus of firemen and its comically impersonal treatment of Herr Biedermann, Frisch's purblind Everyman, also owes as much to Brecht's alienating techniques as to the theatre of the absurd with which Frisch is often linked. *The Threepenny Opera* and its vein of subfusc, social-satirical opera-bouffe encouraged the slapdash sense of improvisation in Brendan Behan's *The Hostage*, as well as in Peter Weiss's *Marat/Sade*. In England, episodic—not to say piecemeal—historical form, introducing a variety of perspectives by the juxtaposition of scene, generated Robert Bolt's

---

[1] 'Gedichte aus dem Messingkauf': 'Die Beleuchtung' (in *Versuche* 14) trans. J. Willett, *The Theatre of Bertolt Brecht* (London, 2nd ed. 1960), p. 162.

[2] This concept is discussed by Brecht in his Notes to *The Threepenny Opera*, to be found with D. Vesey's translation of the play in *Bertolt Brecht, Plays*, vol. 1 (London, 1960), p. 179.

faintly dialectical romance *A Man For All Seasons*, Peter Shaffer's *The Royal Hunt of the Sun*, John Osborne's derivative *Luther* and John Whiting's merely sensational *The Devils*. To continue to list such titles would reinforce the argument that the influence of Brecht may have done as much harm as good.

However, the exploratory work of John Arden has been not only assiduous in testing the Brechtian conventions, but also intelligently original. Arden has pressed into use every external device of any consequence that he found in Brecht, and in particular has perfected by repeated experiment a 'ballad' style of his own in a sequence of startling plays from *The Waters of Babylon* and *Live Like Pigs* to *The Workhouse Donkey* and *Armstrong's Last Goodnight*. The song addressed directly to the audience, which unexpectedly breaks the emotional continuity of the play in order to comment harshly on character or situation, induces in performance a parodic awareness of the theatre situation and a dialectic of feeling in the auditorium. An alienating device such as this would be purposeless if there were nothing in the play that needed it: it is Arden's affinity with Brecht's ambivalent, not merely cynical, view of society that leads him to refuse his audience the easy response. Like Brecht's, Arden's characters are never obviously likeable; nor do his problem situations invite quick solutions. In effect, his dialectic is devised with his conception of a play.

This is most apparent in *Serjeant Musgrave's Dance*, where Arden first evokes in minute detail the brutal realism of his dark, Victorian, Northern town, caught in an English winter, gripped by a strike and threatened by a recruiting squad. From this firm beginning, elements of farce, the ritualism of the soldiers' drumming, stylized *gestus* in character and impersonal folk-songs combine to prepare the audience for the shock and paradox of the last act. The fierce pacificism of Musgrave is taken to its logical conclusion, shown in its crude inhumanity and violently turned upon the spectator himself. In this extraordinary act, Arden creates his argument in directly sensuous terms, as Shakespeare does in his problem comedies, and a steadily accumulating sensation of sights and sounds questions the former image of the puritanical pacificist. The act meets all of

Artaud's requirements for a theatre of cruelty and constitutes a prime example of 'total theatre' in which content and technique are interdependent—as they are in the best of Brecht.

Yet *The Happy Haven*, Arden's symbolic farce about gerontology (as opposed to old age), more amply and consistently demonstrates his determination to test in unison the Brechtian devices, although it has yet to be recognized how well this play manages the task. Jonsonian characters, narration, songs, a *commedia dell'arte* vigour of style, depersonalizing masks, even the demand for an Elizabethan open stage, all work together to a uniform purpose. Perhaps only farce could accommodate the whole gamut of these devices; unfortunately it may also be the farcical elements which render the play's moral theme too objective and its impact too uncertain.

'Complex seeing' has therefore been fairly teased by the small host of Brecht's imitators, and it is clear that his dramatic mode must be anticipated by the *structure* of the play, as Brecht's own successful pieces show.

Galileo presents a great scientist, but one who will steal another man's invention, treat his daughter abominably, publicly renounce his beliefs before the threat of the Inquisition, and grow fat. *Mother Courage* presents a courageous woman who is also the common profiteer who haggles for a price while her own children's lives are at stake. *The Good Woman of Setzuan* presents the tender-hearted whore who is too good to last, until she pretends to be her very unsentimental cousin who must put her financial affairs right by ruthless business methods. Or in *Herr Puntila and his Man Matti* we see in a single character, the farmer Puntila, a man who is both generous and selfish according to whether he is drunk or sober. In such plays, whether by structure of character or of scene, Brecht refreshingly challenges his audience with the contradictions of life in a clash of primary colours.

The contradictions, however, produce unpredictable results for their audience, results that Brecht himself could not control in spite of revisions in the text after he had tried out his effects in practice. Didacticism through alienation was his idea of the theatre's purpose, but the consequent inconsistencies are the puzzle of Brechtian drama.

Arguments which continue to surround *Mother Courage* are the natural outcome of the mixture. Courage is a tough but pathetic old woman who lives through the havoc of the Thirty Years' War. The conduct of her life is relevant to the practice of war generally: she steals, lies, makes a profit out of scarcity. She is carried along on the tide of the misery of others. At the best, one would think, she could be a grotesque character for comedy; at the worst, a painful object lesson in vice. She is something of both, but this is only the beginning of her complexity. Brecht's intention is to show us war through the frame provided by one individual life; yet the audience's cathartic desire to see both its terror and its pity in the end defeats all attempts by the author and the actress wholly to alienate the part and have us judge for ourselves.

In Eric Bentley's account of Brecht's own production of this play in Berlin, this reliable witness and confessed admirer of the author's talent demonstrates that 'alienation is an instance of the principle: *reculer pour mieux sauter*',[1] and in *Mother Courage* he suggests that it actually adds to the emotional content of the drama. Thus while Courage's dumb daughter Kattrin secretly dresses herself in Yvette's gaudy clothes, thereby expressing a pathetic wish to live in greater luxury than her spare existence will ever allow, the Dutch cook sings lustily, 'A mighty fortress is our God', and what starts as a joke 'gradually reinforces the pathos it begins by checking'. Ronald Gray adds further testimony to this: 'Do what Brecht might, he could not rewrite the tragic scene, in which (Courage) loses her son Swisscheese, in such a way as to destroy all sympathy for her in her grief.'[2] She leaves the play with the song which she sang when she made her first entrance; but to avoid the sentimentality of such an ending, bright military music is simultaneously introduced to drown the singing and neutralize the pathos. Yet by this device, as Bentley says, 'Brecht also succeeds in enriching the drama of the scene. It becomes more moving.' In the last moments of a play, especially, this might be a fatal miscalculation. A parallel effect is to be found at the end of O'Casey's *Juno and the Paycock*,

---

[1] E. R. Bentley, *In Search of Theater* (London, 1954), p. 154.
[2] R. Gray, *Brecht* (London, 1961), p. 100.

where Juno's pathetic prayer is brutally contradicted by the coarse drunken singing of Joxer and Boyle; but O'Casey wanted our emotion. The misunderstandings about dark comedy are the likely consequence of such counterpoint in performance.

Brecht was anxious that his techniques should suppress the natural wish of the audience to identify itself with a serious character, without the need for comic distortion. Identification would prevent the audience from thinking. The suffering of the character was to move the spectator, but he was to remain free to laugh about those who weep on the stage, and weep about those who laugh.[1] Yet this theory was constantly in conflict with his practice, for Brecht was fighting against the irrepressible impulse toward shared feeling. A dramatist must trade on the spectator's ability to put himself in the shoes of the characters, for this is at the bottom of all dramatic communication. Shakespeare made a tragic hero foolish or proud or evil or otherwise repelling, in the knowledge that his character could still be human enough to be tragic, that his audience would remain willing to share the final agony of nemesis. In the drama of Bertolt Brecht, all efforts to promote a cold and rational response while at the same time presenting an intensely human drama produced an inevitably tragicomic response, and theory became gratuitous.

In sum, the contrapuntal structure of his drama encouraged both repugnance for Macheath the thief and parody of capitalism, and affection for Macheath the philanderer defying the law; it encouraged both repugnance for Galileo the social coward and affection for Galileo the man. Alienation as a production method, like comic 'relief' in Shakespearian tragedy, served to strengthen rather than to weaken any incipient emotionality in such equivocations and it increased such ironic tensions as the plays possessed. As well as being an object lesson, Courage can be a comedy or a tragedy queen; she is each of these. Martin Esslin, a recent critical biographer of Brecht, sums up the position in these words: 'He sought to spread the cold light of logical clarity—and produced a rich texture of poetic ambiguity.'[2]

---

[1] See Brecht, 'Vergnügungstheater oder Lehrtheater' (1936), *Schriften zum Theater*, p. 64, quoted in M. Esslin, *Brecht: A Choice of Evils* (London, 1959), p. 115.

[2] M. Esslin, *ibid.* p. 236.

Whatever tricks of an anti-illusory nature are employed by the Berliner Ensemble in the performance of Brecht's plays, illusion rapidly reasserts itself. The bare white stage, set only with the paraphernalia of skeleton properties, is quickly forgotten. The actors' convention of merely 'pretending' to be their characters is soon assimilated, as it was in the masked drama of Aristophanes and the *commedia dell'arte*. The audience quickly adjusts itself to startling interpolations of song and narrative, until each break in continuity can surprise no more. The dream world of illusory theatre develops and proceeds as before, and pathetic overtones arise wherever there is a hint of sentiment. Even though the episodic drama is in no need of creating suspense, Brecht supplies enough thrills in one play to satisfy any melodramatist of the last century. The real novelty, if it is novelty, lies elsewhere—in the double vision of Brechtian theatre, indeed its kaleidoscopic vision.

For Brecht, theories were always 'working definitions', his plays '*Versuche*', attempts. In his last years he felt the need to take a new position, and in the light of experience began to qualify his views. In answer to a question put by Friedrich Wolf in 1949, he had this to say:

It is not true, though it is sometimes suggested, that epic theatre (which is not simply undramatic theatre, as is also sometimes suggested) proclaims the slogan: 'Reason this side, Emotion (feeling) that.' It by no means renounces emotion, least of all the sense of justice, the urge to freedom, and righteous anger; it is so far from renouncing these that it does not even assume their presence, but tries to arouse or reinforce them.[1]

There is a fine honesty here, but a damning one too. We are to recognize the stupidity of war and at the same time feel sorrow and indignation. But just before his death in 1956, Brecht modified his 'Short Organum for the Theatre' of 1948. He accepted that the actor could not avoid some self-identification with the character:

The most likely result is that truly rending contradiction between experience and portrayal, empathy and demonstration, justification and criticism, which is what is aimed at.

[1] From 'Formal Problems Arising from the Theatre's New Content', *Theaterarbeit* (Dresden, 1952), trans. J. Willett, *Brecht on Theatre* (London, 1964), p. 227.

The contradiction between acting (demonstration) and experience (empathy) often leads the uninstructed to suppose that only one or the other can be manifest in the work of the actor (as if the Short Organum concentrated entirely on acting and the old tradition entirely on experience). In reality it is a matter of two mutually hostile processes which fuse in the actor's work; his performance is not just composed of a bit of the one and a bit of the other. His particular effectiveness comes from the tussle and tension of the two opposites, and also from their depth.[1]

There is value in 'the tussle and tension'. Indeed, it is arguable that Brecht's real strength as a dramatist, his power in the theatre, will remain this kind of counterpoint of thought and feeling.

When little Shen Te, the pathetic prostitute of *The Good Woman of Setzuan*, or Grusha, the selfless servant-girl of *The Caucasian Chalk Circle*, wins the sympathy of the audience on a thoroughly stylized and distanced stage (and even equivocal characters like Galileo and Azdak strongly invite it), we can recognize the kind of ambiguity of feeling which grows familiar as the drama of the century develops. Add to this the openwork, episodic shaping of the epic manner, and the result is a rare comic medley of logistic and affective juxtapositions. The Gods who praise Shen Te for her good deeds desert her in her poverty and despair, and comically take their leave for heaven. For the sake of a pathetic, fatherless child, pathetic Grusha is comically wedded to a man she thinks moribund ('The son of that peasant woman is just going to die. Isn't it wonderful?'), but he is quick to rise from his death-bed in the truly farcical tradition when it suits him. This hilarious scene is cut short in its turn by Grusha's unhappy realization that she is now irrevocably married to a man she does not love. Thus farce and melodrama succeed each other. The epic construction lends itself to bursts of feeling and to the irreverences of a comic burlesque which 'mocks and imitates at one and the same moment'.[2]

[1] Brecht, 'Appendix to the Short Organum', trans. J. Willett, *ibid.* pp. 277-8.
[2] M. Esslin, *Brecht: A Choice of Evils*, p. 222.

ANALYSIS: 'MOTHER COURAGE', SCENES 5 AND 11

Only through examining in action the great detail and particularity
of Brecht's dramaturgy is it possible to arrive at any just estimate of
his strength. It is this particularity in his most representative play,
Mother Courage and her Children, which will enable general audiences
in the future to enjoy the stimulus of his dialectical skills when
theories about epic alienation have been forgotten. Convention,
after all, is not something imposed on a play, but is organic and alive
and constantly being modified with each new play and each new
production which strains and tests it. When in *Mother Courage*
Brecht has imagined its detailed life closely, effects of dogmatism are
not felt, and audiences enjoy a healthy, pragmatic theatre.

Brecht chooses as his background for this play the horrors of a
meaningless war of religion which rolled back and forth over Europe
and seemed endless in its futility; the remote period of the Thirty
Years' War, 1618–48, encourages our sense of its universality; the
focus is, however, always on the particular scene, constantly upon
Courage and her possessions, upon a mother, her three children and
their wagon. When in scene 6 General Tilly's funeral ceremony is
heard offstage, against the impressive pomp of the funeral march
and the slow drums, the old woman is seen taking inventory. With
superb condescension she offers the dead commander a word of
sympathy as one professional to another:

I feel sorry for a commander or an emperor like that—when he might
have had something special in mind, something they'd talk about in times
to come, something they'd raise a statue to him for. The conquest of the
world now, *that's* a goal for a commander, he wouldn't know any better...
Lord, worms have got into the biscuits.[1]

And according to Brecht's production notes,[2] she says this with a
laugh. The worms in the biscuits display the seamy side of war, the
side of immediate importance to those who have to live through it.
This is not to be story-book history, but history from the underside,
reported with grim humour, as it affects ordinary people. Courage

[1] Trans. E. R. Bentley, 1955.
[2] Trans. E. R. Bentley and H. Schmidt, *Encore*, May–June 1965, vol. 12, no. 3.

got her name because she drove through a bombardment—but only to sell fifty loaves before they went mouldy: 'War is a business proposition.' The death of Tilly is 'a historic moment', says the Chaplain—but for Courage 'it's a historic moment when they hit my daughter over the eye'. This kind of refocusing, this Shakespearian change of tack, is persistent throughout the play. The result is cynical comedy, making of Mother Courage a split character, an anti-heroine, who is at once the image of human endurance and the 'hyena of the battlefield' making a sordid livelihood out of war. And her wagon is seen in every scene as the squalid emblem of her dirty trading while at the same time it appears to roll on for ever like human life, managing somehow to survive the accidents of a hostile environment.

Double vision

The details of scene 5 finely illustrate Brecht's ambivalent effects. This sharp vignette of a scene seems to summarize at a mid-point of the play the kind of life Courage is leading, and what her attitude means. The scene does not further the plot in any way, but the care with which Brecht revised it indicates the importance he attached to it as a revelatory, definitive moment in her progress.

The stage itself is split, as if to divide the audience's attention between the pathetic image of a ruined farmhouse on one side, with all the waste and suffering it suggests, and the wagon busily servicing its customers on the other. The two sets of values implicit in this division are to be seen in contradiction throughout the scene. The placard announces that the wagon has crossed 'Poland, Moravia, Bavaria, Italy, and again Bavaria', and by its narrative form conjures up with the dry impersonal tone of a history text some vast, endless journey back and forth over meaningless frontiers. It continues with a reminder of 'Tilly's victory at Magdeburg'—but what image is there of victory on the stage? Rather one of butchery. It concludes with a characteristic innuendo, that this victory 'costs Mother Courage four officers' shirts'. Blood and business are equated. And always in the distance behind the scene is heard the incongruous sound of a military band, brassily playing a rousing victory march, a touch of gaiety in a world of hate, a false guide through utter chaos.

So, before ever a word is spoken, the audience is granted some previous knowledge of the action and its mood. A sense of the opposite will inform everything seen. The dialogue with its contrasting tones immediately accentuates the antithesis, each player offering a conflicting *gestus* in his role. The attacking, raucous voice of Courage is heard first, shouting above the noise of the band, and her subject as usual is money: 'What, you can't pay? No money, no brandy!' She is busy selling irrelevancies like schnapps in the middle of the devastated village. Over at the wagon she is haggling with two soldiers: the army is curiously nameless in the play and it speaks aggressively without individualized inflexions, 'I want my brandy!' With equal self-interest one of the soldiers, who has a stolen fur coat across his back, is demanding reward for his labours. Tilly has allowed only an hour for organized looting, that proper part of soldiering which contrasts the values of war and peace, and the man can only suppose that his commander has himself been 'bought off'. So all ranks are out for what they can get, and a soldier or an officer is no better or worse than Courage herself. Together this little group at the wagon represent one squalid element of the war's effects.

Even while they are speaking, the eye is taken to the other side of the stage, where the Chaplain staggers out from the farmhouse crying for help: 'I need linen!' This cry focuses on one instance of individual suffering in a universal situation. The Chaplain's action suggests at least an altruistic attitude, and the second soldier (Brecht insists that it is the one who has already had his brandy) goes to his aid; perhaps the army is not all bad, at any rate when it is not thirsty. In the tension between Courage's negative and the Chaplain's positive position, the audience is presented with a thinking perspective on the scene. But the interruption precipitates a fight between Kattrin, the dumb girl, and her mother: Kattrin's compassion adds a dimension to the range of virtue represented by the second group. But of course Courage is 'not tearing up my *officers*' shirts for *these* people'... 'they have nothing and they pay nothing!' Kattrin continues to struggle wildly to reach the shirts.

Our eyes are back on the farmhouse. The Chaplain is carrying in a peasant woman. Why didn't she get away and save herself? One gasped phrase tells the story: 'Our farm—!' Not heroism, but the facts of life, lie behind this. The farm is their means of survival, no less. The expressionistic manner is very much present in this kind of structuring, and here in another sharply selected detail Brecht advances one more attitude, with one more kind of suffering. And, reinforcing our sense of the irrelevance of the cause of the war to the cause of the people, he has the soldier from a Catholic army dismiss the rights of these peasants because they are Protestants. He is immediately contradicted by his companion, who points out that the peasants are Catholics too. The first soldier shrugs the matter off— 'In a bombardment we can't pick and choose'—and this cursory, academic little discussion is brought to a quick end. So much for religion. Religion and morality are irrelevant in the amorality of war, and the victims are faceless.

The discussion is heavily ironic, the more so when it is reduced to empty words by a cry of pain from another peasant the Chaplain is bringing out of the house: 'My arm's gone.' That is the simple, human argument, beyond talk. The Chaplain calls again for linen, and in the pause all turn and look at the only one who can supply it, Mother Courage.

Two mothers

At this point in the first version of the play, Brecht had the old woman bow before such persuasion and tear up her shirts. In the final version, she remains adamant, and the antithesis between human and material values is transparent. Her 'rummaging' for linen in the first version was an act of instinct and humanity; her 'stopping Kattrin' in the second is an act of will. She 'does not budge'. She cannot afford it, with all her 'taxes, duties, bribes' (the bathos is characteristic). Kattrin is now threatening her mother with a piece of wood and the Chaplain goes to the girl's assistance; caricature of the clergy is suppressed for this scene. The shirts are torn into strips and almost simultaneously we hear two screams: from Courage, 'My shirts, my officers' shirts!'; from the house, 'the cry of a child in pain'. The juxtaposition of the two concerns is exact, and the sounds take our attention in two directions at once. Our compassion and our indignation jostle for first place.

Kattrin is inspired to new energy, and she now turns spontaneously towards the screaming of the child. By her quick movement she articulates what she could not with words, and assumes the natural function of her mother. Now Courage has a new reason to restrain her daughter, but Brecht has us recognize the torment of her conflicting interests by her line (also in the final version), 'Go easy on my expensive linen!' It shows her torn between two wishes, and helps us to see the ridiculous pathos of her new position as objectively as before. The scene, for all its speed and brevity, has taken our attention back and forth between its two poles, and now at last it has Courage centre-stage, caught between the two drives of her life, the wagon and her child. Brecht in his notes would have her run back and forward in an alienated movement, until Kattrin has gone and the shirts are torn up. When the girl runs from the house with the baby in her arms 'like a thief', she circles around the wounded and away from her mother. Courage, angry and distracted, can only abuse her pointlessly, until the old woman turns to the soldier and shouts,

Don't stand about gawking, go back there and tell 'em to stop that music. I can see their victory without it. I have nothing but losses from your victory.

Almost laughable in her dilemma, she, like us, finds the mockery of the martial music more than she can stand, and her final vituperation at the top of her voice might well be addressed to an invisible General Tilly himself.

Yet no one on the stage is listening. The Chaplain is at work on the wounded peasant: 'The blood's coming through.' Kattrin is squatting near the wagon as if sheltering under its ugly roof—it is, after all, her home. She is rocking the baby in her arms and 'half humming a lullaby' with the grotesque noises of her dumbness. She is a peaceful centre on this busy stage, oblivious of her gesticulating mother, a pool of dumb happiness in the middle of misery, her human gesture and her humming in direct contrast with the war and its gaudy music as it reaches its crescendo. Kattrin must hug the child like a mother and bounce it up and down as if it is *her* booty.

Brecht has employed all the effects of eye and ear to make this brief episode a dialectical epitome of war, pitting one theatrical statement against another. But he is also intent upon making us feel that his little scene is only a snatch of a persisting story. He breaks the incipient pathos when Courage sees that the first soldier is trying behind her back to make off with a bottle. She remains consistent in the face of a consistent war, and at once she assumes her familiar stance. She retreats from the area of human suffering and protects her livelihood by leaping like a 'tiger' (Brecht's word in his production notes) and snatching the fur coat off the man's back in payment. She rolls it up and throws it into the wagon triumphantly, at the same time as Kattrin lifts the baby high in the air in a triumph of her own. This is almost a comic anticlimax, and the action seems to return to the start. The scene comes full circle as the audience withdraws from the immediate situation and is returned to the business of survival. And as if to emphasize that what we have seen is only a glimpse of the whole, that this corrupt and corrupting war will go on for many more years, Brecht concludes the scene inconclusively with a call from the Chaplain on the other side of the stage: 'There's someone still in there!' The placard is of course still reading, 'Forever on the move, the little wagon crosses Poland, Moravia, Bavaria...'

This is structural alienation working well, making an audience alive to several points of view at once, the constant change not permitting a single focus on one aspect of a character, nor on one scene, but on antithetical centres of interest. Thus emotion is present, even illusion is present, but the mind is engaged by the senses, and we relive the scene to rethink it, not the reverse. The penultimate scene of the play, that of the siege of Halle, is, nevertheless, brilliantly *misconceived* for alienation, but is so powerfully emotive in itself that no audience will ever wish it otherwise.

Counterpoint and Hysteria

One mother

In scene 11, the stage is again divided between the wagon and a farm-house, but this time Courage is absent—it is night and she is away in the village about her trade. Kattrin is alone and asleep in the wagon. The melodramatic thrill of this climactic episode is initiated when a lieutenant and three soldiers grope their way on to the stage urging that 'there mustn't be a sound'. They have come to the farm in search of a guide to take them across the fields to the besieged town of Halle. They knock and an old peasant woman opens the door. A hand is clapped over her mouth and the soldiers drag out her old husband and their son. They threaten the youth with their pikes if he will not show them the path. He resists—he, a Protestant, will not help the Catholic enemy (a gesture of generosity towards youthful idealism by the author!). So the soldiers threaten their cattle instead, and the peasants promptly capitulate. When the son has led the soldiers off, the father sets a ladder against the farmhouse and describes the scene for the audience: 'The army is ready to attack— God have mercy on the town and all within!' Thus far, Brecht has efficiently narrated in feasible stage terms an exciting, but common-place, piece of theatre.

With the spectator, the old peasant and his wife wait in suspense, and Brecht in the interval reveals their state of mind. They rationalize why they should do nothing to warn the town:

— The watchman 'll give warning.
— If there were more of us...
— There's nothing we can do, is there?
— We can't get down there. In the dark.

All they will do is pray, and with typical anti-clerical mockery, Brecht has the old woman in a quavering and whining voice intone a prayer to the God they have just betrayed. Our response to this travesty can be only derisory. But Kattrin is praying too, and when she hears that the peasants' son-in-law and his four children of tender age are in the town, it is she who answers the prayer, and the scene springs to life again.

The dumb girl, not without fear for herself as well as for the inhabitants of the town, climbs the ladder to the roof of the farm-house and begins to beat a drum taken surreptitiously from the wagon. This drum becomes her voice, speaking, like Lear's thunder, almost personally as she hammers it for some three or four astonishing minutes. 'The stone begins to speak.' The audience watches and listens with horror and delight, noting each individual reaction to the noise; and in the sound of the drum they hear the girl's answers.

The peasants, far from being overjoyed that their prayer is being answered, are terrified for their skins: 'Heavens, what's she doing?' ...'She's out of her mind.'...'Get her down, quick!' But Kattrin only pulls the ladder up after her and drums the more. The lieutenant has run back and he now threatens the girl. At this point, friend and enemy, Protestant and Catholic, have joined forces against Kattrin's humane action. But she drums on. They offer to spare her mother, the lieutenant giving his word as an officer. Kattrin does not hesitate and only drums the harder. Her action is bigger than personalities; she is saving people, not persons. Next, the old peasant of his own volition offers to chop at a tree in the hope of drowning the noise of the drum. It is of no use: Kattrin wins the competition in noise, the total of theatrical sound is doubled, and the tension increased. Now it is the peasant's wife's turn, and she more astutely suggests that they smash the wagon itself. Of her own experience, she knows the value of the means of subsistence, and for the first time Kattrin pauses in her drumming and makes 'noises of distress'. By this effect, Brecht has the spectator realize that the wagon is like the farm and the cattle to the peasants, and that the loss of livelihood is no better than the loss of life. But Kattrin's grand gesture is greater than economic necessity too, and the drumming begins again, louder than ever. At this moment, the young peasant, who has been half-heartedly aiming blows at the wagon, drops his piece of wood and shouts encouragement to the girl; he is her echo on the stage level and signifies again Brecht's acknowledgment of youthful idealism. He is viciously struck down with a pike. Through tears and exhaustion Kattrin drums wildly, like a mad thing. But the soldiers have brought up a musket; they set it on forks and level it at her on the roof. The noise of her crying and the fury of her drumming have reached their height, and we hear nothing else in our ears for one long moment before the gun is fired. 'She gives the drum another feeble beat or two, then slowly collapses.' The lieutenant and the old peasants have a brief moment of triumph.

In the silence which follows the crescendo from the drum, we breathe again to assimilate the quality of her self-sacrifice, until faintly in the distance we hear the noise of cannon and alarm bells from the town. The lieutenant, according to the production notes, 'beats the ground with his fists like a child'. 'She did it.' And in the silence after this scene of prolonged excitement and suspense, one which uses all the effects of nineteenth-century melodrama, the audience might well be asking whether Kattrin has not stolen the show from Courage. Unwittingly, perhaps, Brecht has allowed the girl's positive regard for humanity, with all its warmth of sentiment, to destroy the dialectic of the play and substitute unthinking persuasion. He has allowed a single and very moving character to embody all the virtues, and thus to reduce the scale of his world-wide problem. We supply an optimistic faith that an individual sacrifice will cure all its ills. Neither Shaw nor Pirandello ever went as far as this: the Saint Joans appear only to remain enigmatic, uncomprehended, a cause for mirthless laughter. Mother Courage was not there.

Nor can Brecht in his last short scene, however revised, readjust the image. The change in mood and tempo as Courage sits next morning by the body of her daughter, the military music once again barking ironically in the background, can only emphasize the pathos of Kattrin's deed. We even see Courage for the first time in a true role as a mother as she sings a lullaby over the dead child. The touches which recreate the old Mother Courage—the selfish words of her song, her reluctant action when she counts back the money for the girl's funeral, her determination to return to 'business', the detail of blowing her nose with her index finger as she harnesses herself to the wagon, her final effort as she heaves the wheels into motion, alone in the shafts at last—all this only contributes to our vision of her as a mother trapped, not in a prison of her own making, but by the hand of a tragic and ennobling fate. As Eric Bentley says, alienation devices must be 'called into action like a fire brigade' to douche the sympathy of this last scene. And Brecht's notes call for a large number of such externally applied tricks. Whatever a director tries will not make epic drama of this *dénouement*. It will, however, remain first-rate theatre in the best and most ancient of traditions.

ANOUILH

When it is no longer the Parisian fashion to denigrate Jean Anouilh for his refusal to affirm that his *Antigone* was a play 'committed' either to the French Resistance or to existentialism, the dramatic strength of his talents may be recognized. The London critics may then be encouraged to look at him more carefully. For he is well in the running to be the natural successor to Pirandello. He touches here and there on the grim game of mask and face—we remember General St Pé in *The Waltz of the Toreadors*, the Mother and her lover Vincent in *Point of Departure*[1] and many others—do not all his old roués wear their masks uncertainly, if rakishly? He reverts to questioning our need to accept reality—Anouilh's *Traveller without Luggage* prefers not to regain his memory, and Gaston's situation derives directly from plays like Pirandello's *Henry IV* and *As You Desire Me*. The dream world of the Prince in *Time Remembered* and of Georges in *Dinner with the Family* (Act I in this is all Pirandello) is set in direct opposition to the humbler, if not seedy, truth. By the superimposition of *marivaudage* on the dialogue of *The Rehearsal* and in the last act of *Colombe*, which takes us 'behind the scenes', Anouilh even seems to adopt a little of Pirandello's theatrical trickery from *Each in His Own Way* and *Six Characters* to suggest the fiction of human behaviour. *The Cavern* is wholly derivative.

Having said this, one must acknowledge that Pirandello brings more weight to bear on his plays and pursues his arguments to remorseless conclusions, though Anouilh's lighter touch and

[1] The titles of Anouilh's English versions have been used where they are likely to be more familiar to the reader.

apparent cynicism often tend to conceal an equally committed interest in problems of truth and reality. This kind of dramatic echoing is fairly common in these days of international theatre, and the differences between the Italian and the Frenchman are of more importance than their likenesses.

Pirandello repeatedly contrives an inversion of the mental image we derive from the play, deliberately disrupting its stability. Anouilh selects a contraposition from which we are to view his subject, necessarily upsetting our mood. Pirandello has us pirouette dizzily, where Anouilh has us leap acrobatically from one position to the next. Again and again his *pièces noires*, his *pièces brillantes* and his *pièces grinçantes* (respectively 'black', 'sparkling' and 'grating' plays) are just saved from melodrama by his throwing a harsh ironic light on to an unsophisticated pathos. In *Point of Departure* he demonstrated how an over-simple love story between two young people could be made unstable by calculated counterpoint, not like the simplicity of the love of Othello and Desdemona subverted by conscious evil in the person of Iago, but by introducing the callous insensibility and the corrupt but comic attitudes of Eurydice's mother and her lover, by the outrageous memories of the hotel waiter under whose eye the lovers spend a night in Marseilles, by the pressure of the past on the future. In *Ardèle*, the characters revolve in cynical circles round a woman whose spirit is by implication pure; a paradoxical edge is lent to the drama whenever we are reminded that her body is twisted as their minds are twisted. Colombe the dove is caught in the net of unfeeling society, but her tragedy, like that of General St Pé in *The Waltz of the Toreadors*, is presented to us in terms of the rudest farce. We may suspect at times that the farcical interpolations are introduced a little easily, and this is especially true of the uproarious troubles of the General with his mistress and the grotesque intrusions of his wife in the last-named play.

In his progress from the 1930s to the 1950s, Anouilh has, by trial and error, transmuted his private anger to the public elements we now expect to find in his particular theatrical concoction. He has done this often with more of a nimble insight into what the theatre can carry, and how an audience can be manipulated, than his predecessor. His 'sense of theatre' may keep him on the boards when Pirandello is read only in books. This is a dangerous criterion in itself, of course, and Anouilh's constant risk is that his own developed technique will become 'well-made' in the service of the *boulevard* theatre.

Like Pirandello, he usually found it necessary to invent a 'fairy-tale' world of make-believe in order to win our consent to his ideas, and to lend him freedom to arrange them in a way that would make nonsense of them in a naturalistic convention. His frequent choice of the twilight 1910s for his style and setting, even his occasionally facile resort to Greek myth, may lie in his wish to 'play with his characters, with their passions and their actions'. As he explains, 'to "play" with a subject is to create a new world of conventions and surround it with spells and a magic all your own...',[1] and he does this with more obvious theatricality than Pirandello. His early *pièces roses* ('pink' plays) are unmistakably of the genre of artificial comedy. *Thieves' Carnival* is launched with this kind of bold, if somewhat cheap and easy, flourish:

HECTOR (*passionately*). I want to inhale the perfume of your hand! (*He bends over Eva's hand, and surreptitiously draws a jeweller's eyeglass from his pocket to take a closer look at her rings...*)

EVA. Till tonight. (*She goes.*)

HECTOR (*weak at the knees*). My beloved...(*He follows her out of sight, then comes downstage again, putting away his eyeglass, and mutters with icy self-possession.*) A good two hundred thousand. And not a flaw in the lot.

There can be no mistaking the nature of the play that is to follow, any more than we can miss the opening note of *Twelfth Night*,

> If music be the food of love, play on...

or of Wycherley's *The Gentleman Dancing Master*:

> To confine a woman just in her rambling age!

Anouilh will refer again and again to this flighty, frivolous manner, but usually when he is about to make a particularly poisonous state-ment or compel his audience to undergo a particularly gruesome

[1] Quoted in E. O. Marsh, *Jean Anouilh, Poet of Pierrot and Pantaloon* (London, 1953), p. 189.

experience. It may appear as a comic character with a sinister charge, like General St Pé's harridan of a wife, or Robinet, Desfournettes and du Bartas in *Colombe*; as an acrid comment on the scene, like the presence of Toto and Marie-Christine in *Ardèle*; or as an hilarious situation, like the midnight meanderings in the same play, or the tearing of the money in *Ring Round the Moon*.

Remarkably, Anouilh saw a profit in keeping the same light touch for certain moments in his *pièces noires*. Notably in *Point of Departure*, he employs an admixture of farce as a glittering foil for his pathos. The same ironic edge will not be missed where the gentility of Florent's way of life is balanced with a revolting and ridiculous father for Thérèse in his earlier play *Restless Heart*; nor in the lazy drifter of a father and the mocking brother Lucien granted to Julia in his later *Fading Mansions*. In these back-handed Cinderella stories Anouilh is feeling towards the peculiarly mettlesome mixture of his post-war plays. There is to be more sugar-coating on the pill and more iron at the centre, so that, once in the mouth, the flavour is to taste all the more putrid. The contrasts between single characters or groups are not gentle like Chekhov's but more obvious and acute.

A brief example at the tail-end of *Point of Departure* will indicate the singular tone the comic element produces in these earlier plays. Heavily charged emotionally—we should say 'over-charged' if it were not for the refining action of the irony—the final scene shows its hero Orpheus as youth in deep despair: his Eurydice has been killed in an accident. He is being goaded by M. Henri, the death figure, to the suicide which will reunite them. The weight of the play is behind this scene, and the mood of the audience is wholly sober. With a striking ingenuity, Orpheus's feelings are explored and exposed by their contradiction, and their meaning communicated in the main by Orpheus's father. The father, speaking now selfishly, now sensually, now rhetorically, his words empty of any understanding of his son's condition, is given the part of counsellor for life's defence. He is all clown:

FATHER. ...the man who is talking to you has suffered. Drunk life to the very lees. He often kept silent, bit his lips till the blood flowed, to stifle his moans. His companions of the festive board little dreamed the

torture he sometimes bore...Betrayal, scorn, injustice...You sometimes wonder why my back is bent and my hair prematurely white. If
you but knew how heavily life lies on a man's shoulders.

(*He pulls at the cigar without success, looks vexed and flings it away with a
sigh. M. Henri goes up to him and holds out his cigar-case.*)

M. HENRI. Another cigar?

FATHER. Thank you...

The clichés he uses mark him down as hollow and fit only for
derisory laughter. His lachrymose self-portrait as white-haired age
stooped by the troubles of an unjust world cannot be taken seriously,
since we see him thoroughly enjoying himself smoking someone
else's cigars and revelling in the opportunity to make a confessional
speech. His hypocrisy makes us laugh, but also throws us angrily
into sympathy with the silent Orpheus, and when, rightly or wrongly,
the latter accepts death's proposal, we feel we know more precisely
his state of mind. When we talk of Anouilh's sense of theatre, we
partly have in mind that he knows the exact quantity of salt to rub
in the wound.

The *pièces brillantes* and *grinçantes* he has offered us since the war
hold within them the ideas of his earlier plays, and exploit the
techniques of *rose* and *noir* in unique conjunction. In *Ardèle*,
Colombe, *The Waltz of the Toreadors* and *L'Hurluberlu* in particular,
he calls on the artificial world of his lighter comedies to give himself
the greater freedom for irreverence; the angry protest against the
cruelty of existence of his 'tragedies' remains to provide his dramatic
impetus. The farcical and the pathetic are counterpointed in perfect
balance, a balance so pleasing that one suspects that Anouilh has
reached the limit this form will allow him.

The blackness of the black plays, whose passionate, idealistic
attack on man's animality and hypocrisy inclined too easily to
sentimentality and melodrama and often to the simple romantic and
irresponsible negation of life, has been relieved. Anouilh now makes
his apologists of idealism blatant hypocrites like Orpheus' father
and the grotesque Mme Alexandra of *Colombe*:

MME ALEXANDRA. It's very profound! But don't you think it's a little
hard, dear poet?

ROBINET. It's hard, but it's the truth, dear lady. And it's our duty to be hard. We mustn't hide the truth, never...

MME ALEXANDRA. Dear poet, that's blasphemy!...I believe only in the ideal! I want to sound a great clarion call. I want to show them my faith in self-denial, in youth, in all that is fine and beautiful in love!

The cold douche of farce is offered as a prophylactic against the inadequately objective view, and claims our more active and intelligent participation. The violence of the farce combined with the sensationalism of its subjects may not leave us with the warm, smouldering glow we experience with Chekhovian comedy, but it leaves us burning and crackling merrily.

ANALYSIS: TRAGICOMIC COUNTERPOINT IN
'ARDÈLE' AND 'COLOMBE'

'Ardèle': interactions

Ardèle and *Colombe* are chosen in order to investigate the effect of the later Anouilh on his audience. The first, once likened by Roy Walker to a 'grotesque quadrille of amatory partners', is at pains to establish its fantasy in a variety of ways. The excessive number of its lovers, with the jigsaw plotting that must result if the play is not to collapse, should lower our naturalistic defences. Its element of social high comedy, found in the persons of the Countess, her husband and her lover, suit admirably with its mellowed period, '1912 or thereabouts'. Its free sprinkling of typed characters with their raw language and wild situations of a lower tradition, in the old General with his scarecrow hag of a wife Emily and his 'ripe, juicy peach' of a chamber-maid, in the Count's relationship with his 'monkey darling', his 'little dove', his 'lambkin' of a little sempstress, are disarming. The increasingly funny echo of the General's Christian name Léon by the cry of the peacock in the garden, with its strident sound adding at the same time an overtone of horror, and the mounting incongruity of the two imps Toto and Marie-Christine, children who eavesdrop at the inappropriate times and shockingly ape the adults, are at first in the lightest vein. In this jumble of theatrical conventions, we may not be surprised that, as the pivot of the play, Anouilh has supplied *two* hunchbacks as true lovers: this is just beyond the bounds of credibility, and we are to be forgiven if we realize too late that we should not have laughed. But there is yet another pair, Nicholas and his elder brother's wife Nathalie, to convey to us the sense of guilt: they, like Ardèle and her lover, play in the manner of the realistic *drame*.

Clearly this is a play that at every performance is in danger of fragmentation, and it represents Anouilh's most daring experiment in testing the possibilities of the stage and juggling with our responses. Its success rests upon the extent to which the variety of characters, the ill-assorted styles of making love, and the mixture of realistic and farcical manners of writing are related. The statement of the play is to emerge by the contrasts between the characters, the interactions of its parts, and the revolutions of feeling we sustain. As in all of Anouilh's plays, at its core is a bare simplicity—that those we think of as tainted may in fact be pure—but the author turns all his energy towards shocking us into a full recognition of his platitude. Amid the ludicrous decorums of the Countess, the clowning of the Count and 'fishlike' Villardieu, the bedroom titters and the groping in the dark, Nicholas and Ardèle are struggling tragically for a dignity among the undignified. Nicholas may have failed, but Ardèle may well have succeeded, for she, the unseen player, measures them all: 'Aunt Ardèle is Love.'[1]

Before the amazing transitions of feeling of the last act, we make a series of comparisons between one character and another, and between one set of standards and another.

Age is judged by youth, and experience by innocence. The General is fighting a losing battle against senility and sterility, and he knows it; he declares he is like an old tree: '...I blossom every spring. It's a fine show, but the trunk, alas, is hollow.' He fears the unspoken comment of Nathalie his daughter-in-law, a girl of twenty:

NATHALIE. It is not for me to judge you.
GENERAL. And yet I feel you are in some way my appointed judge. The Lord knows why.

[1] Trans. L. Hill (London, 1951).

Yet Nathalie, the accuser, is not innocent herself, and later she tells her lover that she is afraid that someone will suddenly call her name as Emily calls her peacock husband. They have a lesson for each other. Even Toto his youngest son, aged ten, criticizes him by echoing in his squeaky voice his blandishments to the maid. When Ardèle, an elder sister and a hunchback to boot, sends him a message by the Count that he revolts her, the General cannot understand it: 'Ha, that's good! That's very good! She is in love with a hunchback, and it's me she finds revolting!' Though he cannot understand, we can. In the chain of relative values Anouilh is constructing, the old man, for all our laughter and all our sympathy, is at the earthy end of it.

The Countess philanders with her lover while at the same time she is madly jealous of her husband's attentions to his mock-suicidal mistress down in the village. In her turn she comes under fire when she rashly offers Ardèle her advice from her familiarity with the world's ways: '...I am younger than you are, but I know so much more about life. Will you let me give you some advice? (*She listens a moment at Ardèle's door, then straightens, tight-lipped with fury.*) Ardèle, how dare you!' And the Countess utters the remark which Anouilh has been working to have us ask and answer ourselves: 'What can she possibly know of love?'

Nicholas and Nathalie, the adulterers, are the last to be weighed in these treacherous scales. Unlike Ardèle's other critics, Nicholas allies himself with her, and sees in her defiance of social convention the enactment of his own extremity: 'Aunt Ardèle! It's Nicholas. Stand firm! Laugh at the world! Laugh at what they are pleased to call scandal! Love whom you want to love, and don't listen to them! If they didn't tell you you were deformed and too old, they'd say you were too young...' He is pleading his own cause, but ironically he is incapable of seeing that his position is not Ardèle's, for the kind and quality of his love are inferior, as in the issue it will appear.

These dramatic logistics are, like Pirandello's, expertly organized, but they are insufficient in themselves to urge upon us a strong and committed passion. This is to be done by the shifts in convention and style, in tone and feeling, that he brings about at the crisis.

'Ardèle' and 'Colombe'

'Ardèle': modulations

If we are right in supposing that in this play Anouilh has perfected his device of counterpointing pathos and comedy, then in his last act it is we who are to be probed and tested by our seesaw reactions to his effects. In this act he shows his instinct to be essentially Pirandellian. We may trace briefly its sequence of dramatic styles and its transitions of feeling.

The act opens with a mimetic summary of most of the relationships expounded in the previous two acts, with Toto, the precocious child, as apparent puppet-master. His appearance on the gallery which serves the bedrooms causes Nicholas, seeking a midnight rendezvous with Nathalie, to hide. Toto makes sure that the General is safely in bed, then tiptoes back to his room 'laden with hats, walking-sticks, furs and coats', all the paraphernalia of dressing up, tokens of the adult world. The Count, soaked through in spite of his raincoat, his straw boater and his umbrella, enters stealthily from the garden and prepares to escape to his room, but in the light of the bronze Cupid, which stands symbolically at the foot of the stairs, his wife sees him. All the elements of this furtive activity in the night are those of horse opera. Comic characters in a ridiculous situation make themselves more ridiculous, and we respond at the lowest level of appreciation.

The short exchange between the Countess and the Count which follows raises this level by a fraction only. The Countess veers between sarcasm and a false sympathy in order to discover what her husband has been doing. When this fails, she strikes another pose, and addresses him with the coy and winning tone that has in the past presumably subdued Villardieu: 'Gaston, had you noticed that we had virtually stopped speaking to each other? I have felt for so long the need of a quiet talk with you.' As she smoothes out the phrases and proposes a clandestine meeting in a teashop or the station, we are, as earlier, reminded how ludicrous it is that a wife should need to speak like this to her husband, and that the remote conventions of the artificial *ménage à trois* call for the derisory laughter of the comedy of manners:

COUNT. ...Think of Marie-Christine. You have no right to risk a
    scandal...

The Countess's coquetry, the Count's scandalized strictures, their exaggerated guilt, the absurd earnestness of their argument, are all in the strongest tradition of the Molière of farce, rather than of Marivaux and de Musset. Then an angry Villardieu appears, and the Countess with a startled cry runs into her room. When this is capped by the appearance of Ada the maid in her nightgown on her way upstairs to the General's study, where the old man immediately follows her, we are truly back to the tone of bedroom farce of the scene's opening.

Only for a brief interval. A very sober Nathalie now descends to Nicholas the romantic idealist, and with her first words the mood has changed:

> NICHOLAS (*in a whisper*). . . . You are here—at last.
> NATHALIE. Yes, my darling.

At first we may be inclined to respond to this as we do to the Count and Countess, or to the General and Ada, but we are quickly corrected. Nicholas's dark comment, 'You are my brother's wife!', is spoken in a tone which must modify our attitude. A deep pathos, passionate and bitter, rapidly discolours their interview.

In contrast to what has gone before, the latest manner is wholly realistic. This is suggested by the solemn tones, the limping tempo, and the new note of uncompromising criticism: 'They are ugly, all of them.' Nathalie's confession of her reasons for marrying Nicholas's brother Maxim is sincere and earnest, and this love duet, unlike the others, is forlorn, humiliating and hopeless: fate has laid none too light a hand on this relationship. The dry ironies grow stronger as the pace increases and as Nathalie feels their love to be as 'ugly and horrible' as Ardèle's: she confesses to having abandoned herself to Maxim in spite of her hate for him. The change in her reflects our own response when we see Ardèle's lover ('the hesitant figure of a man, misshapen, wrapped in a big hooded cloak') seek and enter her room. The farce is submerged in disgust, and we are once more 'guilty creatures sitting at a play'. To clinch the effect, the terrifying figure of Emily the General's wife emerges shrieking his name. She and Nathalie might be the same woman, having the same distaste for physical sex, at different stages of its obsession. A moment of sheer sensation brings to its crisis this sequence of incongruities.

The seriousness of the scene between Nicholas and Nathalie is soon modified. All the contrasts are embodied as the whole company from the ludicrous General to his grotesque wife fills the stage. Even the peacock joins in. We are whirled back to the fantasy in which the scene was conceived, and we are near to laughter again. Only Aunt Ardèle and her lover are absent.

Two shots interrupt Emily's extended hysterical accusations against her husband. In a second, the whole fantastic fretwork has been collapsed by this simple symbol of tragic reality: Ardèle and her lover have shot themselves. In this highly contrived context, these shots wake us as after a dream: a realistic death is shocking in fantasy, and here we are brutally assaulted: but only to be asked to laugh again by the crazy efforts of the Count, the General and Villardieu to break down Ardèle's door: 'this must almost be a clown act'. In fact, we cannot laugh. Yet their stupidity, their lack of human compassion, is firmly transmitted by having the reality condemn their behaviour as a mockery.

Nathalie and Nicholas are alone again, now our spokesmen: 'You see, we don't even have to kill ourselves now. These two who were made for the world's laughter, they have done it for us.' The former prisoners, the hunchback lovers, have become the arbiters in this trial of sexual relationships. Incongruously they set the only standard of perfection, and we have been forced to accept it. We, the former judges, have been convicted in our own court. Having thus confounded us, Anouilh brings down his curtain in a mood of absolute mockery. 'Two grotesque little dwarfs', Toto and Marie-Christine dressed in adult clothes, mimic the game of sex we have been analysing emotionally. They telescope the love–hate quarrels of their elders, and the inherent pathos of the subject is finally shown as a monstrous burlesque. Anouilh ends his play with the Pirandellian mixture of the spit and the guffaw that brings the curtain down on *Right You Are If You Think So*.

This play has added interest for us because of its introduction of symbolism into an already crowded image, and this symbolism turns

on the invisible presence of Ardèle. She is the only positive character
in the play, but she is never produced for examination and she is
defined only by the negation of the characters we do see. In this the
play worries us rather like a sermon: for it is easier and stronger for a
dramatist to speak a negative 'don't be like this' than a positive 'do
be like that'. Anouilh knows that sinners are more exciting than
saints. By hiding Ardèle away he deftly avoids the danger of making
his symbol unreal and uninteresting or of having to make her too real
and therefore unsymbolic. He avoids putting pure virtue on the
stage, because he knows that goodness tends to be seen as priggish-
ness, and this is a risk to his theme too great to run. Perhaps he
guessed that her spiritual beauty might be marred by showing her
deformity. He knows his audience well enough to lock the lovers in
the room, hint at the romance of an elopement and then, as a
romantic if not symbolic reinforcement, shoot them in adversity.

'*Colombe*': preparation as hoax

A short exegesis of *Colombe* will demonstrate the outrageous extent
to which Anouilh will go to find a symbolic pattern for his view of
life. For *The Rehearsal*, the play which followed *Ardèle*, he hit upon
the formula of presenting his subject as if it were set in the tinsel
world of Marivaux: its characters rehearse their parts for *La Double
Inconstance* at the opening of the play, and their situation is deliberately confused with the plotting of the play-within-the-play.
Anouilh made an essay at this kind of device in *Dinner with the
Family*, where a hired actor and actress play-act the parts of
Georges's idealized mother and father to mark the difference
between wish and actuality. In *Point of Departure*, four years later,
Lucienne and Vincent are again provincial actors, and when they
find themselves automatically speaking about their love in lines from
de Musset's *On ne badine pas avec l'amour*, it is strikingly suggested
that their attitude is a second-hand rhetorical gesture. In all these
plays, the theatrical climate is illusory and bogus.

The young girl Colombe is absorbed by the sham *fin de siècle*
magic of the theatre: its atmosphere of extravagant melodrama,
inducing the amoral behaviour of romantic fiction, at once corrupts

her, embarrasses us with laughter, and provides an extreme contrast to unromantic reality. In the person of the doyenne Mme Alexandra we see the gay, tyrannical hypocrisy of middle age and the degradation of worldly success to which Colombe may descend: Mme Alexandra is the Colombe who will be. In the settings, back-stage and on-stage, we see where the two realms of fact and fiction overlap: in the last act Colombe's story is even played out in crude terms by her counterpart Mme Alexandra. At the same time the fantasy of theatrical life gives the author that margin of licence to paint certain of his characters with his former glaring colours of grotesquerie.

The characters of the lovers in *Colombe* are thin and, by comparison with that of *Ardèle*, the plot is thin too. A stern and idealistic young man, Julien, marries Colombe, a pretty flower-girl. When he goes into the army, she is left with his actress mother, and Colombe in her turn goes on the stage. When Julien returns, he discovers to his horror that his Colombe is no longer the sad Cinderella, the little dove, he left behind. That is all. But from what we know already of Anouilh, his plot is the merest peg on which to hang a multicoloured coat, and the exposition and tracing of the theme, the mixing of the audience's feelings, and the form of their development give the play its values. The trite becomes novel because the process is novel.

The theme is simply stated early in the play:

JULIEN. The world's a much harder place than you believe.
COLOMBE. I know.
JULIEN. I want you to...to try to grow up a little, and take life more seriously.
COLOMBE. Yes.
JULIEN. If you don't, you'll become one of Mother's kind of people: never happy without pleasures.
COLOMBE. I know. You've explained it before.
JULIEN. It's the world of pleasures you'll see now. It'll all seem so new, so dazzling—
COLOMBE. Yes.
JULIEN. But it's all false, my darling—you must realize that.
COLOMBE. Yes, I'm sure.[1]

[1] This is not from a translation, but from a 'version' of the original, done by Denis Cannan (London, 1952). There are no substantial differences of intention in the excerpts quoted.

So she counters his warnings of evil with a giggle, '*à un petit rire*'. This contest between respectable principle and primitive simplicity is enacted through the play. Interestingly, even here the author is misleading us: we must rethink the moral position from the start. Julien sounds priggish and prudish in our ears, and we react against the Puritan and in sympathy with the natural girl. Yet it is this girl who, in tormenting Julien, is to torment us when we try to fix her in the kaleidoscopic pattern.

Mme Alexandra, who 'can never attend to family matters unless she's playing a mother at night', initiates the device for the restatement of the theme. She is presented as a brilliant planet round whom all others are satellites. At her first entrance she flashes across the stage followed by a little host of attendants, and after one curt remark is gone again. We greet her with the laughter which dissociates us from her florid attitude to life and does not allow us to take her seriously. We listen to her artistic pretences as she makes suitable noises for the approval of Robinet's new play, but it is transparent that she is all *poseuse* and utterly self-centred:

ROBINET. I will begin: 'O moon so wan, my heart's chill friend in death—'
MME ALEXANDRA. Superb! Beautiful beyond belief. 'My heart's chill friend in death.' I know exactly how I shall say it. (*She has never stopped looking at herself in the mirror. Suddenly she shouts.*) Lucien!
HAIRDRESSER. Madame?
MME ALEXANDRA. Look at this! You've made me look like a poodle...

This little episode visually confirms the earlier suggestion of the theme, but the line of our response remains uncertain as we struggle to assess the woman. Her flamboyance is disarming, but although we are as innocent in the theatre as Colombe herself, we no longer accept it uncritically, as wide-eyed Colombe is doing. When Colombe appears at the end of Act I beautifully dressed by the personal care and attention of Julien's brother Paul (Armand in the original), 'bejewelled, transformed' and 'forgetting everything in her ecstasy at the glory of her reflection', our identity with Cinderella is not so strong, and our sympathy for the husband, helpless before her innocent enthusiasm, is growing:

> COLOMBE. Oh, Julien—is it me? Is it me?
> JULIEN. Is it my wife? Colombe, I don't know any more...

'*Colombe*': counterpoint and violence

Anouilh can mount his hobby-horse from either side. Having slyly misdirected our judgment, he has us pursue the tragicomedy of life by tossing us freely between Julien and Colombe, the rivals for our affection. Julien is the deserving poor, but such an unpleasant young man. Colombe holds the glittering riches, but we are never sure that her apparently naïve cruelty is not calculated. The evidence is not presented forensically as pro and con, but sensationally as ruthless pathos mingled with beguiling farce. The comic balance is ours to assert, if we can.

In the second act, the kaleidoscope begins to revolve. The farcical note is struck resoundingly by the ludicrous flirting of Lagarde, an actor (du Bartas in the original). With a 'wide-brimmed hat, an elegant cane, a flower in his button-hole', he is as affected as Mme Alexandra. The ridiculous is drained to the dregs by the stylized repetition of Lagarde's formula for the seduction of Colombe, 'a drop of port, nibble a biscuit' after rehearsal—which is echoed by Desfournettes the manager and Robinet the '*poète*'. Colombe accepts these approaches so lightly that we can only place her in fairyland and refuse to admit evil of her. We are reminded of Lamb's comment on the comedy of the Restoration: he

could never connect those sports of a witty fancy in any shape with any result to be drawn from them to imitation in real life. They are a world of themselves almost as much as fairyland...They seem engaged in their proper element. They break through no laws, or conscientious restraints. They know of none...It is altogether a speculative scene of things, which has no reference whatever to the world that is.[1]

[1] Lamb, 'On the Artificial Comedy of the Last Century' (1823).

This scene concludes with an exchange with Paul, during which Colombe shows herself to be an accomplished actress:

PAUL. . . . when we come to rehearse the scene of farewell, will you really feel unhappy?

COLOMBE. Not really. But the tears will come into my eyes just as if it were life.

We are sober again, wondering indeed whether it is not Colombe who is seducing Paul. We are ready to apply our normal standards of judgment when Paul offers us his estimate of her at the curtain: 'You devil. You dirty little devil. . . '

The procedure has been first to set her at a distance, deceiving us with all the patter of the conjurer, then gently to bring her nearer for closer inspection. Now on guard, we see Colombe through the passionate eyes of her husband who has returned. The switches in style alternate more rapidly, now that by the use of Julien our eye is hard on the object. With Julien predisposed to jealousy, the third scene[1] at its beginning quickly evokes pathos, and the reunion between Julien and Colombe is presented sentimentally. Out of context, this episode would be cloying, since Anouilh goes as far as he dares in lubricating our tender emotions; in context, Colombe remains on trial, and we, like Julien, are torn between submission and revolt.

It is a stroke of pure theatre when Anouilh follows this uncertain mawkishness with a repetition of the bizarre farce that characterized the previous scene. Lagarde, Desfournettes and Robinet appear once more in succession, each with a new excess of seductive prattle: 'Are you there, my little mousey?'. . . 'Are you there, my little wolfie?' They are cut short only by the presence of the husband. Their comic appearance in a situation of traditional farce makes laughter again irresistible, and even Julien's justifiable anger must to a degree become risible, since he has automatically fallen into place in the pattern of the conventional triangle. He is the traditional cuckold, fit only for further scorn as his temper grows warmer. This farcical mood is increased by the particular stage arrangement

[1] Act II, sc. ii, in Cannan; Act III in the original.

devised for the scene: the stage is divided between Colombe's dressing-room and the back-stage passage, so that while Colombe is being interrogated, a silent, gesticulating group of buffoons eavesdrop outside her door.

In the issue, one cannot be sure that this effect comes off. For Julien is still at times the cold, realistic centre of the action that develops, and as he and we attempt to ascertain whether or not Colombe is a little cheat, his new tone of disgust, a tone wholly inappropriate to farcical comedy, spreads through the theatre. Our attempt to reconcile this with the unassimilated pantomime in the back-stage passage demands an effort which is untenable. Anouilh resolves the position with a device which reproduces the effect of the pistol shots in *Ardèle*:

> JULIEN (*striking her suddenly across the face*). You whore! You grubby little whore like all the rest!...

That blow and that word, shockingly of the real world, bring to an abrupt end the buffoonery on the stage, and smother the free, garish colouring of the first three scenes. This is the first of two crises of feeling we sustain in this scene. We begin violently to reorientate our image of the play in order to entertain the ugly sequence between Julien and Paul which follows immediately.

Elements of farce at the end of this act cannot reassert themselves, and perhaps are not intended to: the unnaturally rapid recovery of Colombe at Surette's call for the actors to be on stage, her quick concern for her appearance before the mirror, must seem as unsympathetic to us as Julien finds them himself. We undoubtedly veer towards Julien's point of view, and we are sure that Colombe is the whore he thinks she is. The moment at the end of the act when Julien forces his mouth against Paul's to discover insanely what Paul has to offer his wife is a moment of acute sensation, and the second crisis, as effective in its place as Eddie Carbone's insulting embrace of Rodolpho in Miller's *A View from the Bridge*; its bitterness reflects our feelings.

We are a long way from the play which 'tells a story', the play with a strictly narrative line. We have been taken through an

emotional attack and counter-attack which is better compared with
music than with narrative, and yet which is peculiar to any dramatic
medium. The two women, Mme Alexandra and Colombe, have
embodied experience and inexperience (we dare not talk of Colombe's
innocence now), while the fun and games back-stage, the surface
gaiety and its sinister undercurrents, have forced us to respond with
both feeling and intellect. A simple tale of pretty Columbine and
clumsy Pierrot has become a sharply satirical, violent experience for
an audience.

'Colombe': the play's form emerges

The play's story is over; there is no more to tell. Colombe is corrupt
and the marriage is ruined. No event, however extraordinary, can
reverse our verdict. Yet, surprisingly, Anouilh's curtain rises again.
We may not be able to reverse the verdict, nor may the story be
extended; but it is characteristic that he should devote his whole last
act to making the significance of that verdict more precise by
juggling exclusively with the play's formal patterning. That the
author adopts two disparate methods to illuminate his intentions
and have us review our feelings suggests not so much padding as
that he is straining to give his play an added complexity. He resorts
first to the artifice of the ironic play-within-the-play, and concludes
with a 'flashback', suggestive of the play-that-might-have-been.

The English version by Denis Cannan appeared a few months
after the French. It presumably had the blessing of the author and
perhaps at the opening of its final act enjoyed the 'elfish' inspiration
of its producer, Peter Brook.[1] It is this version which uses a clever,
noticeably Pirandellian, trick in the presentation of the play-within-
the-play. We find ourselves looking at the stage of Mme Alexandra's
theatre from where the back wall would be, while Mme Alexandra,
Lagarde, Colombe and Surette, their backs to us, act *La Maréchale
d'amour* to an imaginary audience we cannot see. We are given the
odd impression that we are looking towards ourselves, the audience
that had been looking at this same stage during the second act. At
once we are aware that conclusions we reached earlier were those of

[1] Cf. H. Hobson, *The French Theatre of Today* (London, 1953), p. 29.

a fiction deriving from a fiction, and that we too were playing a part. It compels us to suspend our judgment by separating us from the play of Julien and Colombe by several removes: what was pathetic then must become like the sad event of years ago that today we smile over—perhaps wistfully, perhaps more wisely, perhaps with unconcern. This effect of chill distancing is enhanced by our seeing all the dead apparatus of back-stage: the reverse sides of the flats and ground-rows, the wire that supports a cardboard moon, the stage-hands in the wings, the waiting actor who reads a newspaper. If this were not enough, the scene is spoken in stilted verse in complete contrast with the earlier dialogue.

Under conditions which must incur our criticism of the scene to be played, we are offered a burlesqued résumé of Julien and Colombe's story. Mme Alexandra plays the wife surprised with her lover by her husband. She is a Colombe who, through the prismatic lens of the romantic theatre, has been awakened to passion by a true love:

> Is't me? I only know
> A girl stood here before, so long ago
> And yet, an instant hence; now woman stands,
> Possessed of new-found wisdom...

War intervenes, and the lover and the husband depart with a heroic flourish, prepared to forget that 'in the clash of war...wives scarce wed may play the whore'. The lady and her confidante are left wondering whether they should remain faithful to lover or to husband:

> Shall we thus mourn, and let our beauty fade
> In loveless chastity?

Abruptly they depart in a gondola for 'mirth and pleasures gay'.

Once more we have been forced to mock Julien's little tragedy. We reject the imaginary audience now applauding the false romanticism and gay abandon of the scene: in doing so, we reject a little of ourselves. Nor are we alone: immediately the play is finished, Lagarde confirms that our view is his: 'Phew! What a damn silly lot of swine out there tonight!' Which is, of course, a venomous remark addressed indirectly to us. Yet, because of the convention of the play-within-the-play, we cannot be insulted, but remain receptive to the second and final irony which Anouilh has yet to inflict.

Before this arrives, and the more to disconcert us, he presents us with yet another Colombe, perhaps the only real one, disarmingly unaffected, but emphasizing the character of Julien's jealousy. She explains that she was happier in his absence:

> ...I cleaned the rooms as if it were a game, and I put a basin of water in the sunshine and stood in it naked, to wash myself—and what did it matter if the old man opposite was getting a treat through his binoculars? It was a natural joy to both of us, a present from God as much as the sun on the trees.

Their duologue has the effect of modifying the 'before-and-after' shape of the play. The *naïveté* of the inexperienced Colombe we first knew had become, it seemed, a cunning and sophisticated laxity; the sympathy we had felt for her charm had hardened to a colder, dispassionate assessment of her weaknesses. Now her naturalness returns and with it our understanding. As she says, her head has been so stuffed with his 'sacred opinions of right and wrong' that her childlike heart has dried up. Thus, just when Anouilh is ready to play his last card, we are again hung in the balance between sympathy for Julien and understanding of Colombe. Surette confirms Julien's disgust at the female principle, while Mme Alexandra confirms Colombe's distrust of the male.

The flashback that concludes the play is introduced solely as a new measure for audience participation. By an easy transition of music ('on entend un piano lointain, fantomatique...') and lighting ('la lumière baisse jusqu'au noir'), with some preparatory suggestion in the dialogue, we rehearse the first meeting of Julien and Colombe. This scene has been criticized as unadulterated sentiment offered as a sop to a jaded audience. It is true that Anouilh writes the sequence in an understated language which is deliberately sickly. Its simplicity may be illustrated by the closing lines:

JULIEN. Now our story begins. I'll never forget what you've given up for my sake.
COLOMBE. Oh, it's been too quick—I'm sure it's been too quick. It can't be the real thing, can it?

JULIEN. I think it is. And I think it will last. (*He kisses her. She leans tightly against him.*)
COLOMBE (*a whisper*). My darling!...Now I am sure of it...for always.
JULIEN. For always....Not a second less.
(*They kiss, and*)

The curtain falls

This certainly is an idealized demonstration of love at first sight; but the words, the embraces, are only different in degree from the burlesque tone and manner in which Mme Alexandra and Lagarde had opened the act: this curtain with this kiss is a convention of the type of theatre Anouilh travestied. Because of the play-within-the-play, we are doubly the sceptical audience we were: we simply do not respond sentimentally to the sentiment with which the words are spoken. To believe that the author intended us to, would contradict the total meaning of the play, not to mention his others.

This last device is used to cap the climax of bewilderment in which we find ourselves: weighed against the indecisions that troubled us before, set against our knowledge of the two years of marriage that are now fact, and the parting of Julien and Colombe that resulted, this tailpiece can be only ironic. In itself a simple enough reversal: in context, irony is a term rather too narrow to convey the complexity of its effect. The wink between the author and his audience is certainly implicit here, but into these last exchanges Anouilh has also squeezed his statement of value, disagreeable as it may be. We are still not to apply standards of moral right and wrong to our hero and our heroine; but in the corners of our minds we hear whispered an anguished and a passionate plea for human understanding in a world where nothing remains sacred.

Is this a *statement* of values? The effect of this curtain, as of other devices, on the play is to press its feeling upon us as if we had lived the experience ourselves: we are forced to participate beyond our natural will. It is achieved by Anouilh's ingenious tragicomic counterpointing, by the ironic discomfort in which we find ourselves when we attempt to assume comedy's attitude of omniscience.

Counterpoint and Hysteria

TENNESSEE WILLIAMS

Tennessee Williams has always written freely about his life, his feelings and his way of making plays. We can sense some of the spirit behind his drama when he writes biographically in a programme note,

In St Louis we suddenly discovered there were two kinds of people, the rich and the poor, and that we belonged more to the latter. If we walked far enough west we came into a region of fine residences set in beautiful lawns. But where we lived, to which we must always return, were ugly rows of apartment buildings the colour of dried blood and mustard. If I had been born in this situation I might not have resented it deeply. But it was forced upon my consciousness at the most sensitive age of childhood. It produced a shock and a rebellion that has grown into an inherent part of my work.

Williams calls it a 'bitter education', and his work reflects strikingly the American condition, found generally throughout serious American drama: in a world of prosperity and of unlimited opportunity for prosperity there remains the great immovable doubt that the central values are not as yet discovered. As O'Neill said in 1946, 'the United States, instead of being the most successful country in the world is the greatest failure...because it was given everything more than any other country. Through moving as rapidly as it has, it hasn't acquired any real roots. Its main idea is that everlasting game of trying to possess your own soul by the possession of something outside it too...'[1] Galbraith's affluent society has a moral 'imbalance' as well as an economic one.

Equally important to recognize for an understanding of the nature of Williams's peculiar sensationalism is the background of influences on a young man embarking on the career of a playwright at the end of the 'thirties. The American indigenous theatre is at the most only fifty years old. It missed the Ibsenite vogue of inquisitive realism, and until recently it lacked a broad tradition of playing and playgoing. Serious drama on Broadway had for years been losing the fight against the evils of commercialism, the star system and the prohibitive costs of production. The song-and-dance routine of the

[1] Quoted in E. R. Bentley, *In Search of Theater* (London, 1954), pp. 233-4.

musicals, plays of 'homey' sentiment about the American way of life, the bedroom farces and the cheap thrillers had their content inevitably dictated by the taste of the majority. Williams had to enter the jungle of big business, and he has never quite ceased to play it at its own game.

Nevertheless, he would have been well aware in the 'thirties of the watery trickle of serious drama off Broadway, from such as Eugene O'Neill with the Provincetown Players and Clifford Odets with the Theater Guild. The plays of these writers and others were essentially social in character and content, aiming at a frank realism of dialogue and subject, grinding out plays about sex and prostitution, about miscegenation and the Negro problem, about morals and divorce, about social issues and strikes. There was always a certain romance in the realism of this pre-war theatre, and especially in the drama of O'Neill, the greatest single influence of the time. O'Neill used local colour and dialect, but with a fury suggesting that an honest representation was not his first concern. His settings achieved novelty in aiming at originality, and, as in *Desire under the Elms*, realistic drama soon slid into melodrama. His special interest in psychopathology, as in *Strange Interlude*, in 'the duality of human character', as in *The Great God Brown*, and in the subtleties of self-delusion, as in the pipe-dreamers of *The Iceman Cometh*, became an obsession. These comments on O'Neill's romantic realism could as well have been written about Williams.

At the same time the American theatre must be grateful to O'Neill for furthering in practical terms the American concept of the 'art' theatre. He did much to promote the limited successes of a presentational drama deriving from Gordon Craig, Max Reinhardt and others in Europe: he made repeated excursions into dramatic symbolism, and his technical curiosity about the use of mask and monologue, expressionistic character and chorus, myth and mood play, was insatiable. At the other end of the scale, his more naturalistic plays of neuroticism gave new opportunities to the 'Method' actors of Lee Strasberg's Group Theater. Again, in this, Williams's own symbolic and naturalistic mixture can find useful precedent.

Unlike O'Neill's, however, Williams's plays have been all of a piece, and his earlier plays were trials for his later ones. The frightened Matilda of *You Touched Me*, a girl unwilling to face realities, provided a pattern for Laura of *The Glass Menagerie*: Matilda 'has the delicate, almost transparent quality of glass' just as Laura 'is like a piece of her own glass collection too exquisitely fragile to move from the shelf'. Mrs Hardwicke-Moore, who is *The Lady of Larkspur Lotion*, a prostitute with grand illusions about a Brazilian rubber plantation, about men friends and a coat of arms on the wall, is a prototype for Blanche of *A Streetcar Named Desire*, as is Miss Lucretia Collins of *Portrait of a Madonna*, her hair 'arranged in curls that would become a young girl'. Miss Collins is, like Blanche, removed to an asylum. *Baby Doll* is made up of two one-act plays from *27 Wagons Full of Cotton*. *Orpheus Descending* is a revision of *The Battle of Angels* of seventeen years earlier. Williams in his revisions and self-parodies is rather like a man gnawing at his own vitals.

He speaks through his overheated settings, usually inspired by New Orleans and the South. In *A Streetcar Named Desire* 'the houses are mostly white frame, weathered grey, with rickety outside stairs and galleries and quaintly ornamented gables...The sky that shows around the dim white building is a peculiarly tender blue, almost a turquoise, which invests the scene with a kind of lyricism and gracefully attenuates the atmosphere of decay.' The old house in *Baby Doll* is appropriately dilapidated and in its attic we see 'dusty late afternoon beams of light through tiny peaked windows in gables and a jumble of discarded things that have the poetry of things once lived with by the no-longer living'. The accent is on the decaying and the seedy, always with a strong hint of ironic symbolism. The Wingfield apartment in *The Glass Menagerie* 'is in the rear of the building, one of those vast hive-like conglomerations of cellular living-units that flower like warty growths...The apartment faces an alley and is entered by a fire-escape, a structure whose name is a touch of accidental poetic truth, for all of these huge buildings are always burning with the slow and implacable fires of human desperation.' The yellow stains on the walls behind torn wallpaper, the hot porches on which sweaty people sit drinking cans of beer in the late evening, such images are for him the recurrent metaphors for his dramatic vision.

Music of all kinds, from old gramophone records of the 'twenties, from the juke-box and the Mardi Gras, to the 'hot trumpet' and the 'blue piano', almost any noise can, as in the cinema, subserve his characters' states of mind, sometimes with ironic accentuation, sometimes adding a simple dimension of memory. As Tom of *The Glass Menagerie* says, 'In memory everything seems to happen to music.' When the sounds are harsh they suggest external realities; when they are soft they identify a thought or gently echo an idea identified before, binding the play together.

To apply still more pressure, Williams treats stage-lighting in a highly conventional fashion. He selects a character for special attention by the use of spotlights, like the silent Laura in her pool of light in the supper scene, or he sharpens the image of a character like Blanche who goes mad to the accompaniment of 'lurid reflections' on the walls, 'grotesque and menacing'. Colour tones make an insistent contribution, like the sky in *Summer and Smoke*, 'a pure and intense blue like the sky of Italy as it is so faithfully represented in the religious paintings of the Renaissance', or in *Cat on a Hot Tin Roof* where 'the set should be roofed by the sky; stars and moon suggested by traces of milky pallor, as if they were observed through a telescope lens out of focus'.

Symbolic characters and properties assert themselves, some garishly, like the blind Mexican woman in *A Streetcar Named Desire* chanting 'Flores para los muertos', 'flowers for the dead', or like the poker players dressed in their primary colours who watch Blanche taken away, like the stuffed canary in a cage in *Lord Byron's Love Letter*, the goat in *The Rose Tattoo*, the statue of Eternity in *Summer and Smoke* and the trapped iguana in *The Night of the Iguana*; some more subtly, like the boisterous family of lusty infants or like Brick's crutch in *Cat on a Hot Tin Roof*, like the rose silk shirt in *The Rose Tattoo*, like the fancy lampshade which Mitch strips from the naked bulb in *A Streetcar Named Desire*, like Laura's boot and her glass menagerie. The ramifications of meaning that Williams devises by such means seem inexhaustible. Nor does he hesitate

to call up a surfeit of theatrical pathetic fallacy, the weather of
nineteenth-century melodrama: heat, wind, thunder, all the rage
of heaven or of the diseased minds of his characters.

These effects add up to an impressive hothouse theatre to
accommodate those who people his world: mostly neurotic and
lonely women, immoderately romantic, leaning hard on a Southern
gentility which can no longer support them, caught in the toils of a
society which will not easily admit weaklings. There is a great
compassion behind the conception of such people as Laura the
cripple and Amanda her mother, Serafina the widow and Maggie the
cat, Baby Doll Meighan and Blanche Dubois, and 'rapaciously
lusty' Maxine and saintly Hannah in *The Night of the Iguana*. They
are not held up for ridicule, nor to satisfy our salacious curiosity
about those who live on the fringes of life. They are exposed because,
in the words of Peter Hall, 'they are symptoms of the stresses and
strains of modern living'.[1] No other dramatist has so persistently
used female characters through whom to communicate with his
audience.

Williams's career to date is that of a man concerned to say one very
big thing only, to say it over and over again, and to say it with all the
strength of the agencies of the modern theatre working together: that
life is never what it seems, but that it must be faced. The failed
writer who sympathizes with the unhappy prostitute 'of larkspur
lotion' is asked his name at the end of the play, and he speaks in
what seems to be a tone of gentle irony: 'Chekhov! Anton Pavlo-
vitch Chekhov!' With Ibsen, too, Williams saw that irreverent
society, if not life itself, could shatter the individual's romantic
image of reality. With Strindberg he saw people torturing each other
and themselves in their impulse 'to avoid fluidity and differentiation
and to exist and function as one interfused mass of automatism', as
he says with usual aplomb in *The Glass Menagerie*. And he wrote the
following remark in his preface to *Cat on a Hot Tin Roof*: 'We're all
of us sentenced to solitary confinement inside our own skins.' In this
he speaks with the voice of Pirandello. Williams, it seems, attempts

[1] P. Hall, 'Tennessee Williams: Notes on the Moralist', *Encore*, no. 10 (London,
Sept.–Oct. 1957), no pagination.

to sum up for his compatriots much that has been expressed before in the best of modern theatre.

To make his points in the theatre Williams ultimately relies on an accumulation of many little ironies, but these are superimposed upon one powerful and sustained tension which arises from the roots of his conception of life. If Laura's long-sought-after 'gentleman caller' in *The Glass Menagerie* had not been already engaged to be married, we might have known that her disappointment had to come in some other way. In a situation where her mother will not see her own illusions for what they are, any breath of normality would have swept that glass menagerie from its table. Yet, amazingly, we are pleased to find Amanda a devoted mother for all her insensitivity to her daughter's sufferings: she is both comically clumsy and pitifully anxious for Laura's happiness.

The suffocating atmosphere of the Wingfield home is reproduced in *Summer and Smoke*, in which Alma, all soul, is the inhibited virgin daughter of a minister of religion, fighting against her natural affection for a wicked charmer, the son of a doctor, all body. Again we might have known that, by the time when finally she can restrain her desire for him no longer, he too has become inhibited. As Alma says at the crisis, 'You've come around to my old way of thinking and I to yours like two people exchanging a call on each other at the same time, and each one finding the other one gone out, the door locked against him and no one to answer the bell!...The air in here smells of ether...' Sexual ideals are rubbed against hard reality; there is no final communication between people: and a clear conflict is depicted which allows of no compromise.

From *Camino Real* and *Cat on a Hot Tin Roof* onwards, all the apparatus of his theatre strains under the weight of an increasingly metallic and mechanical contrast of attitudes. *Camino Real* of 1953 is his fling into fantasy, 'the construction of another world, a separate existence', as Williams says in his Foreword, and it strangely anticipates in its formless, kaleidoscopic visions many elements of the theatre of the absurd: Kilroy with his golden boxing gloves is Albee's exemplary Young Man in *The American Dream* and *The Sandbox*; the mad fiesta foreshadows the concluding rebellion of the insane in Weiss's *Marat/Sade*; the Streetcleaners who carry away those who die of despair might have been the invention of Samuel Beckett for a play about hell on earth.

With the exception of *Baby Doll*, which introduces a new frivolity in the child-play between Baby Doll and Silva Vacarro, the Sicilian with a strong sense of humour, Williams never recaptures the simplicity of *The Glass Menagerie* or the subtlety of *A Streetcar Named Desire*. *Cat on a Hot Tin Roof* overreaches itself to play off a trio of self-delusions against one another: in Big Daddy the rich merchant, strong in everything except the courage to accept the fact that his cancer is more than 'a little spastic condition'; Brick his homosexual son crippled with drink and with shame, living out an impossible marriage, challenged by a virile brother with a teeming family; and Maggie his oversexed wife, who can find no way to breach her husband's defences. The play soon becomes a riot of sensational exchanges in which his paralysed characters taunt and accuse and torture each other into a condition of mental stalemate, like George and Martha in Albee's *Who's Afraid of Virginia Woolf?*

By contrast, scenes in *A Streetcar Named Desire* yield little gems of a somewhat less hysterical irony. While we may admit that Stella's simplicity and single-minded sexual acceptance of Stanley Kowalski is of questionable psychology, and that Stanley's unsubtle and ape-like approach to life is crudely painted to provide a glaring foil to Blanche, nevertheless Blanche herself probably remains Williams's most notable creation. It is because she is such an amalgam of contradictions and because all the barbs are directed at us through her alone that the comic-pathetic note is sounded so frequently through the play. She is a woman of refinement of attitude as well as of manners, while she is also a sensualist tippling in private and teasing the other sex. She lies and evades, and yet in her effort to bring a touch of magic into her life, she speaks for us too. She is too sensitive to be able to reject her fantasies in the midst of the ugliness she finds around her, and in this we understand her and want to shelter her, while we also criticize her and want to change her.

The chiaroscuro of Williams's action is as well sampled in scene 7 of the play as anywhere. It is the scene of preparation for her birthday supper and to it she has invited Mitch, the man she hopes to marry to escape from it all. The birthday cake and the flowers stand on the table, and Blanche is in her bath singing happily,

> It's only a paper moon, / Sailing over a cardboard sea,
> But it wouldn't be make-believe / If you believed in me.

On stage Stanley is telling Stella of the lies Blanche has been telling Mitch about her life at the Hotel Flamingo. As his voice grows more insistent and Stella is stunned into silence, so Blanche's song wells to the point where 'in the bathroom the water goes on loud; little breathless cries and peals of laughter are heard as if a child were frolicking in the tub'. Then Stanley tells Stella that he has informed Mitch of the whole story of Blanche's background, and that he is not now to be expected at the party. Blanche grows more and more jocular through the bathroom door, until she is answered with angry sarcasms from Stanley:

STANLEY. Blanche! Oh, Blanche! Can I please get in my bathroom?
 (*There is a pause.*)
BLANCHE. Yes, indeed, sir! Can you wait one second while I dry?

Stanley then caps his performance by announcing to Stella that he has bought her a bus ticket to take her away from New Orleans. At this moment Blanche bursts from the bathroom with a gay laugh:

A hot bath and a long, cold drink always gives me a brand new outlook on life! (*She looks through the portières at Stella, standing between them, and slowly stops brushing.*) Something has happened!—What is it? (...*The distant piano goes into a hectic breakdown.*)

The counterpoint in the song, the bathing and the happy comments, with the presence of the cake on the table, heighten the horror of Stanley's revelations. The double world in which Blanche is living is epitomized. The ingredients exert a perfect tension on the scene, a tension maybe of the villain preying on his victim, deriving from the simplest of melodramatic formulae; and yet while we weep for Blanche, she has, we know, earned her deserts. We know that we share with her the instinct to live in some sort of consonance with circumstances. A quality of inevitability lifts our response from that of a merely sordid pleasure in the cruelty of the scene.

Notwithstanding Tennessee Williams's command of the theatre, and a lighter tone in his most recent plays, certain doubts about the quality of his work are not unfounded. His drama gravitates to sensationalism and melodrama because he does not trust his audience to accept his ironies without their being overstated. He paints in primary colours and avoids the shades between wherein we mostly lurk ourselves. He risks sacrificing that quality of universality which belongs to the restraint and innuendo of real suffering. He too often mistakes the theatrical for the dramatic and again and again overloads his vehicle. He feels he has to stress the pain of reality on the one hand and the hopelessness of the aspiration to overcome it on the other, until his stresses grow destructive, and, sensing insincerity in the drama, we sit there like a professional audience witnessing a conjurer with a ragbag of tricks.

One has greater reservations about the recent work of Edward Albee, a writer who shares, at least, Williams's warmth of feeling for his creatures and some of his methods. At first associated with the theatre of the absurd because of his pointedly sardonic short plays, *The Zoo Story* and *The American Dream*, Albee has now found a dramatic *milieu* of the self-tormented in which he can move easily with his gift of writing a dialogue of smouldering tones. But in his florid but static melodramas, in the naturalistic *Who's Afraid of Virginia Woolf?* and *A Delicate Balance* and in the heavy-weight symbolism of *Tiny Alice*, he repeatedly risks losing comic objectivity.

Virginia Woolf is the most successful, and at least his cynicism leaves an audience twitching. The fierce, hot mixture of love and hate with which George and Martha sustain their marriage also for long periods sustains an icy play. But a practised symbolism which was more acceptable within the convention of the absurd is obtrusive in a play of psychological realism, and when it is disclosed that this (untypical) American couple also (incredibly) sustain their hopes by a futile dream of having engendered 'a beautiful, beautiful boy'— presumably an extension of the American dream which, it has been suggested, started with Horatio Alger's popular heroes—the medium is overstrained. If the venomous, neurotic deflation of one another's self-esteem just allows a transition to pathos in the third act, the final charade in this play of charades kills conviction. The imaginary son must suffer an imaginary death in an imaginary car, and as a result the play acquires neither a final tragic momentum nor a final comic bite. The theme of truth and illusion remains the author's private property, and the play deflates itself. *A Delicate Balance*, which reveals the delicate balance of sanity behind the delicate balance of family relationships—a substantial theme—is written self-consciously in a watery Eliotese without Eliot's command of rhythm and stress, and if it displays a greater control of the flamboyant tone, it at the same time sinks into mere domesticity, Chekhov without flesh and blood.

BECKETT AND THE ABSURD

In the mid 1950s the comic *danse macabre* was at its height in Western Europe. The work of the Irishman Samuel Beckett and the French-Rumanian Eugène Ionesco for the French theatre lies in direct line from that of Strindberg and Pirandello and Anouilh.[1] They are of the same breed in method, and occasionally in feeling. Their plays go to the limits, take all the risks, in the theatrical tactics of stimulus and response. They are of their time, not only in their pursuit of grisly symbols across a macabre stage, but also in their search for a new language, a new *poésie de théâtre*, which will speak the ambivalences of feeling of the post-war years.

Paris has been the hothouse of their experiments, and this latest genre has been identified by a blanket name, 'theatre of the absurd', one which is not always appropriate to the forms of theatrical hysteria associated with it. The plays of Beckett, Ionesco, Arthur Adamov and Jean Genêt are its centre-pieces, but it is only by accident that they all work in the French language and by convenience that they all present their plays in Parisian *avant-garde* theatres. Of the four, only Genêt is French by birth, and he has no

---

[1] In the present academic hunt for sources, influences and echoes, the violent dream plays of Frank Wedekind and the nonsense drama of Alfred Jarry, beginning with *Ubu Roi* in the 1890s, have been frequently named. It is difficult to believe that this shapeless material proved much of a guide to a meticulous artist like Beckett.

particular love for his countrymen. Each is different in particular technique and aim, and in no sense are they a school or a movement. They do not collaborate, and it is now apparent that their different purposes have taken them in different directions. None of them is young—absurdism is not a form of juvenile high jinks—and they have no reason to present a united front to the world.

They share, however, a common starting point. All seem to agree that the world they see, the world they are concerned to depict, shows little sense of direction; the *reason* in life is obscured and events occur and are accepted without apparent meaning.[1] Under these circumstances, if a tile falls off a roof and kills me, it is much the same as if an atomic bomb had been dropped. Of the tile, the only complaint I can make is that it should have fallen on you and not on me; an atomic bomb would have been less partial. And perhaps the only fact in either case that the human intelligence can grapple with, albeit inadequately, is the fact of death itself. The theatre audience is to be treated to the direct experience of this absurdity, inoculated first with laughter. But, as when we go to the dentist, even if we know that laughing gas or some other anaesthetic is to be administered, there remains the strongest suspicion that the operation will be painful. The experience of this toothache level of drama is echoed by Didi in *Waiting for Godot* when he discusses the Crucifixion: 'One of the thieves was saved. (*Pause.*) It's a reasonable percentage...' As a thinker without beliefs, the chance of being saved rather than damned strikes Didi only as a problem in arithmetic, and he is appalled by the shortness of the odds.

Beckett and Ionesco also present a horror greater than that of little faith. Waiting *alone* holds terrors which are unimaginable. The

[1] Friedrich Dürrenmatt wrote in 1954, 'Tragedy presupposes guilt, despair, moderation, lucidity, vision, a sense of responsibility. In the Punch-and-Judy show of our century, in this back-sliding of the white race, there are no more guilty and also no responsible men. It is always, "We couldn't help it" and "We didn't really want that to happen". And indeed, things happen without anyone in particular being responsible for them. Everything is dragged along and everyone gets caught somewhere in the sweep of events. We are all collectively guilty, collectively bogged down in the sins of our fathers and of our forefathers. We are the offspring of children. That is our misfortune, but not our guilt: guilt can exist only as a personal achievement, as a religious deed. Comedy alone is suitable for us.' *Problems of the Theatre*, trans. G. Nellhaus (New York, 1958), p. 31.

tramps in *Godot* constantly fear separation, although when they are together they share a mutual dislike. Winnie in Beckett's *Happy Days* may be buried for life up to her neck in sand, but because her Willie is there, even for the most part mutely, she is happy; she has her nail-file and her lipstick, emblems of her sexuality, signs of life; and she can talk. King Bérenger, Ionesco's little Everyman, appears in *Exit the King* (*Le Roi se meurt*) to face death and dissolution. But no help can be expected from his court, his queen or his mistress, who find his concern with dying laughable. At the last he must face the unknown naked and alone. The absurdist's complete image of despair is one of solitude and silence.

Yet purposelessness, waiting, solitude and silence are all the very opposites of drama. To depict them on the stage must invite theatrical boredom: the word 'drama' derives from the Greek δράω, 'I do', and the verb is transitive—'I do *something*'. Thus all these dramatists are remarkable for their degree of practical success. What must therefore concern us is the originality of their techniques of communication. These techniques of the absurd are not an overnight phenomenon: ways of unsettling an audience, giving them the *experience* of fear and shock, have been steadily developing through the century, with some post-operative injections from Antonin Artaud's theories for a 'theatre of cruelty'.[1]

These methods are based upon those of comedy, indeed on those of farce. Perhaps farce as a genre will now be recognized as the fundamental form it has always been. Farcical techniques are now devised primarily as a means of breaking down resistance to the horror of the content; and they use Pirandello's 'feeling of the opposite' in order to twist the knife in the wound. Beckett, who admits a debt to the vaudeville of Chaplin, forces an audience to laugh helplessly at suicide, mortality and despair, and induces a kind of blasphemy against its sensibilities. By a variety of verbal, aural and visual devices, Ionesco takes the curtain up on a ridiculous scene, until in plays like *The Lesson* and *Rhinoceros* we are trapped in a menace we did not anticipate. Harold Pinter's early variant on this was to begin with a scene so commonplace that the play's

[1] See *The Theater and Its Double*, trans. M. C. Richards (New York, 1958).

8-2

sinister repercussions came as an unpleasant surprise. Genêt presents his material as a charade, talking in terms of the double make-believe of plays-inside-plays, in order to have us see inescapable mirror-images of ourselves. In *The Blacks*, his black actors play both black and white characters until we have the sensation of being told what a Negro thinks a white thinks about a Negro. The sensation, again, is not pleasant.

In this visionary world of farce, tempo can accelerate madly, as in Ionesco's *The Chairs*, or slow down to the point of strain and torture, as in *Godot*. The action can be unpredictable, Pozzo can go blind, Lucky can go dumb, death can be sudden, the tile can fall. The theatre has come full circle since Ibsen and the nineteenth century. Life is not a well-made play; it is angular, startling, unmotivated, irreverent. In imagination, time and space, cause and effect, can be quite illogical—one wakes in the night to discover that what had seemed five minutes has been five hours. This is a fully conventional theatre of the imagination to shake us into recognizing the real business of existence. It is 'uncommitted' in any social or political sense, but rarely 'absurd', since to show us that living is absurd can only be a disquieting experience.

The arguments that have surrounded *Godot*, the outstanding example of dramatic nightmare, have arisen partly because in this play Beckett has refused to make a definitive statement of his purpose. He has, instead, used the medium to portray a common attitude, whether or not we care to acknowledge its universality. He will have us ask questions, but will not supply answers. We commit ourselves without the author's committing himself. To some extent this accounts for the state of high excitement with which we watch the play: we are driven at a rate of acceleration which is exhilarating, and the clashing colours of existence speed past us. We find the destination approaching too fast, without having observed the signposts of disaster. Yet, paradoxically, this effect is achieved through creatures who suffer a slow, slow death by waiting.

A second source of excitement in the play lies in the operation of its parable. An extended metaphor, it makes itself felt at several levels. It compels us to complete an equation and find for ourselves the *tertium aliquid* at which the play only hints. We are shown a universal setting, the drab muck-heap to be found on the fringes of any human habitation. The characters answer to names of strangely international currency, and their speech is as lively and as apparently inconsequential as most trivial conversation. Its hang-dog pauses seem to occur and recur illogically, though with the odd power of giving alarming emphasis to the most commonplace word or the most colloquial phrase. For the duration of the play we relive and assess and blench at the life of vague anticipation which excludes suspense, the life we may generally expect at home and not in the theatre: on the surface of the play, we are to be entertained in watching others plagued by time, time that hangs heavily. Like many people, the characters are waiting for something to turn up, sensing meanwhile that nothing very helpful will. When something or someone does turn up, it is difficult to recognize or beyond their power to control. So they turn again to their feeble jokes and their petty quarrels, and limit their interest to matters that press most nearly, matters which are intimately personal and which can at least be understood, matters which chiefly concern their animal bodies. The very idea of waiting is burlesqued, like the idea of living in Beckett's bald mime *Act Without Words I*, or the idea of dying in *Endgame*.

Beckett's 'waiting' is in a kind of purgatory, an 'abode of stones ...in spite of the tennis', as Lucky says. There, immobility is the real nature of life: 'Let's go... *They do not move.*' This is a dramatization of time, not *Troilus and Cressida*'s 'injurious time' with its 'robber's haste', but 'that double-headed monster of damnation and salvation'[1] which compels us to be born and then to die without a by-your-leave. Within these relentlessly deterministic limits, how much freedom do we have? In Richard Coe's words, 'the freedom of the slave to crawl east along the deck of a boat travelling west'.[2] Or in Pozzo's parting speech:

Have you not done tormenting me with your accursed time? It's abominable. When! When! One day, is that not enough for you, one day like any

[1] S. Beckett, *Proust* (London, 1931), p. 1, quoted in R. N. Coe, *Beckett* (Edinburgh, 1964), p. 18. Beckett's theme of time, especially in the novels, is helpfully discussed in Coe's book. [2] R. N. Coe, *ibid.* p. 58.

other day, one day he went dumb, one day I went blind, one day we'll go deaf, one day we were born, one day we'll die, the same day, the same second, is that not enough for you?...They give birth astride of a grave, the light gleams an instant, then it's night once more....On!

At the end of *Godot*, Pozzo seems to be the only character who is aware of this condition; and in his sudden outburst he also illuminates for the audience the lives of Didi and Gogo. This imprisonment of the mind Beckett represents physically in *Happy Days*, by Winnie buried in the sand, and in *Play* by three characters confined in urns, arguing their human concerns, sex in general and adultery in particular. In both plays the talking goes on mechanically, and increasingly seems to be heard like a record played at the wrong speed; only the spectator sees the ludicrous situation of the characters, their death in life.

In *Godot*, we see the vindictive environment in which the tramps live, while Didi worries whether they have come to the right place, or on the right day, and the oblivious Gogo takes his pleasure in teasing his companion about place and time. Beckett's device of the second visit of the Boy, whom the audience sees as one and the same although he claims to be another, helps to induce the uncertainty that Didi also feels. Time stands still, yet the tree grows a leaf or two. Nothing has changed, yet Pozzo and Lucky are blind and dumb.

The allegory of the play thus carries the interest of a detective story, but one in which the clues are found in ourselves and the discoveries are about ourselves. Didi and Gogo, Pozzo and Lucky, are each a part of ourselves. There is an excitement in recognizing truths in what seems to be a grossly fantastic morality play; there is another excitement in finding how we differ from our representatives on the stage, where we expose or conceal a greater or lesser share of Didi or Gogo or Pozzo or Lucky. The play stimulates in its negation of our illusions and in its affirmation of our confident denials. As in the play, so in ourselves, there is Christ and anti-Christ, and its near-blasphemy tends to act as a homeopathic purge. The play is too indirect and ambiguous to diminish itself with the nihilism with which it is sometimes charged: it is a medicine that produces startling symptoms of the disease it treats.

The special feature of *Godot* that must interest us in this study is its manner of presentation. 'The saddest play and yet the funniest,' declared the English press. Beckett chooses to paint his urgent portrait of life-in-godlessness in the lowest and simplest terms for which he has a precedent. As we shall see, he writes an overdrawn music-hall or vaudeville sketch,[1] with its comics and their cross-talk dialogue of cohesive and suggestive rhythms, a concoction of mimicry and fooling. They speak the compressed behaviour-language of the circus, and sometimes of the primary farce of the *commedia dell'arte*. When Beckett's clowns think, they press their foreheads; they say goodbye, but they do not move; they peer into their bowlers and exchange them; they greet each other by falling into one another's arms. Gestures such as these can surprisingly articulate many common attitudes: we lose our self-assurance when we lose our hat, and we dare not commit suicide with the indignity of our trousers down. What is right in this ingenious way of speaking is the general ridicule it also calls down upon creatures who behave in this way—we must laugh at their antics before we weep at their madness. It combines the surreptitious attack on the spectator with a redoubling of its satirical implications: an economy of means to secure an outrageous end. Beckett has invented a screen of laughter through which to conceal and filter his nightmare; the clowning exhibits the life-and-death tensions of the fool on the high wire; the bowler is part of the circus-ring mask behind which to conceal the sensitive tissue of a human face. The laughter is that of hysteria, a paroxysm that suggests a serious mental disturbance.

'WAITING FOR GODOT':
AN ANALYTIC NOTE ON PERFORMANCE

The experience of playing *Waiting for Godot* not only insists upon a genuine act of re-creation, but also serves to identify the qualities of an unusual dramatic poem. It is a play which reveals little of its

---

[1] Elements of vaudeville generate a prickly irreverence in other recent plays, like John Osborne's *The Entertainer*, Brendan Behan's *The Hostage* and Félicien Marceau's *The Egg*. Eliot's *Sweeney Agonistes* may be the ghost that haunts them all.

nature in the reading. It was written with a fully active stage in mind, even an open stage, if its frequent asides and appeals and general address to the audience may be taken as evidence. Certainly its own spirit of tragicomedy emerges only in the theatre.

Since its first production in the Théâtre Babylone in 1952, conceptions about this unique play have been crystallizing, not to say solidifying; it is all too easy to talk oneself into a belief about the text of a play apart from the performance of it. The theatre must ever remain humble before the fact of the experience. It is not helpful, for example, to subdivide the characters into four Everymen on a scale of virtue and vice, intelligence and stupidity, hope and despair. On this count Didi scores highly as the one who has a soul, a brain and a faith; and Pozzo comes bottom as the one who shows most cruelty, is the most selfishly designing and the most pessimistic of the four. Beckett is not measuring people nor creating characters like this. In performance, the play strikes a surprisingly natural chord in a large number of hearts. Could Beckett have anticipated the extent of warm identification and sympathy between the audience and each of the characters in such apparently alienating drama? Circus clowns are loved. The abysmal trivia of small talk and small behaviour, the mundane business of feeding, clothing and defecating, with its tiny elements of envy, self-satisfaction, pain and ridicule—these are Beckett's raw material of communication with an audience.[1] These details in a world troubled by loneliness and insecurity and mutual need supply the actor with colour for his character and for his relationships with others. They characterize the spirit of the play, its brand of theatre poetry. If it is a play with a purpose, but not one with a message, its qualities of insight are those of a piece of sharp reporting.

In practice the insights result from the play's vigorous burlesque of such commonplace details. In a convention of the mock-serious, what follows when abject despair is travestied? The gentle, anglicized pathetic tragedy of English productions—presenting a pair of Chekhovian tramps caught in Helzapoppinland—was no more than a pretty dirge for mankind. A tidy, under-played, naturalistic treat-

[1] Harold Pinter has seized upon something of this expressive 'triviality'.

ment smothers the play. Its allegory operates fully only under two conditions: first, that the audience is not allowed to be so close to it that its characters seem to be real people and, second, that the full spirit of its ballet-like movement, the broad evocative vocabulary of gesture, mime and dance in which it is conceived and written, is not dwarfed and confined. Its non-literary effects are specifically designed to explore and expand its theme. We must not be invited to feel narrowly at the end of a performance, 'So that is what it is like to be a tramp in France, or Ireland, or wherever it is.' The mode is of spatial communication: Beckett repeatedly calls for the grotesque gesture between actor and actor, and dynamic movement between actor and spectator, to create both his comedy and our sense of his symbolism. Production must not fetter and gag the clowns in *Godot*, or it will deny it its meaning.

There is plenty of evidence in Beckett's writing that his mode of laughter is intended to be that of the circus, the guffaw. From Molloy with his short, stiff leg to Clov's staggering, mechanical routine with the ladder at the opening of *Endgame* and the antics of the player in *Act Without Words I*, who is flung on to the stage, tumbles and gets up, only to perform the whole pattern again, Beckett recalls the circus. Pozzo with his whip and his rope might be taken for the ring-master bellowing his orders. Even the names, Didi, Gogo, Pozzo and Lucky, are those of the circus, echoing Grock and Coco and Nikki and other typical eccentricities and diminutives. Didi and Gogo actually end one of their little 'canters' of dance and repartee with a fragmented argument about the poor entertainment:

> —It's worse than being in the theatre.
> —The circus.
> —The music-hall.
> —The circus.

A study has already been written which enumerates the occasions when the kind of tumbling familiar in the circus occurs in stage directions; some forty-five of these indicate that 'one of the characters leaves the upright position, which symbolizes the dignity of man'.[1]

[1] M. Esslin, *The Theatre of the Absurd* (London, 1962), p. 35. The study is N. Gessner's *Die Unzulänglichkeit der Sprache* (Zürich, 1957).

The microcosm of the circus ring is amplified by a somewhat more sophisticated style of farce. Didi and Gogo have much in common with the comic *personae* of the *commedia dell'arte*. Theirs is a stage for improvised drama. In this Beckett has returned to the roots of theatre, making a charade or a pantomime of both his play and the lives of his characters. They not only seem to wear the masks of circus clowns, but they behave like mummers who develop their parts in performance by the impact of one upon another, like so many billiard balls which take paths partly unpredictable. And behind the comic mask the actor is released and freely exaggerates his points to the audience, as when one takes a comic beard or a false nose at a party. The actors are freed from the bondage of realistic characterization, and their 'masks' make anonymous and in part universal the idea of antipathetic friends in Didi and Gogo and interdependent enemies in Pozzo and Lucky. This freedom is not, paradoxically, at odds with our sense of the clowns as characters fixed in their roles: the paradox on the stage represents precisely Beckett's philosophy of illusory freedom. The repetitive structure of their dialogue, always returning to a version of 'What are we waiting for?...Godot', for all their animation as clowns, indicates their predictability.

In performance, it is evident that Beckett's lines were written for fully gestic acting, written with gesture and movement in the conception of the parts, the expression in the sound of their words trailing—in the way that Molière created much of the dialogue for his farcical comedies and comedy-ballets. At times, particular business recalls the *lazzi* of the *commedia*: the looking, shaking, tapping, feeling, smelling that accompany business with the boots and bowlers; gazing into the distance with the hand screening the eyes; looking about wildly as though information were inscribed on the landscape; pacing up and down in agitation; gesticulating like a spectator encouraging a boxer; embracing and recoiling; the stylized gestures of reflection, concentration, brooding, huddling together, cringing; the weightily vocalized sighs of relief; circling about Lucky; the mimicry by Gogo and Didi of Pozzo and Lucky; violent kicking; the brandishing of arms; approaching and retreating with catlike steps; searching with nose to the ground; mutual salutations repeated over and over; gestures of recognition ('they look long at each other, recoiling, advancing, their heads on one side, as before a work of art, trembling towards each other more and more, then suddenly embrace, clapping each other on the back'); feverish movements, hurried exits, bouncing entrances; and so on. In all this business *Godot* is classical and remote, although within this framework of style, of course, it is perfectly possible to differentiate between the attitudes of one character and another.

Much of such business survives in the circus today, and one would not have to look far to discover where Beckett found Gogo's game with his boots, or Didi's with the flea in his hat. Beckett's contribution is to pair the troublesome boots with the troublesome problem of the Gospels, and to interrupt Didi's musing on the immortality of the soul with the flea, just as, when Lear asks Poor Tom, 'What is your study?', Edgar acknowledges the confusion in man of the spiritual and the bestial in his reply, 'How to prevent the Fiend, and to kill vermin.' And Lucky's entrance at the end of a length of rope whose other end is not at first seen is both a circus joke and a grotesque visual representation of the soul's predicament.

In this there is a form of immediate communication to the senses. This is particularly true of the business with the bowler-hats. The bowlers not only transform the actor, again like a comic mask, but also give him a second, a bizarre, tongue, as they have done for numerous comics from Chaplin and Laurel and Hardy to the buskers still seen in Piccadilly. The language of the bowlers is extensive. Their tilt can suggest amazement, indifference, amusement or disposal to sleep. With their aid, the tramps can meet and part. The bowlers can suggest derision at the mention of Godot, or strengthen the immobility of 'I'm going'. A gesture with a bowler embraces a 'reflection' or a 'concentration' or a comment to the audience. It marks a moment of self-satisfaction or a mutual agreement: 'That's the idea, let's contradict each other' or 'That's the idea, let's ask each other questions.' It can be used for knock-about as when Didi and Gogo juggle with their own and Lucky's 'thinking' hat. This reinforces by mockery one of the strongest effects in the play: after Pozzo has stressed that Lucky cannot think without his hat, its removal at the crescendo of Lucky's diatribe brings about his collapse and with it the most eloquent silence in a play full of silences. Only so much of the 'dignity'—and reality—of man is tolerable.

Yet Didi and Gogo are also, to use the terms of music-hall and vaudeville, the 'straight' man and his comic 'feed' in a 'two-act'. One delivers a heavy recitation while the other belittles it: Didi discourses on the Bible while Gogo, hobbling around him on one foot, punctures his pretensions. One proposes a riddle which exasperates the other, who indeed reflects a little of the spectator's own confusion: 'One out of four. Of the other three two don't mention any thieves at all and the third says that both of them abused him.' Thus many of the important duologues are conducted in the pattern of patter we cannot avoid associating with the ir-relevancies and antics of a frivolous medium, even when the topics raised are serious ones:

> DIDI. Hope deferred maketh the something sick, who said that?
> GOGO (*tearing at his boot*). Why don't you help me?

and

> DIDI. Gogo.
> GOGO. What?
> DIDI. Suppose we repented?
> GOGO. Repented what?

and

> DIDI. Gogo.
> GOGO (*irritably*). What is it?
> DIDI. Did you ever read the Bible?
> GOGO. The Bible...(*He reflects.*) I must have taken a look at it.

This manner of cross-talk is echoed through the play, and is assumed every time we hear the final recognition:

> GOGO. Let's go.
> DIDI. We can't.
> GOGO. Why not?
> DIDI. We're waiting for Godot.
> GOGO. Ah!

And Gogo's '*Ahs*' must variously express surprise, disgust, acceptance, recognition, anguish, but never joy.

Their conventions of speech and movement lift the characters from the possible naturalism of their rubbish-dump, roadside setting. Stylizing is felt even in the slight exchanges which convey their little self-doubts:

> GOGO. What did we do yesterday?
> DIDI. What did we do yesterday?
> GOGO. Yes.
> DIDI. Why...(*angrily*). Nothing is certain when you're about.

It is also felt in extended statements of their mood, dramatically divided between the two of them and explored in dialogue that truly belongs to Eliot's 'third voice of poetry'. One of many such occasions is when they decide upon suicide by hanging:

> DIDI. Go ahead.
> GOGO. After you.
> DIDI. No, no, you first.
> GOGO. Why me?
> DIDI. You're lighter than me.
> GOGO. Just so!
> DIDI. I don't understand.
> GOGO. Use your intelligence, can't you.
>
> (*Didi uses his intelligence.*)
>
> DIDI (*finally*). I remain in the dark.
> GOGO. This is how it is. (*He reflects.*) The bough...the bough...
> (*angrily*). Use your head, can't you?
> DIDI. You're my only hope.
> GOGO (*with effort*). Gogo light—bough not break—Gogo dead. Didi
> heavy—bough break—Didi alone. Whereas—
> DIDI. I hadn't thought of that...

Here is a verbal incisiveness of repartee which is at the same time mobile like a weird ballet. Beckett's is an exact textual control of the spectator's eye and ear, enlivening and illuminating while it distances its ugly meaning.

The detail of tone, gesture and business supplies a rich mode of symbolism, a neat shorthand for theatrical communication. It answers Artaud's call for a total theatre employing all the faculties of actor and spectator,[1] and it fulfils Eliot's wish to recapture the vitality of the English music-hall.[2] But Beckett's way of talking to an audience is only familiar in this way in order to accomplish monstrous ends. His design is to perpetrate a gigantic hoax, a form of disarming ridicule parallel to the burlesqued ceremony with which Molière mocked the University of Paris in the finale of *Le Malade imaginaire*, the comedy-ballet in which the fool Argan receives his degree from physicians, apothecaries and surgeons who dance and sing with incongruous reverence. Once we recognize Beckett's code, we begin the decoding with a flow and purpose of intense imaginative activity, immediate and meaningful. The shocks of varied tone and tempo, the isolation of a line by pause or stichomythic crescendo, are not 'tricks', as early comment on the play suggested, but an insistence of style upon meaning.

The following sequence contains a typical variety of such effects:

DIDI. Let's wait till we know exactly how we stand.

GOGO. On the other hand it might be better to strike the iron before it freezes.

DIDI. I'm curious to hear what he has to offer. Then we'll take it or leave it.

GOGO. What exactly did we ask him to do for us?

DIDI. Were you not there?

GOGO. I can't have been listening.

DIDI. Oh...nothing very definite.

GOGO. A kind of prayer.

DIDI. Precisely.

GOGO. A vague supplication.

[1] 'Practically speaking, we want to resuscitate an idea of total spectacle by which the theater would recover from the cinema, the music-hall, the circus, and from life itself what has always belonged to it. The separation between the analytic theater and the plastic world seems to us a stupidity. One does not separate the mind from the body nor the senses from the intelligence, especially in a domain where the endlessly renewed fatigue of the organs requires intense and sudden shocks to revive our understanding.' *The Theater and its Double*, trans. M. C. Richards (New York, 1958), p. 86.

[2] In 1923, Eliot wrote on the death of Marie Lloyd, 'The working man who went to the music-hall and saw Marie Lloyd and joined in the chorus was himself performing part of the act; he was engaged in that collaboration of the audience with the artist which is necessary in all art and most obviously in dramatic art.' *Selected Essays*, 2nd ed. (London, 1934), p. 420.

DIDI. Exactly.
GOGO. And what did he reply?
DIDI. That he'd see.
GOGO. That he couldn't promise anything.
DIDI. That he'd have to think it over.
GOGO. In the quiet of his home.
DIDI. Consult his family.
GOGO. His friends.
DIDI. His agents.
GOGO. His correspondents.
DIDI. His books.
COGO. His bank account.
DIDI. Before taking a decision.
GOGO. It's the normal thing.
DIDI. Is it not?
GOGO. I think it is.
DIDI. I think so too. (*Silence.*)
GOGO (*anxious*). And we?

At the beginning of the run, Didi and Gogo are recovering from a moment of passivity, having just found it unsafe to hang themselves: they will wait to see what Godot says instead. They begin by slipping into vaudeville jokes and clichés, 'strike the iron before it freezes'... 'take it or leave it', which they point and intone with comfortable conviction. From these they draw strength and regain dignity, until they are on their feet for 'A kind of prayer'...'Precisely'. The impetus of self-confidence lifts them into their cross-talk act, bouncing them downstage for a 'performance'. Pace, pitch and gesture build to a crescendo which itself makes mock of the social attitudes in the lines, as well as of the limited vision of God implied behind them. At the peak, with their bowlers in the air, they suddenly remember their doubts and themselves. Beckett's '*silence*' at this point is indispensable for the actors' performance and for the sense of the piece. They return their hats slowly to their heads, they sag at the knees, and they assume their former postures of lassitude. The short bursts of life by which Didi and Gogo shift from one convention of playing to another are present variously throughout the performance, and enact a pattern of life that is touched with breezy moments of hope, agreement, glee, or false resolution, little moments of excitement that light up their dull existence. Didi and Gogo enact the clown's awkwardly dignified progress across the circus ring before he trips over his own feet, falls on his face and picks himself up. If he has the strength. In all this, Beckett is making a travesty of an average lifetime.

Pozzo too is a clown. Secure with his tidy possessions, substantial and autocratic on his camp-stool in the first act, he seems to know what he is about and where he is—'on my land'. But he too has a part in the horseplay. His pleasure is in eating and drinking, noisily and selfishly; he enjoys his pipe and he enjoys delivering his lectures to the indifferent audience of tramps. From this he descends to the agonized whines with which he announces that he has lost first his vaporizer, then his pipe, and lastly his sight. In the second act, Pozzo spends much of his time supine on the stage with the tramps using his paunch as a pillow, or ludicrously supported by the pair of 'caryatides' who prop him up like crutches. In this way the cruelty of his image is exactly tempered.

In conditions of the circus, it is impossible to see Lucky as the pathetic slave he seems in the text. In any case, he too has his moments of satisfaction, as when he swings at Gogo with his boot; perhaps he responds to Didi's line, 'He's bleeding', with an unexpected grin across his hanging white features. Again, mechanically moving his arms as he lowers and lifts, lowers and lifts, the items of his master's equipment, Lucky creates the guilty response of laughter that belongs to this play. And if we look closely at his Joycean tirade, it is not a gabbled piece of nonsense, a race against the actor's fatigue, but careful dramatic writing. Lucky represents in series the men who set up to instruct us in our way of life, and in voice and gesture he mimics first the parson warning us of hell-fire, then the lucidly obscure lecturer who draws upon an endless line of authorities to make his indeterminate point, then the sportsman advocating the cult of the body, then the strangely Cockney businessman who advises us to measure the facts, and lastly the prophet and poet foreboding doom. It is only at the end of Lucky's harangue that the author calls for the garbling which results from muddling up all the vignettes. The spectator delights in his own half-recognition of these unfinished sketches, and enjoys catching at the semi-articulate phrases, and his attention is to be broken only when Didi and Gogo break it upon Lucky's last hysterical outburst. Thus Lucky, too, claims an ambivalent response.

Beckett constantly works for this ambivalence. The mixture of horror and farce is written into every major piece of business. Characteristic is the '*terrible cry*' which announces the first entrance of Pozzo and Lucky: this sound is crazily marked by the mad rush of the tramps to escape '*the menace*', and by Gogo's frantic return for the carrot and the boot. Undercutting is typical of each key detail of the play. Pozzo's ferocious self-introduction with his 'PPPOZZZO!' is countered by Didi's pitifully apologetic 'I once knew a family called Gozzo. The mother had warts—'. Or Gogo staggers ludicrously as he tries to show Didi the leg that was hacked by Lucky, but on presenting the wrong one he is horrified, as we are, by Didi's order, 'The other, pig', Pozzo's words and voice reminiscent of a less convivial relationship. Or Gogo's painful cry, 'God have pity on me!...On me! On me! Pity! On me!', is succeeded by the slapstick of the collision between the blind Pozzo and his guide Lucky. Beckett gives the play its final twist at the close: determined upon a final solution, Gogo takes the string which supports his baggy trousers for use as a hangman's noose, whereupon they drop hilariously about his ankles.

The director of *Godot* must decide how strongly he must place the stress on these jokes in order to achieve a balance: the uglier the nightmare, the wilder the farce and the more digestible the mixture. The only doubtful element, other than the audience's capacity to swallow these shocks, lies in the shape of the play, its image in time. Here Beckett's control can be subjected only to the test of performance. Can an audience endure the long-drawn-out progress from anxiety to panic? The shape and tempo of the whole are governed by Didi's passage from reasonable discontent to his misgiving at getting no satisfactory replies from the Boy at the end of the first act; and then from his alarm at failing to recognize Gogo's boots and to recall the tree at the start of the second to the consternation of his most direct speech in the play, 'Astride of a grave and a difficult birth...' Didi, the most choric of the four figures, offers the only certain signals for the *development* of the play's total feeling. If the audience come away from the performance wondering whether they have not laughed more and more inappropriately at Didi's plight, Beckett and his director have gauged accurately how far the spectator's thinking can be made to contradict his feelings, and, fascinated and scandalized, he has been introduced to a new order of experience.

AFTER 'GODOT': IONESCO, GENÊT AND PINTER

Beckett's *All That Fall* was a gentle extension of the human qualities in *Godot*; *Endgame* was an astringent retreat. The former presents the story of a fat, rheumatic old Irishwoman, Maddy Rooney. It enacts her painful walk to meet her blind husband at the station, the strain of waiting for a train that has been delayed, and the struggle back home in bad weather with the blind man on her arm. The sense of huge anticlimax is dramatized here as in *Godot*, but the play retains the interest of a human allegory in its trancelike, condensed journey through a life of unanswered questions. Again, 'unaccommodated man' is shown living his bizarre existence: it is 'one great squawk and then peace', like the hen killed on the road. Presented for radio with the quaint, distorted sounds of farm animals, of the weather, a bicycle, a car and the train; its events curiously ridiculous; its language just missing the normality of conversation but allowing an Irish fluency ('sometimes I feel you are struggling with a dead language'), *All That Fall* creates its mood with the *Godot* mixture of feelings rather more carefully stirred, its suggestions pointing more compassionately to the struggle of existence.

Endgame would seem to be a recession. Maddy Rooney conveyed a singular kind of majesty; Hamm the tyrant waiting for his end is all degradation. The mutual dependence of Hamm and Clov, lacking the music-hall give-and-take of Didi and Gogo, suggests only misery, a life made up of a series of empty moments, where the most hopeful event is to ask for the pain-killer. In Nagg and Nell, Hamm's 'intolerable progenitors' imprisoned without legs in two dustbins, we see Hamm's own future—that of an animal, living in sawdust, fed upon biscuits. The allegory has grown so remote as to be almost meaningless; the humour so desiccated that comic balance is lost; the audience so numb that there is little participation.

Chayefsky wrote of his *Bachelor Party*, 'I wanted to show the emptiness of an evening about town, and emptiness is one of the most difficult of all qualities to dramatize.'[1] It is especially difficult if the convention is naturalistic. But Chayefsky's convention permitted some individualizing of character; Beckett has invented a theatrical form where life can be as dull as a recurring decimal. If he sets his play in an unrecognizable setting, grants his characters no individuality and for a plot has them pass their time passing their time, an audience will be watching a representation of a universal limbo. He shows in *Godot* how to dramatize the meaning of time, telescoping it to scare us, extending it to make us lose our bearings, by its very absence making us crave it. But *Endgame* offers us no recognizable time zone and we are not implicated in the crime of being born. In *Godot*, the Boy we have just seen can declare he was not there, and we are aware that the tramps' pinpoint of temporal life has been lost in a dramatic eternity. We 'give birth astride a grave, the light gleams an instant, then it's night once more'. Shall we go? We do not move. Like the hero of Pirandello's *Henry IV*, we are to know that life can be like a 'stopped watch'. As in Dylan Thomas's *Under Milk Wood*, we feel life recurring timelessly through a single day, until day fades into night and the life of a community merges into death. In Samuel Beckett, we hear the crusty voice of old Dan Rooney in his blindness, 'If I could go deaf and dumb I think I might pant on to be a hundred. Or have I done so? (*Pause.*) Was I a hundred today? (*Pause.*) Am I a hundred, Maddy? (*Silence.*)'

All That Fall and *Waiting for Godot* are something of a measuring rod in the Western drama of the absurd. Eugène Ionesco had begun writing plays in the genre before Beckett, but his work showed less restraint than Beckett's at his best, and was therefore prone to the greater failure of a disintegrated audience. How much ridicule can

---

[1] P. Chayefsky, *Television Plays* (New York, 1955), p. 263.

a dramatist pour over his characters and their situation without destroying that necessary link with an audience's reality? If an audience can perceive no relationship between the stage and themselves, or if an audience laugh so much that *belief* remains suspended, the play lapses into an extended knock-about charade. To call upon the extremity of absurdity to make one's point is to risk all in a monstrous gamble. Ionesco has a talent for presenting his characters as imbecile clichés in the context of a serious dissertation, as immobile puppets in a world that is alive with constant threat. *Grand guignol* violence surrounds the unconscious victim, and, as in *Exit the King*, the walls rock ironically round his doomed head. It is the method of classical comedy grown cruel, and its satire grown hysterical.

The Chairs offers a quick illustration of the method. His theme is serious in the extreme, one recurring in Ionesco: that, stifled by banalities, we ache to express ourselves, to forge a link with another person, to discover the artist within ourselves, to lower the mask and speak our minds. Unhappily, many can never do this, lacking the power, the opportunity and the language. How does Ionesco present this idea? Not by a realistic picture of someone struggling to find himself, perhaps like Solness in Ibsen's *The Master Builder*, or Konstantin in Chekhov's *The Seagull*. He shows us two old people, but absurdly old—they are each ninety years of age—so that their very wish to articulate is eccentric and their message derided. Significantly, they live on an island in a river, isolated from their fellows, thrown upon each other.

Crazy characters are established in a crazy world, and in the development of their situation there can be no subtleties that are not subtleties of visual and verbal rhetoric and magniloquence: there can be only the one given position for the concept and one deployment of its parts—hence Ionesco's early fondness for the one-act play form. All else is anticlimax. He must prepare the joke and then crack it, holding his face and his breath until the laughter comes. It is remarkable that he could sustain his jests to the extent that he did. In *The Chairs*, the old couple have invited guests to hear the statement to the world the old man wishes to make before he dies. They begin to arrive, but we do not see them. They are figments of imagination, products of a wish. With each new arrival a bell rings, a door swings, conventional noises of greeting are made, and a chair is placed. More and more guests arrive, until at the climax the stage is full with chairs packed together, the host and hostess ludicrously running hither and thither. As with the furniture which the Gentleman in *The New Tenant* admits into his apartment, or with the fantastically extended conversation of Mr and Mrs Smith in *The Bald Prima Donna*, the author stretches his absurdity to breaking point.

At this stage in the structure of his drama, Ionesco seems uncertain how to turn easy laughter towards the dark mood in which his subjects are conceived. As in *The Lesson*, he holds his top note for too long. In *The Chairs*, a professional orator is finally brought in to address the 'gathering', but when the old man and his wife have jumped to their deaths through the windows, this man in flamboyant cloak and top hat discloses that he is a deaf mute. Nothing can cap the climax of the chairs themselves. No one can say whether these last details of the suicide or the disclosure can sober us and leave the force of the irony which is clearly intended. Unlike the violent shocks of reality which conclude *Henry IV*, *Six Characters* and *Ardèle*, effectively prepared by some touchstone of realism in the plays, in Ionesco caution of this kind is thrown to the winds, our image of the drama rocks groggily, and may never achieve stability.

In later years he has gone on to write the ghastly social comedies of *The Killer* (*Tueur sans gages*) and *Rhinoceros*. In both of these, his Kafka-like sense of the nightmare of fear that lies hidden among a community of people has grown stronger, and its horror has been brought more into the open. Yet the more urgent his statement, the more hilarious his manner. *The Killer* depicts Bérenger, Ionesco's little man now grown more human ('his behaviour should seem sincere and grotesque at the same time, both pathetic and absurd'[1]). Alone he sets out to save his community from the hatred at its heart, from the dwarf who has been ravaging the city. As he talks, his enemy says nothing, but only chuckles enigmatically at his efforts.

---

[1] Ionesco, *Plays*, vol. III, trans. D. Watson (London, 1960), p. 99.

Poor Bérenger's bookish ethics and arguments become meaningless, and at the end he stands exhausted and indifferent to evil in spite of himself. Tragedy is presented as comedy again in *Rhinoceros*, which takes up and continues the earlier theme. The play begins with a startling incident by which a human being is strangely translated into a rhinoceros. This fantastic peculiarity rapidly becomes the dreadful normality as more and more people are caught up in the epidemic. With the physical transformation comes a more frightful change: the human mind, at first full of rationalities and excuses about moving with the times and peacefully coexisting with the rhinoceroses, is caught up by the herd instinct and becomes animal. Ionesco's plays have the power to make sense, if at a loosely political level, certainly at a personal level. He is writing of the death of the soul. When they touch us on a raw spot, as they frequently do, they are cautionary tales indeed.

Ionesco has taken to task those who believe that only a socially committed drama can be justified.[1] He speaks scathingly of 'that complicated shallow-pate, Jean-Paul Sartre, who makes of his personal passions a sort of objective truth and wants to impose it on others'. For him the twentieth century is too various for didacticism: 'Things are simple and clear only to Brechtian Boy Scouts.'[2] But he is increasingly committed to his obsession with mortality and what he calls 'the finite condition of man' ('*la finitude*'). This theme has been present in his drama all along. The marriages depicted in *The Bald Prima Donna* and *Amédée or How To Get Rid of It* are those of a living death. In the second, the growing corpse with which the Buccinionis have been living for fifteen years is the cancerous guilt of their dead love. Death by proliferation is the fate of the Gentleman who immures himself among too much furniture in *The New Tenant*. In *The Future Is In Eggs*, such a death is also the result of the social burden placed upon Jacques and Roberta, who must procreate the race to the satisfaction of their kin—which they do by laying baskets and baskets of eggs. Death in *The Killer*, as we saw,

[1] See especially 'The London Controversy' in his *Notes and Counter Notes* (London and New York, 1964), pp. 87–108.
[2] Ionesco in an interview with Carl Wildman, *Plays and Players* (London, April 1965), p. 50.

is the grinning dwarf who haunts the beautiful, the ideal 'radiant city', and by his silence wins the battle of wits with Bérenger. *Exit the King* dares to present on the stage an image of dissolution itself. The death of King Bérenger is announced at the start, and this disturbing information is repeated at intervals. For one and a half hours we watch him dying, a clown and a figure of tragedy:

GUARD (*announcing*). The king is passing!
DOCTOR. We shall miss your Majesty greatly! And we shall say so publicly. That's a promise.
KING. I don't want to die.
MARIE. Oh dear, look! His hair has suddenly gone white. (*The King's hair has indeed turned white.*) The wrinkles are spreading across his forehead, over his face. All at once, he looks fourteen centuries older.
DOCTOR. Antiquated. And so suddenly too!
KING. Kings ought to be immortal.
MARGUERITE. They are. Provisionally.
KING. They promised me *I* could choose the time when I would die... I've been trapped. I should have been warned, I've been trapped.[1]

Bérenger is seen passing through each mortal stage toward the inevitable, displaying first intellectual indifference, then emotional anxiety, and finally a collapse into abject bestiality. At the last, he simply disappears; what more final? For Ionesco, man in his mortal condition is a puppet, puppetry is death, and life a comfortless comedy.

Arthur Adamov, a less successful practitioner of the absurd, began by translating his own troubled state of mind into inadequately dramatic form. *La Parodie* presents two characters, each an aspect of man, the active and the passive, rivals in love with a shadowy girl called Lili. The active man feverishly meets her at rendezvous which are imaginary; the passive man lies in the road merely waiting for her to pass. We are to wonder 'Which way is better?' in an indifferent world. *Professor Taranne* is a Kafkaesque picture of a highly respectable scholar who is one day surprisingly accused by the police of indecent exposure, but who increasingly manages to accuse himself of the crimes he is trying to rebut. These plays deal in the mad jests of bad dreams.

[1] Ionesco, *Plays*, vol. v, trans. D. Watson (London, 1963), pp. 36–7.

Since 1955, Adamov has written a more 'committed' drama of social purpose. His major plays, *Ping-Pong* and *Paolo Paoli*, are saved from the didactic malaise by their farcical complexion. In *Ping-Pong*, the whole concern of the characters is with pin-ball machines, and in terms of these, and these only, Adamov ingeniously sustains a full-length play which touches on art and science, work and management, human ideals and personal feelings:

VICTOR. . . . I maintain, against all the evidence, that to suppress the top flippers was an act of folly.

ARTHUR. Listen, Victor—you know me, you know it's not like me to place much value on success. But give the matter a moment's thought, I beg of you. . . *you* ought to be able to see that in a well-constructed machine the bottom flippers have got enough force to send the ball up to the top, and consequently, even if the player is deprived of the top flippers, he's by no means reduced to passivity. The period of waiting is longer, I agree, but it's a thrilling period, during which he watches not only. . .

VICTOR. My dear Arthur, there's no need for you to give me a detailed account of a discussion which I listened to in full at the Old Man's office.[1]

The passion with which Victor and Arthur discuss such minutiae is all the more ridiculous when we reflect that the object of their attention, the pin-table, is only a mechanical toy. The central characters in *Paolo Paoli* are merchants and businessmen who trade in butterflies and ostrich feathers, further belittling topics as trifling as the pin-tables. But in this play the presentation is realistic, the argument is conducted in an actual historical context and, in his somewhat cerebral way, Adamov is able to range over such matters as the economic cause of the First World War and satirize the social and political system in the French Third Republic before 1914.

In the progress of Beckett, Ionesco and Adamov toward this one frontier of the absurd, the drama may go very little farther. But the absurdist's assault of the actor on the spectator goes on. In technical originality, Jean Genêt points to another way, one equally extreme: the way of mock ritualism.

[1] Trans. D. Prouse (London, 1962), pp. 65-6.

The story of Genêt's early years as an illegitimate child has been told graphically in Jean-Paul Sartre's book *Saint Genêt, comédien et martyr*.[1] Genêt was sent to a reformatory for theft at a tender age, and spent many subsequent years in and out of prison. Sartre the philosopher finds in his protégé a single phenomenon through whom he can argue his case for existential man, and he writes as if we must all share the responsibility for his condition. Genêt owes a great deal to his distinguished sponsor, but on balance the biographical approach to his work proves to be a distraction from the real business of Genêt's theatre, just as a reading of Strindberg's lurid life story tends to obscure his dramaturgy. When Genêt has so far repudiated society that he repudiates his audience and abandons any attempt to manipulate existing theatrical conventions, then his critics may have reason to take their eyes off his stage.

His plays are advanced exercises in theatrical communication, all the more because he is aiming insults and often obscenities at the conventional morality of his audience. *Deathwatch* is a statement of the reason and beauty in murder, and to make it Genêt attempts unsuccessfully to create the atmosphere of dream by an excessive stylization of gesture and movement, the use of violent and clashing colours and deadened voices heard in the impersonal stone setting of a prison cell. The action nevertheless remains too personal and fails to create a recognizable mirror-image of a self-satisfied community. *The Maids* shows a very considerable advance in technique, and the author hits on a promising direction in which to proceed in later plays. Solange and Claire are the two maidservants of a wealthy mistress. By a comedic trick the spectator is introduced to the game they play when madame is away: they pretend exaggeratedly to be mistress and maid themselves, free to express their feelings of power or servility, and of erotic hate or love. In their make-believe roles they are able to magnify for the spectator, as by a magic lantern, the inner tensions of mind in a class society. It is a cleverly structured piece, Genêt's first attempt at a play-within-a-play, in which truth and half-truth can merge acceptably in a personal ritual. Thus he can shock and delight within the framework

[1] Paris, 1952.

of a single action. Peter Weiss's *Marat/Sade* owes more to this manner than to that of Brecht's epic theatre, but lacks Genêt's unity. If the play-within-the-play of the persecution and assassination of Marat had been integrated with, and given the panache of, the madness with which the inmates of the asylum mirror their audience, Weiss's view of Marat's purpose would have been fulfilled, 'To turn yourself inside out and see the whole world with fresh eyes.'[1]

With *The Balcony* and *The Blacks*, Genêt consolidated his gains, and worked his vein of theatrical image-making to the limits of consent. The fantastic brothel of the first act of *The Balcony* opens the play as, again, a bizarre trick upon the spectator. 'The Bishop' is imposing in his huge mitre and gilded cope, sitting centre-stage in a yellow chair; his ceremonial speech is part of the deception; but before long his robes are removed and he stands in his underwear, punily reduced to life size (the reverse process of the robing of Pope Urban VIII in Brecht's *Galileo*, and more pointedly comic and satirical). Thereafter, the procession of clients, the Bishop, the Judge and the General, lends the brothel the function of a theatre, as Mme Irma the keeper explains:

They all want everything to be as real as possible....Minus something indefinable, so that it won't be real. (*Changing her tone.*) Carmen, it was I who decided to call my establishment a house of illusions, but I'm only the manager. Each individual, when he rings the bell and enters, brings his own scenario, perfectly thought out. My job is merely to rent the hall and furnish the props, actors and actresses.[2]

[1] In his Introduction to the English translation of the play, Peter Brook's justification for the mixture of ingredients takes us directly into the alienated world of dark comedy: 'Weiss not only uses total theatre, that time-honoured notion of getting all the elements of the stage to serve the play. His force is not only in the quantity of instruments he uses; it is above all in the jangle produced by the clash of styles. Everything is put in its place by its neighbour—the serious by the comic, the noble by the popular, the literary by the crude, the intellectual by the physical: the abstraction is vivified by the stage image, the violence illuminated by the cool flow of thought. The strands of meaning of the play pass to and fro through its structure and the result is a very complex form: like in Genêt, it is a hall of mirrors or a corridor of echoes—and one must keep looking front and back all the time to reach the author's sense' (New York, 1966).

[2] Trans. B. Frechtman (London, 1958), p. 35.

When a revolution annihilates the leaders of the state, the clients of the brothel take on the public roles of their private fantasies, and Genêt ingeniously manages to transmute the sexual insights into social ones. Illusion, he is saying, is both personal and institutional, and has its function throughout society in all its phases from peace to war.

Structurally illogical, *The Balcony* tends to lose its coherence as a theatrical experience, but, like 'The Murder of Gonzago' in *Hamlet*, or the milliner's-shop scene in *Six Characters in Search of an Author*, its internal pantomime is used to measure the reality of the world around it. The style of the play-within-the-play, heightened visually and aurally, throws into sharp critical relief the absurd limitations of our public roles. It was a short step from Genêt's device of a play-within-a-play to his use of a mask-within-a-mask. When he chose to write another play of Chinese boxes, he wrote for a cast of Negroes, in the knowledge that the colour of their skin would itself be a primary social mask upon which he could impose others. To enable *The Blacks* to work, he sought an even more ritualistic framework and style, and gives a first indication of this intention in his subtitle, 'a Clownerie'.

To encourage a fiercer reaction from a live audience, he insisted that it must be white; even if there were only one invited white spectator 'the actors will play for him'; and other spectators would presumably see through his eyes. This duel with the audience is felt at the outset in an insulting direct address in speech and gesture, and is present throughout the performance. The reaction of black to white, and white to black, is also reinforced by the form of the drama: the audience is at all times to be aware that the stage is peopled with black actors playing the parts of blacks, and also that those who seem to be playing the parts of whites are still black actors, their skins showing clearly beneath white masks. Thus, on the stage itself, insults thrown from black to white, or from white to black, reflect the reaction of actor to spectator or spectator to actor. In addition, the division of the stage into acting areas on different levels visually heightens the tensions implicit in the text, while the mock ceremonial style of dance or blasphemous litany enables the author to distance the shocks he administers to the audience.

These inducements to participation are more than a Pirandellian device. The spectator becomes acutely alert to the reality of racial problems by being thrust into an engaged, self-critical position. With the central incident of the play, the ceremonial rape of a (pretended) white woman by one of the black actors, the tensions between black and black, and white and black, provocatively accentuate the racial and social issues like a challenge. For although the theatre is accepted implicitly as a place of illusion, the hatred of the black actors for the white spectators is represented as real, and when the audience is told that offstage a racial revolution is really in progress, what before seemed real by the intensity with which illusion endowed it, now makes the events offstage a frightening 'actuality'. By contrast, Genêt's next play, *The Screens*, a title unusually describing a technical device and not the substance of the drama, is a storm of promiscuous acting conventions, symbolic screens, doll-like characters and architectural stage levels. The ritualistic theatre of *The Blacks* has become centrifugal and chaotic, its uncomfortable sensations those of a mirror cracked into a thousand splinters.

Genêt's influence is unpredictable; it may well prove to be greater than Brecht's. His concept of a theatre of explicit make-believe is capable of infinite extension, and is applicable to all manner of subjects; in its way it offers the imaginative release with which the Elizabethan theatre encouraged its experiments. Meanwhile, in England, a more controlled playwright, Harold Pinter, has been digging over the territory newly claimed by the absurdists, and offers to be the best comic talent in English since Shaw. Like his predecessors, he practises a new illogicality, yet one pregnant with the logic of feeling that belongs to the subtextual world of tragicomedy. As in the novels of Kafka and the plays of Beckett and Genêt, a sphere of normal human relationships can become quick and sinister and violent. Pinter appears to move into another dimension of drama and by his skills seems to grant his audience new faculties of apprehension.

Pinter's experience as an actor in repertory has taught him to write for actors, their voices and their bodies, and he studiously allows that degree of freedom for improvisation which makes every performance alive to its own audience. Only the hidden pulse of his lines, the stops and hesitations, the carefully judged turn of his phrases, each embodying its own precise attitude, ensure that the author keeps his hand on the mood and direction of the play. His lines are alive because each character is alive to the presence of others on the stage. Pinter was at one time damned as a playwright of so-called 'non-communication', but he never writes a monologue proper (even in *The Caretaker*), and it would be nearer the truth to say that every Pinter character is communicating too much, but furtively, subtextually, ironically, through the audience which completes the circuit of communication. Take away the third party, the spectator, and there is no Pinter.

In each play commonplace people and their commonplace attitudes start him on his series of revelations about human relationships. Once alive to the links on the stage, the spectator finds them a compulsive matter of watching for every slight move, listening for every innuendo, and he is forced to give them the kind of attention given to a pause or a glance in Chekhov. In *The Homecoming*, Ruth is the enigmatic wife of a teacher in an American university, who has brought her home to London to meet his family; Lenny is her rough diamond of a brother-in-law who interrogates her by indirection:

Eh, listen, I wonder if you could advise me. I've been having a bit of a rough time with this clock. The tick's been keeping me up. The trouble is I'm not all that convinced it was the clock. I mean there are lots of things which tick in the night, don't you find that? All sorts of objects, which, in the day, you wouldn't call anything else but commonplace. They give you no trouble. But in the night any given one of a number of them is liable to start letting out a bit of a tick. Whereas you look at these objects in the day and they're just commonplace. They're as quiet as mice during the day-time. So...

He is trying to intimidate her by the tone of his voice, and it is evident by a sudden remark a moment later that he is also probing for a specifically sexual response: 'Isn't it funny? I've got my pyjamas on and you're fully dressed?' The spectator is aware of the emphasis in his tone; here it is Ruth who does not complete the circuit. The silence and secrecy of woman in a male world are the subject of the play.

Part of Pinter's effect arises from his seemingly casual idiom and the inflexions of his repetitive colloquialisms. As in life, the inconsequential has its repercussions; in the theatre these can be electrifying. A clock can be re-experienced ludicrously, frighteningly, because it is so intimate a part of living. When Davies, the tramp in *The Caretaker*, urges that he cannot carry on without a clock:

> See, what I need is a clock! I need a clock to tell the time! How can I tell the time without a clock? I can't do it! I said to him I said, look here, what about getting in a clock, so's I can tell what time it is? I mean, if you can't tell what time you're at, you don't know where you are, you understand my meaning?...

he does it as a way of testing his host's friendship, and to intimate to us that he is alone and in some despair. When Lenny talks to Ruth of the clock that ticks in the night, not taking his eyes from hers as he speaks, the scene is both of the theatre and of the nervous world we know.

We are never told the motives of a character in a play by Harold Pinter, but, as in life, we can have powerful presentiments about those with whom we are half-acquainted. In a programme note to the Royal Court production of his two early one-act plays *The Dumb Waiter* and *The Room*, he wrote:

> A character on the stage who can present no convincing argument or information as to his past experience, his present behaviour or his aspirations, nor give a comprehensive analysis of his motives, is as legitimate and as worthy of attention as one who, alarmingly, can do all these things.

As in Beckett, a character's actions can be surprising, his fortunes can change without warning, and the purpose of it all be hidden and mysterious. Seen by an outsider, this is startling and amusing, until he reflects. *The Dumb Waiter* introduces the audience to two restless gangsters, Ben and Gus, who await their orders in a hotel basement. The dumb waiter in the wall suddenly clatters into motion, and in alarm Gus timidly takes from the hatch a piece of paper:

BEN. What is it?

GUS. You have a look at it.

BEN. Read it.

GUS (*reading*). Two braised steak and chips. Two sago puddings. Two teas without sugar.

BEN. Let me see that. (*He takes the paper.*)

GUS (*to himself*). Two teas without sugar.

In terror, and unable to decode the hidden message, they try pitifully to fulfil the order, anxious to avoid discovery. But other, more extravagant, orders are sent down, until the mechanical dumb waiter becomes an unfeeling monster. At the curtain, Ben is told to kill the man who is about to come through the door. Amid our laughter, we are shocked to see that it is Gus, and the play ends abruptly.

Pinter's sense of theatre is firmer than that of any other absurdist. His audience is made to feel, through an exquisite friction of nightmare and normality, the earthy need for security, recognition and acceptance of some kind. But society, by expecting us to conform to its ways, can destroy the very security we seek from it. His first long play, *The Birthday Party*, is a comedy of menace which tends to sacrifice credibility to the horrors of the subconscious. In a squalid seaside boarding-house, a very proletarian Everyman named Stanley has buried himself from the world, without work, and without washing himself. Unexpectedly a Jewish businessman named Goldberg and an unfrocked Irish priest named McCann, agents of our imperious society, come to claim him. In the sinister scene of Stanley's birthday party, in which a terrifying game of blind-man's-buff is played, Goldberg and McCann reduce their victim to speechlessness. On the next day they dress him in 'striped trousers, black jacket and white collar', and he is marched off in a bowler-hat as an animal to the slaughter, a man without identity. The device of the party itself, in which the stage is in darkness to communicate Stanley's fear to the audience, skirts failure, and our terror at the last act is uncertain.

However, the extension of Pinter's work from plays about solitary, frightened, working-class figures suggests that his theatrical instinct is now more sure. His is not a socially committed drama: he

is occupied with people in any sphere of life and presents them in
direct theatrical images: not, for example, writing about love, but
about lovers and what they say and do. He generalizes only through
particularities. He increasingly writes a vertical, rather than a
horizontal, drama, engulfing his audience in the tensions of distrust
between his characters. In *The Caretaker*, the brothers Aston and
Mick who entertain Davies in their house are quite opposite in
temperament. Aston is introverted and gentle; Mick is extroverted
and aggressive. But each has his own way of teasing the old man, of
undermining his pride and confidence. Thus Aston's way of saying
'You must leave' is to bring him a pair of shoes.

ASTON. Pair of shoes.
DAVIES (*turning*). What?
ASTON. I picked them up. Try them.
DAVIES. Shoes? What sort?
ASTON. They might do you.

> (*Davies comes down, takes off sandals and tries the shoes on. He walks
> about, waggling his feet, bends, presses the leather.*)

DAVIES. No, they're not right.
ASTON. Aren't they?
DAVIES. No, they don't fit.
ASTON. Mmnn. (*Pause.*)

As Aston executes his method of dismissing Davies, so Davies tries
to find a way of saying he does not want to go: his arguments about
the fit, the laces and afterwards the colour of the shoes intimate to us
his anxiety. Yet Davies is also playing a game, that of insinuating
himself into the house without offending either of his hosts, and the
tensions are doubly in earnest. The brothers are never seen alone
together, so that the spectator never knows their true minds but
only senses their collusion. Thus between them they succeed in
reducing Davies to despair.

In more recent plays like *The Collection*, *The Lover* and *The
Homecoming*, Pinter displays a closer interest in the most testing of
human relationships, that between the sexes. Indeed, in these plays
we may recognize a line of development in English drama through
The Country Wife, *She Stoops to Conquer* and *Man and Superman*.

In *The Collection*, a chess-board control of his quartet of lovers shows a command of dramatic form, and the duologues explore all possible links between elegant husband and wife, sophisticated homosexual and lover, every relationship except the one which would disclose the truth. This Pinter denies us as Pirandello might have done. *The Lover* skilfully and delightfully plays the same game of sexual manoeuvring, but with only a husband and wife in four roles: a faint echo of Kate Hardcastle and Marlow in *She Stoops to Conquer* when Goldsmith resorts to burlesque in order to expose the two faces of sex.

The Homecoming is surely Pinter's most profound play to date. It is brilliantly conceived for form and meaning, never abandoning his standards of controlled innuendo. The subject of the play, the real place of woman in as ociety of male hegemony, the brutish need for her and her incredible strength, profits from Pinter's oblique manner and his scrupulous non-sequiturs. Its framework—we hesitate to use the term 'plot' of a Pinter play—is the return home from America of the educated son, Teddy, as we saw. With him is his elegant wife Ruth. In the old family house in North London, she finds herself surrounded by working-class men: Max, the foul-mouthed father, a retired butcher with animal manners; Sam the uncle, sly and treacherous; brother Lenny, a dandy and a pimp; and brother Joey, stupid and lecherous, a demolition worker who boxes as a hobby. Not a pretty family gathering to greet a young woman. Each man manoeuvres until he is in a position to use the woman for his own narrow ends, but Ruth abundantly demonstrates the adage that woman is all things to all men, and a repulsive picture it is. When her abasement seems conclusive, it is then that the audience realizes how firmly she has entrenched herself, and that the men are her servants, not she theirs. Shaw would have approved, especially since Ruth, like Ann Whitefield, says very little, no more than she must.

The last triumph of the male conspiracy is to demand that she pay her own way as a prostitute, and to this end they offer her a flat in town. For some moments she makes no response to this shocking proposal; she sits with the enigmatic expression on her face that we see through most of the play. Finally she speaks.

RUTH. How many rooms would this flat have?
LENNY. Not many.
RUTH. I would want at least three rooms and a bathroom.

Her cool leap over all the moral evasions we might expect of a married woman is exactly in key with the supra-naturalistic tenor of the play, which appropriately ends in a tableau with Ruth's sensual · self at the centre and the hard-boiled father whimpering at her feet. She is the mother, the wife, the mistress and the whore. Thus she emerges from the engrossing rhythm of bluff-and-be-bluffed, elude-and-trip.

The correspondence between the fabulous province of Franz Kafka's mind and the nightmares of Beckett and Pinter grows more striking. Modern man falls helplessly before the inscrutable power of Klamm in *The Castle* or Leni in *The Trial*, just as before Godot or Goldberg or Ruth. Time stands still as he becomes preoccupied with his own soul and feels the ridiculous paralysis of living in infinity and eternity, like Joseph K. or Maddy Rooney or Didi. In the teeth of coincidence and the unknown, the laws of nature crumble, while a hostile and obscene universe arbitrarily transmogrifies him into louse like Gregor Samsa in *Metamorphosis*, or puppet like Lucky or Davies, or into the despicable animal of Hamm or Stanley or Max.

From Chekhov to Pinter sixty years later, we might guess that a highly original phase in the history of comedy has been completed. In the 'sixties the comic dramatist leaves us alone and giddy in a spinning world: it is very funny, but quite terrifying. And he has proved Dr Johnson's contention that there can be no certain limit to the modes of composition open to the dramatist.

5

THE DARK COMEDY

'...Such, then, is the love of the heavenly Aphrodite, heavenly
in himself and precious alike to cities and to men...And this,
Phaedrus, is all I have to say, extempore, on the subject of love.'

The next speaker...should have been Aristophanes; only as
it happened, whether he'd been overeating I don't know, but
he had got the hiccups so badly that he really wasn't fit to make
a speech.   PLATO: *Symposium*

INVOLVING THE AUDIENCE

To understand modern tragicomedy, we must first understand
afresh the role of an audience in the theatre. The suggestion that
drama is a structure of shifting relationships between character and
spectator in the course of performance asks for closer definition. It
means rather more than that the interplay between the actor and his
audience brings the play to life.

Every human being is an actor *manqué*: nor do we need the psychologists to tell us this. Besides the faculty of laughter and the
faculty of thought, he has also the faculty of taking the part of
others.[1] He reproduces within his imagination situations and circumstances which are not his own in order to comprehend the life
about him. From the early years he learns to enter into the thoughts
and feelings of those he sees outside himself, and in this way he
civilizes himself, and his mind and spirit grow. This is perhaps the
supreme faculty he brings with him into the theatre. The spectator's
willingness to identify himself with characters on the stage, or to
have feeling for conditions that are not his own—temporarily to
understand them, perhaps later to reject them—is the dramatist's
greatest asset, his means of reaching out to an audience to win it or
repel it. A word coined by the psychologists has been borrowed by

[1] The idea that 'man is a role-taking animal' is helpfully discussed by Ian Watt, *The
Rise of the Novel* (London, 1957), pp. 201–2.

dramatic criticism to express these qualities in the spectator: 'empathy'—and in the most conventional of theatres from Aeschylus to Bertolt Brecht a degree of empathy has been the starting-point, and provided the norm of theatrical experience, in the construction of a dramatic pattern of feelings. We must first understand *by sharing* the mind and situation of Agamemnon in order to feel any significant pathos afterwards; in the same way, we must understand Macbeth in order to feel any significant repulsion afterwards. These are fundamental elements of theatre which still persist in the changed conditions of twentieth-century drama. Even Brecht was working from such assumptions for his iconoclastic drama when he asked us to think of

a sister lamenting that her brother is off to the war; and it is the peasant war: he is a peasant, off to join the peasants. Are we to lose ourselves in her agony? Or not at all? We must be able to lose ourselves in her agony and at the same time not to. Our actual emotion will come from recognizing and feeling the double process.[1]

The spectator may be immersed in the thoughts and feelings of the character on the stage, becoming more and more at the mercy of the puppet-master as his own personality is sunk in that of the puppet; but at this point the other-world of the character, the world of his environment, may be brought into focus. Then the character's responsibility towards others, his place in a family, his relationship to a social group, moves into the field of the spectator's consciousness. Out of this handling of the innocent spectator some of the true tensions of drama arise. So the case of Shakespeare's Henry V is made our own, and we are as keen as he to make the Dauphin 'blush', before we are made to see through the eyes of Williams, the common soldier: 'But if the cause be not good, the King himself hath a heavy reckoning to make, when all those legs, and arms, and heads, chopped off in battle, shall join together at the latter day, and cry all, We died at such a place...' So Hjalmar Ekdal of *The Wild Duck* obsesses our consciousness until the details and events leading

[1] Brecht, 'Gespräch über die Nötigung zur Einfühlung' in *Die Dialektik auf dem Theater, Versuche 15*, p. 104, quoted from J. Willett, *The Theatre of Bertolt Brecht* (London, 1959), p. 186.

to the death of Hedvig compel us to cut him down to size as a well-meaning but impossibly selfish man.

Or else a social situation is presented as something living for the spectator to observe objectively—until from this impersonal yet identified world emerges the personality of one or other of its victims. This is the pattern of *Romeo and Juliet*. Even in the introspective *Hamlet* the particular sufferings of mind of the protagonist do not make their mark on us until our general sense of mischief and evil in Denmark has been vividly suggested by the presence of the Ghost and by the bland forensic manner of Claudius on his throne. Only after this do we hear Hamlet say

> It is not, nor it cannot come to good,
> But break my heart, for I must hold my tongue,

and a new, vastly more urgent because more personal, issue grips our attention. So Ibsen shows us the world of Nora of *A Doll's House* before the woman herself. So Shaw indicates the madnesses of *Heartbreak House* before Ellie, our curiosity and our mouthpiece, emerges.

Sometimes situation and character are one and the same, and we spend our time in fearful activity fighting within ourselves for the supremacy of the subjective or the objective view. In this way we meet and know Antony and Cleopatra, or Coriolanus, or Alceste, or Solness the Master Builder, or Saint Joan. To examine in any detail the varieties of dramatic structure is to write the history of the theatre: this general mixing of our impulse to identify ourselves with a character, and our impulse to withdraw the better to see him in perspective, provides the common ambivalence of all drama except extreme kinds of impersonal farce, like that of the *commedia dell'arte*. 'No mind can engender till divided into two': Yeats's dictum is as true of the creative audience as it is of the poet.

Encouraging this worthy ambivalence, the theatre is, we remind ourselves, similar to life with its contradictory pressures. Without feeling and compassion we should be ugly mechanical beings; but without reasonable circumspection we should be the fanatics of too many ill-considered enthusiasms. Having both, we see the world warmly, yet in proportion. Not that the drama wishes us necessarily to sustain this sane balance: it will require its moments of un-controlled enthusiasm, and there will be other times for weighing and considering. But it is properly the strength of theatre that it can make us behave like over-energized creatures living a life-span of human activity within the two hours' traffic of the stage. The play is in its way a microcosm of natural life. For its mysterious purposes it can isolate and separate particular kinds of response, of a thinking or an emotional kind, or it can mix and join them. Some of the greatest plays of Shakespeare's maturity or of Molière's best period, as we have seen, are great because of this very mixture. They torment the spectator with the perplexing reality of laughter and tears that he is not unfamiliar with. It is not surprising that in an age like ours, an age we believe to be of greater generosity in moral understanding and finer clarity in psychological insight, we find that our best plays are given to experimenting with this sublunary mixture of attitudes in the minds of men and women.

So the spectator arrives in the theatre today with less prejudice of the kind that restricts the drama's breadth of characterization and situation. In a modern play he will not be so disconcerted if the comedy becomes cloudy with feeling or the tragedy suddenly illuminated by witty breaks of sunshine. But he does expect to be in some agreement with his fellow spectators when he laughs or when he suffers; and if the degree of laughter or feeling, being lessened and adulterated, is not strong enough to overwhelm the individual spectator completely, can the dramatist be sure that his audience, jostled this way and that, will remain united?

It is a generally accepted premise that the playwright must attempt to unite his audience in pursuit of the thoughts or emotions of his play. In tragedy and melodrama this is perfectly possible where our hates and sympathies are turned upon one character or group of characters; in high comedy and in low farce it is comparatively simple to choose the object for ridicule shrewdly, making a character sufficiently gross for an audience to know how it is to respond. A straightforward identification of spectator with character, or with-drawal from character, and a refusal by the author to distract the spectator's attention from this, coupled with the spectator's willingness to bow to his wishes, is the pattern of an easy success. Today, when a play enjoys a long run, it is likely to be a play prepared to embrace an audience strongly and to follow such rules as these. If we applaud a melodrama like Bolt's *A Man For All Seasons* or Miller's *The Crucible*, we do so from comfortable seats. Arguably, Miller's is a *pro*-McCarthy play in that it confirms us in our righteousness.

We shift uneasily before the dialectic of Arden's *Serjeant Musgrave's Dance*, and the case is very different where an audience is not allowed a facile agreement with itself, or, to put this another way, where the mind of the spectator, busy in the attempt to build a firm emotional or rational image of the play, is divided in its loyalties. Panic and rejection may ensue. A writer may hold such an independent point of view that he will not let his play slip into the ready-made formula of preconceived opinion, nor into the convention of established tradition. Eric Bentley rightly suggests, discussing Meredith's convenient proposition that comedy 'is an interpretation of the general mind', that 'comedy might also be the individual's protest against the general mind'.[1] Bentley instances the outstanding example of Shavian comedy which does not speak for the audience at all, but for the audience as Shaw would have it. In this case as in others, the rebel may wish to lead his fellows, but, short of howling to himself in the wilderness, to satisfy his wish he must adopt a measure of theatrical 'deception'. If the issues are truly controversial—and this is not to speak necessarily of political, religious or moral ideas, but rather of ambiguous feeling, such as that prompted by such plays as Strindberg's *The Ghost Sonata*, Jean Genêt's *The Balcony* or the drama of Samuel Beckett, for example—the deception may take the form of tricks of stylization or the use of myth and symbolism to make an unwelcome point obliquely. Whatever conventions are used, it is important that the spectator who might be prepared to scoff must remain to pray.

Thus the unpalatable hypothesis of *The Ghost Sonata* is, as we saw, that we can live happily in self-delusion and yet suffer from the terrible fear of having our illusions smashed and our

[1] E. R. Bentley, *The Modern Theatre* (London, 1948), p. 133.

self-corruption exposed. Genêt in *The Balcony* portrays with immense wit and abandon the Napoleonic complex in human character and society. Men may assume in greater reality the grandiose masquerade of their most private wishes, and we see the frightening picture of what monsters of a bishop, a judge and a general might emerge were human desire given enough licence. To coax the spectator to accept these particularly unpleasant views, it may be necessary to divide him against himself. It may even be necessary to divide a whole audience against itself.

In our own time, many attempts have been made to make the spectators feel, in Diderot's words, 'like those who in the presence of an earthquake see the walls of their homes rock, and feel the earth yawn before them'. Violent ends demand violent means. On the one hand the audience may be righteously shocked and baffled, as they were with Anouilh's *Ardèle* and Beckett's *Endgame*, plays which in the execution seem to lose touch with the spectator. On the other hand, the explosive response to John Osborne's symbolism in *The Entertainer* was a calculated effect, as it was in somewhat less degree in his *Look Back in Anger*. Using the last ugly stages of the senility of the English music-hall as a devastating symbol for England in the 1950s, Osborne's Archie Rice and his bawdy clichés compel us to resent our own laughter, and even each other, as we laugh. One correspondent to *The New Statesman* at the time of the first performance reported on her reaction as a member of the audience as follows:

I am still not sure how we were induced to play the part written for us—to emit that deadly sound of luke-warm laughter, willing but uncertain which gave the cue for Archie's ironic impromptu about bringing the roof down and gave point to the venom behind his surface heartiness. Pretty flat it would all have fallen if we *had* been bringing the roof down, wouldn' it?...Maybe John Osborne knew just how much corn and bawdy h could include and be sure that the guffaws of the randy and the distaste of the squeamish would both be tempered and confused by reverence for the leading player.[1]

[1] E. Morgan, letter in *The New Statesman* (London, 11 May 1957). The leading play in question was Sir Laurence Olivier. We are reminded of Brecht's advice to the acto in his 'Short Description of a New Technique of Acting which Produces an Alienatic Effect': 'he allows the existing divisions within the audience to continue, in fact I widens them'. Quoted in J. Willett, *Brecht on Theatre* (London, 1964), p. 143.

The kind of play we are growing more accustomed to prohibits easy solutions of the problems of 'involving' the audience. In order to recreate the effects of ambivalent life, in order to make us more aware of our minds working through our feelings, the good modern dramatist will insist, by refreshingly questioning illusion and convention in the theatre, that we remain aloof although implicated. There can be no comforting sense of 'belonging to a side' in the experience of his theatre. There can be no relaxation in a play that acquits us by laughter at one moment and then convicts us the next. To place us in this unhappy limbo, the playwright will be busy measuring, expanding and contracting that vital gap between the world of his actors and the world of his audience, between art and life. The characters stand there on the stage—how are we to regard them? As next of kin or as distant poor relations? What if we are unsure? That is the uncomfortable state of mind the writer of dark comedy aims to create. He must control our infinite little decisions of heart and head. We are ready poised to cast our vote, but repeatedly we hesitate. The detachment of comedy is not allowed us, nor the sympathy of tragedy. All the instinctive psychology of the man of the theatre is needed to achieve this particular tension: he must mix sufficient reality to hold our belief with sufficient unreality to have us accept the pain of others. At the point of balance, we are in pain ourselves, and the play is meaningful.

A case of some interest in recent years has been Osborne's brash dramatic adventure in *Look Back in Anger*. Whatever the ultimate judgment passed on this play, diverse reports suggest that in performance it captured its audience. Whether enmeshed by love or by hate, no spectator could escape it. The play caught fire because Osborne diabolically promoted amongst the audience a clash of generations and a clash of classes: it was at once a play hitting out at the older generation and a story of a socially mixed marriage. Stressing the divisions in our society, it criticized its failures. This 'success' was not due to any substantial degree of sympathy conjured for its hero, nor yet did he leave us detached. Jimmy Porter, the young working-class graduate who loves and hates his middle-class wife as he loves and hates the human race, demanded much of our sympathy as an isolated, over-sensitive idealist 'raging against the evils of man', in the words of A. E. Dyson,[1] but he loses it as soon as we see him also as 'a cruel and even morbid misfit in a group of reasonably normal and well-disposed people'.

Jimmy's character, central to the play and primarily directing our responses, is intended throughout to remain an enigma to us. What he says and does, together with the way other characters regard him, so complicates our image of him that we can quickly cease to trust our own judgment. As Dyson has usefully illustrated, Osborne is from the beginning offering us a bold and theatrically daring ambiguity for a character. The stage directions read:

He is a disconcerting mixture of sincerity and cheerful malice, of tenderness and free-booting cruelty; restless, importunate, full of pride, a combination which alienates the sensitive and insensitive alike. Blistering honesty, or apparent honesty, like his, makes few friends. To many he may seem sensitive to the point of vulgarity. To others, he is simply a loud mouth. To be as vehement as he is is to be almost non-committal.

His stage behaviour swerves violently between the honest indignation of a warm-hearted man and the attitudes of a moral egotist. His worst action is to blaspheme against life in hoping that his wife 'will have a baby, and that it will die'; but Alison his wife does have a baby, and it does die; and so he is punished. It is impossible to admire his ugly, self-defensive manner, but perfectly possible to love the man for his genuine misery, as do Alison and her friend Helena, in spite of everything. Simply to retreat from the paradox of Jimmy Porter is to ignore the persistent existence of human ambiguity with which Osborne vitalizes his stage.

This essay has tried to explore a little of the great variety of such capricious and contrary drama which has arisen now that the dramatist has felt the new freedom of the dark comedy. We mock the absurdities of the clowns Didi and Gogo in Beckett's *Waiting for Godot*, who pass their time on the stage fruitlessly 'passing their time', abortively contemplating their future, half-heartedly telling themselves a dirty story and half-heartedly questioning the meaning

[1] A. E. Dyson, 'Look Back in Anger', *The Critical Quarterly*, I, iv (Hull, 1959), p. 318.

of Christ's Crucifixion. We laugh at their antics of mind and body, but under the growing realization that what they are doing is only a modest parody of what we do ourselves; we know before the piece is done that they are ourselves.

Anouilh's hunchback Aunt Ardèle is determined to hold fast to her belief in herself and the purity and disinterestedness of her love for the other hunchback, and she does so in the face of every opposition from her family and society at large, who romantically consider that physical sex can only be beautiful where the body is beautiful too. She deserves, and perhaps gets, all our sympathy for remaining steadfast to her ideals in a world of corruption, since it becomes increasingly apparent that every one of her critics is corrupt in his or her own way; yet we are irked, as the pretty adulterers Nathalie and Nicholas are, by the knowledge that the physically repulsive should thus represent our finest feelings.

Giraudoux's gentle warrior Hector of *Tiger at the Gates* is a man who has tasted the horrors of war. Just before the impending conflict with the Greeks over the rape of Helen, he finds himself a man inclining to pacifism against his own nature, looking in his wisdom for every avenue of escape from the miseries he foresees. He is a full symbol of the modern circumspect mind. But having had his mortal way for the whole of the play, at the very end he lets his control of the situation slip through his hands. In the first flash of anger he has shown, Hector kills his compatriot Demokos; Demokos in revenge declares with his dying breath that it was the Greek envoy Ajax who killed him; the crowd falls on the Greek, and war is unleashed like the tiger of the play's symbol. It is troubling to realize that, like ourselves in more contemporary circumstances, it is Hector himself who must in the end bring war about his head.

Pirandello's mock emperor Henry IV is the man who teases other people apparently by feigning madness, making his friends and his enemies play parts in a game of his own invention, delighted to see how readily they now abase themselves for him. He plays his own part with a light *élan* until he too succumbs to a moment of anger and kills his rival Belcredi. With this momentary act after years of calculated restraint, he sentences himself to play his part of the madman not only for this performance but for ever. Indeed, was he ever sane? His make-believe, like ours, condemns him utterly to a life of self-torment.

The paradox of the excitement of this kind of play-writing, which ought logically to leave us unaffected, but which can enthral us mercilessly, is not easily resolved. Perhaps it may be explained by reference to I. A. Richards's general theory of art, and in particular to his theory of an aesthetic equilibrium within the mind:

We cease to be orientated in one definite direction; more facets of the mind are exposed and, what is the same thing, more aspects of things are able to affect us....At the same time since more of our personality is engaged the independence and individuality of other things becomes greater. We seem to see 'all round' them, to see them as they really are; we see them apart from any one particular interest which they may have for us....To say that we are *impersonal* is merely a curious way of saying that our personality is more *completely* involved.[1]

In making his audience respond by ironies and contradictions, playing off the reason against the emotions and the emotions against the reason, the writer makes us earn our experience the harder way. 'More of our personality is engaged.'

The achievement of such dramatists as we have discussed and especially of Chekhov, Pirandello and Anouilh, each in his own sphere, is to make the audience suffer without the relief of tears and to make it mock without a true relief of laughter. The audience remains at a distance, yet within immediate call; impersonal, yet strangely involved. However, the attempt at a descriptive account of such effects upon an audience was immediately an encounter with the great variety of individual methods and private subtleties employed. In particular we felt that extraordinary theatrical quality of *irony* which is the chief controlling agent of an audience undergoing a play.

[1] I. A. Richards, *Principles of Literary Criticism*, 2nd ed. (London, 1926), pp. 251–2.

Irony as a Controlling Agent

To discuss the mutual support and peculiar inclusiveness and unity of incongruous ingredients is to discuss the methods of mixing them. To recast an image in our minds, to secure a calculated reaction, to achieve a precise control over the feelings running in the auditorium, and to know how much rope we need to hang ourselves—this is the difficult technique of the new comedy.

An audience goes willingly into the theatre, its imagination open to receive without undue question a great variety of impressions. On his part, the dramatist tries to start, sustain and elaborate the pattern of interest that constitutes his play, and his power to develop that interest is the measure of his skill. The alert playgoer will exercise his image-making faculty by his accurate scrutiny of idea and feeling, his eyes and ears finely attuned to the actors' suggestions. The play develops as the stage action shifts the kaleidoscope; suggestion follows and anticipates suggestion as the dramatist refocuses the picture for us.[1] For this the audience's active contribution is essential.

An emotional sequence once begun under these conditions is not easily restrained: it makes its own momentum. There is every danger that an audience will take the play in charge: thus Shylock can grow to be a tragic hero, and Willie Loman can come too close to our hearts for us to criticize the system he symbolizes. To require an audience suddenly to turn from such emotional anarchy and become more detached may call for an uncommon juxtaposition of impressions. On the other hand, to build and then break our comic attitude, as happens in plays as varied as *Pygmalion*, *The Playboy of the Western World*, Pirandello's *Henry IV* and Tennessee Williams's *The Rose Tattoo*, is to intoxicate and then sober an audience which is also reluctant. Both processes demand an equally delicate flexing of the play's fabric to manipulate its audience and induce its embarrassment.

---

[1] See the author's *The Elements of Drama* (Cambridge, 1960), ch. 4. In one sense, all that the spectator sees on the stage is seen ironically, since he is always on the outside looking in. This has been suggested, too, by G. G. Sedgewick, *Of Irony, especially in Drama* (Toronto, 1934).

reorientation of attention in the audience may be decided by a
le turn of mood or tone, even at a verbal level simply, as in
conversation when a stray remark from a stranger arrests us, or when
a new note in a familiar voice makes us start and look. Or it may call
for a complete revolution of convention, wholly altering the drift of
the play, with intent to give us some theatrically traumatic shock.
Both methods may be equally exciting. The superimposition of a
comic tone upon a tragic one was not uncommon in Elizabethan
drama, nor in Molière, as we saw; but the exploitation of 'convention', though not wholly unknown in plays like *Troilus and Cressida*,
is rather a characteristic of more modern times when the dramatist
sets about his task quite conscious of the variety of conventions
available to him. This has been Anouilh's particular opportunity and
occasional triumph; it has been the persistent object of Brecht's
stagecraft. But in some degree 'alienation' by breaking the continuity of mood or style or both is found in the very great variety of
plays that have been mentioned.

Dark comedy is drama which impels the spectator forward by
stimulus to mind or heart, then distracts him, muddles him, so that
time and time again he must review his own activity in watching the
play. In these submissive, humiliating spasms, the drama redoubles
its energy, the play's image takes on other facets, the mind other
aspects, and the spectator 'collects the force which again carries him
onward'.[1] But now progression is more cautious, and he is on guard.
He is charged with a tension as a result of which he is a more alert
and therefore responsive participant. This tension is one of dramatic
irony.

Such tension can be a reinforcement, not a weakening, of the
structure. Wilson Knight in his brilliant essay on *King Lear* is
certain that the tragedy is incomplete without its explosive ingredient:
'This is of all the most agonizing of tragedies to endure: and if we
are to feel more than a fraction of this agony, we must have sense of
this quality of grimmest humour.' He insists that 'the pathos has not
been minimized: it is redoubled'.[2] It is redoubled because Lear's

---

[1] Coleridge, *Biographia Literaria*, ed. Shawcross (London, 1907), vol. 2, p. 11.
[2] G. W. Knight, 'King Lear and the Comedy of the Grotesque', in *The Wheel of Fire*
(London, 1954), p. 175.

suffering is so painful that it has a final authority over our r/
to the play and ensures that the element of comedy is unquesti.
ably of the 'double-faced' kind, and is received as such.

This kind of renewal is particularly noticeable at the climax of a
sequence of disruptive sensations, though often the process is
operating throughout the play. The real climax of dark comedy
may be, not the place in the play where the hero is pressed to a
decision, the villain unmasked, the situation brought to a crux, but
the place where the tensions are so unbearable that we crave relief
from our embarrassment. At the end of *Juno and the Paycock*, we
move with relief towards Juno's prayer, are reconciled by her loss,
and comforted by tears; then, cruelly, O'Casey scourges us with the
drunken platitudes of Boyle and Joxer. We hear their words while
Juno's grief echoes round our brains, till we hear only the mechanism
of our own thinking, and the curtain disburdens us.

It is enlightening to find Bronislau Kaper, the musical director of
John Huston's film of Stephen Crane's novel *The Red Badge of
Courage*, asserting that the continuity of the film would be strengthened, and the audience's view of the major characters defined, by
ironies. He was of course thinking of musical ironies: 'After the
Youth's regiment wins the first battle, the soldiers act happy...But
I come along, and I tell the audience, with sad music, what is so good
about this? I make a little ridiculous the whole idea of one American
killing another American.' The visually gay is in counterpoint with
the aurally cheerless. In the scene in which the Youth writes his
letter home, Huston insists that his fear on the eve of battle is not to
be treated tragically, and he hits upon the sound of the banjo to
touch in the ridiculous: 'We have a funny sound coming from outside while the Youth sits in his tent and writes. A funny sound to a
sad situation.'[1] We saw how Serafina of *The Rose Tattoo* felt her
heart break to the music of the graduation-day band. The playgoer
will not have missed the likeness to the effect of the military march
with which Chekhov's three sisters are bade farewell, nor of the
waltz which heralds the news of the sale of the cherry orchard. We
remember that Hedda Gabler played her wild dance tune just before

[1] L. Ross, *Picture* (London, 1952), pp. 136–7.

her suicide. The villagers danced on Midsummer's Eve while Jean and Julie were alone in Jean's room in *Miss Julie*. Similarly, O'Casey's *The Silver Tassie* welcomes the wounded with a foxtrot and a waltz. Tennessee Williams's Blanche has her unhappy story told while she sings 'blithely' in her bath, and she loses her mind to the music of the 'Varsouviana', in a polka rhythm, the blue piano and the muted trumpet. The bright jazzy musical interpolations in the sordid themes of Shelagh Delaney's *A Taste of Honey* and Brendan Behan's *The Hostage* tend to echo these effects. And Mother Courage heaves her wagon on its way to the sound of fifes and drums. Such means in the film or play can be devised to catch the right tone of the dramatic theme, and start the appropriate degree of tension.

Like the fit of laughter we suppress in church, tragicomic tensions can be mortifying. They can be induced as well by an incongruity of the solemn and the ridiculous as by the sudden quirk of mind that recognizes the ugly beside the beautiful. So, at Cleopatra's death, she can regally, and indeed like a Roman matron, demand her 'best attires', prepare to robe herself for death in words as well as clothes; but this inspired pomp is raised upon the earthy mockery of the clown with his 'worm': 'those that do die of it do seldom or never recover'. The senses are twisted sharply in prelude to the experience to follow. Flights of sentiment undermined by prosaic detail were of course a feature of Shakespearian tragedy at its moments of crisis: the raucous comedy of Capulet and the County Paris on the eve of catastrophe, Hamlet's mockery of himself, the irreverence of the Porter in *Macbeth* and the mad trial in *King Lear*, the simplicity of Lear at the death of Cordelia. The parody of the serious by the 'low life' in *Henry IV*, as identified by William Empson,[1] and the parallelism between the conduct of war and the conduct of love in *Troilus and Cressida*, are equally to be found in modern drama, even where the grey of naturalism is the dominant colour.

If Chekhov allows us to feel some spark of elation in the last act of *The Cherry Orchard* by showing us with what pride and vigour the new generation, in Anya and Trofimov, leave the ineffectual house, we are not allowed to forget that the older generation of Mme

[1] W. Empson, *Some Versions of Pastoral* (London, 1950), pp. 29 ff.

Ranevsky and Gaev are departing in sorrow, spending their feelings only on the useless past, while the oldest generation, represented by Firs, is sunk in oblivion before the curtain has finally fallen. This firm juxtaposition of the generations throughout the play is there to mark the polarity of our response. So, too, in John Osborne's *The Entertainer* and in Anouilh's *Point of Departure*, the divergence of parent and child in their attitudes towards the dramatic issue is devised to force us to reorientate *our* attitudes: the device forestalls the too simple verdict, even prompts an ironic anguish.

In another sphere, we are pivoted upon the sane norm of Aunt Ardèle in Anouilh's play or of Sir Henry Harcourt Reilly in *The Cocktail Party*; in this position we are engaged first by those we may only despise, then by those who elicit sympathy, until the two responses fuse. The behaviour of the General, the Count, the Countess and Villardieu in *Ardèle*, weighed against that of Ardèle herself, is fit only for satirical comedy, because we see them only through our imaginary ideal in Ardèle, just as we tend more and more to see the light inanity of the guests at Eliot's cocktail party through Reilly's objective eyes. But before these plays are over, the rope has grown shorter. We are implicated by the insistent presence of those we were once free to shrug off: Ardèle, in conjunction with a passionate Nathalie and Nicholas, becomes a mine with which to blast the dandlers and flirts; the slight problems of Edward, Lavinia and Celia are made weighty when Reilly, our mouthpiece, decides to aggravate them.

The dark drama is exciting because one pattern of feeling, dramatized perhaps by one character or group of characters, is countered by a contrary pattern from an opposite character or group, or by the same character or group seen in another light. Obliquely the dramatist approaches his goal. By contradiction, Pirandello edges nearer to the 'truth' in *Right You Are If You Think So*: Signor Ponza declares that his mother-in-law, Signora Frola, is mad in thinking that his wife is her daughter; she is in fact his second wife, for his first, her true daughter, actually died in an earthquake, an unhappy event the mother has never been able to accept. This seems convincing until we hear from Signora Frola that Ponza is the insane one, since he actually believes that his wife has died in an earthquake; and they have had to let him remarry the same woman, her daughter, convinced that she is another. Both stories tally, and we are never told the answer.

We want the truth? The truth is that *both* Ponza and Frola are right—for that is the nature of truth. Dark comedy is built with impressions which modify and contradict what has gone before. By the unseen presence of the martyr Celia Coplestone in Act III of *The Cocktail Party*, we are enabled to measure the quality of life in Edward and Lavinia Chamberlayne. This kind of treatment is ironic parallelism with a difference: the final decision is ours, and we are permitted to be responsible adults. In suffering this change of interest from irresponsibility to responsibility, we are leaving behind the kind of comedy in which the spectator wields the satirical weapon with a glee equal to the author's. We unhappily find ourselves sharing the punishment with the victim. The irony is the more incisive and painful because we have felt the peculiar misery of changing sides.[1] We are brought low from the indifferent heights of the spectator to be tumbled on the rack ourselves.

In the two-toned twilight drama we are discussing there can be nothing that might properly be called comic *relief*. The sensation derived from the moment of farce in high comedy, or the element of clowning in romantic comedy, is very different: one effect is but an extension of the other, and relief is found in a sudden sense of irresponsibility. But any sensation of real discord in the *tone* of a play is a felt lack of equilibrium, and is no relief, but only strain. This tension is only to be relaxed by an effort of consent and adaptation from the spectator himself.

I. A. Richards in one place discusses at once the 'catharsis' of tragedy and the irony of Rabelais and Flaubert in such terms as these: 'Besides the experiences which result from the building up of connected attitudes, there are those produced by the breaking down of some attitude which is a clog and bar to other activities.'[2] By this argument he may also be explaining the motive behind Macbeth's

[1] Cf. A. R. Thompson, *The Dry Mock* (California, 1948), p. 19.
[2] I. A. Richards, *Principles of Literary Criticism*, 2nd ed. (London, 1926), p. 209.

Porter and Hamlet's Gravedigger, Cleopatra's Clown and Juliet's Nurse, as well as Ibsen's Molvik, Chekhov's Epihodov, O'Casey's Fluther, and many subsidiary 'comic' characters in Brecht and Anouilh. As the playwright's plotting is clearer, the danger arises of having the spectator's image flow too easily into preconceived patterns of his own making. Thus one way of restraining and yet refreshing his energy is to introduce a discordant note, which, though out of key, will also contribute to the total music of the play.

The traditional reasons given for comic relief seem to have been two: first, and even today the most common, it has been a 'shot of spirits'. So Dryden: 'A continued gravity keeps the spirit too much bent; we must refresh it sometimes, as we bait in a journey that we may go on with greater ease.'[1] It is certainly true that if an audience is taxed too hard, if the play is too demanding of the emotions, and especially if its mood is too grim, the audience itself will supply the relief without hesitation, laughing mercilessly at any detail, however irrelevant, that it can use as an excuse. This has been proved many times with new plays which have made no provision for the natural impulse to reassert the sane balance. But far from proven is the implied corollary that from the retrogressive movement the spectator collects the force which again carries him onward.

The second is the theory of the 'gypsy laughter in the bushes', where the comedy acts as a foil to the pathos, a nineteenth-century view. In David Daiches's words, the comic scenes provide 'an oblique commentary—illuminating by the sudden difference of its point of view from that exhibited in the tragic scenes—on the same kind of human world in which the tragic action takes place. True comic relief completes the picture of the tragic world.'[2] By this interpretation we are certainly able to comprehend the content of what is spoken by, for example, the Porter and the Gravediggers. But it is difficult to believe that that is the only reason for the intrusion of these characters into emotional sequences so carefully built up. Nor does it explain moments of pure farce in O'Casey's tragedy of Juno or Anouilh's tragedy of Ardèle, where the farce would seem

[1] Dryden, *An Essay of Dramatic Poesy*, ed. Arnold (Oxford, 1889), p. 56.
[2] D. Daiches, *Critical Approaches to Literature* (London, 1956), p. 236.

completely to undermine the spectator's emotional attitude and the play's created image.

We must now assume a third explanation which shall include the earlier and the modern drama alike. An explanation in terms of 'from Philip drunk to Philip sober' falls logically into place in this essay. The comic scenes in many of Shakespeare's tragedies serve to enrich the pathos both by measuring the wealth of our feeling on the objective and precise scale of our more normal resilience to emotional experience, and by complicating the significance of the drama with a new and exciting ambivalence of attitude. For how many of Shakespeare's tragic heroes have a divinity we are to accept without question? We are to know their corporeality as we know our own, and we work hard to know it. The comic moments are not happy afterthoughts: as with *King Lear*, a degree of comedy is at the root of the play in its conception. The comedy is there to discolour the bright image in our minds—for at calculated moments we are compelled to give *equal weight* to Lear sane and Lear mad, and to the Porter and to Macbeth, as we are to Serafina the tragedienne and to Serafina the clown, and to Joxer and to Juno. The play may suffer a momentary paralysis, but it leaps forward again because the spectator is alive to more of the drama.

It is worth remembering that A. P. Rossiter, in a brief discussion of that supremely mongrel play *Measure for Measure*, argued that Shakespeare adopted a medieval ambivalence because his experience did not let him rest untroubled: 'The play is a searching analysis, an *empirical* moral investigation—not an application of ready-made Christian *a priori* moral schemes where all the answers are known. Shakespeare does not know the answers. He pokes and probes around, a duke of dark corners.'[1] We might add that many a good dramatist will see it as his task to pass on his empirical but enigmatic knowledge of experience as well as to meet it 'within himself'; to do so may be more a release than a relief of feeling.

---

[1] A. P. Rossiter, *English Drama from Early Times to the Elizabethans* (London, 1950), pp. 146–7 (Rossiter's italics).

THE COMIC-PATHETIC HERO

It is probably helpful in this general conclusion to notice the odd residue of 'characterization' left after the distillation of tragicomedy has taken place.

Traditionally one character has provided the keystone of the structure of the play, whether tragedy or comedy. This commanding position of a towering central character has determined, and still can, where the audience's interest is to be, loving or deriding it. Falstaff or Tartuffe, Hamlet or Harpagon must shine his light bright enough to take the eye and lead it on. But where the audience's affections towards the character are equivocal, as they might be if the action that surrounds him brightens and then dims the spotlight on him, or shows him now in this, now in that colouring, the character, our human link with the make-believe, begins to work upon us to other purposes. His centrality may still epitomize the world in which he lives, as Peer Gynt suggests the forces at work in modern Norway, or as Willie Loman stands for the self-deceptions of modern America in *Death of a Salesman*; but the spectator is participating in the performance in a different way, still concerned and yet vastly more critical. Character is aiding and abetting the disruptive intentions of the playwright anarchist, while the audience grows creative and constructive in its turn.

Bergson, evidently following such strong hints as those thrown out in Strindberg's preface to *Miss Julie*, declared firmly that 'every comic character is a type'[1] presented with one side only towards the spectator, whereas tragic heroes tend to be many-sided individuals. Tragic heroes may well have many-sided, individual characteristics, but of course in the last resort an Oedipus or a Hamlet must be simple enough to 'embrace half the world' if the tragedy is to take on universal qualities. In dark comedy, the comic-pathetic hero, a creature who at the crisis is so human as to remember and hope rather than heed and act, often tends to assume universal qualities through the very individual and contradictory details that go to make him up. In Walter Starkie's phrase of 1926,[2] this character is an

---

[1] Bergson, *Laughter*, trans. Brereton and Rothwell (London, 1911), p. 148.
[2] W. Starkie, *Luigi Pirandello* (London, 1926), p. 247.

'anti-hero'. He is a character capable of suggesting complexity because he has implicitly two or more sides towards the spectator. More than this, he calls for two or more *responses*, positive and negative and all the shades between. A Peer Gynt or a Willie Loman will absorb and quicken us with pleasure and pain in the theatre as we are absorbed and quickened by the mortal of flesh and blood we meet in life.

The argument suggests that, as the structure of tragicomic action grows complex and ambivalent, so must the structure of character: our reaction to the tapestry of varied impressions will ensure it. We remember the thrust and recoil of curbed emotion in contemplating the sad mordancy of Lear's Fool, the pitiful cuckolding of Molière's Georges Dandin, the early portraits of Charlie Chaplin the pathetic simpleton, and the anguished repartee of Archie Rice of Osborne's *The Entertainer* in his seedy palace of varieties, though these instances would at first sight seem incongruously placed together. This kind of double response arises when our initial recognition of the clown in his traditional role of wit and joker is denied and contradicted, when he is shown as capable of suffering the pains of mundane life, pains which would not have mattered to him or to us in his artificial character. The clown can be an Everyman, whether hero centre-stage or merely onlooker. As with Mr Polly's, his pose cannot be sustained if reality comes too close; as with Falstaff, death is the leveller. If we cannot play the hero, we can play the fool, even as Hamlet descends to play the clown to Polonius, Fortinbras, even Laertes.[1] It is the special force of dark comedy to show us that a clown can also be a hero: we see him playing both parts.

We are not discussing those parts inserted to provide such horse-play as we find in *Doctor Faustus*, which has rightly been found suspect, nor those written to provide the music-hall buffoonery of Gobbo-Launce tradition, through to the comic policemen of today. There is a whole category of mixed attitudes which is probably inexhaustible. It must include Edgar, simulating madness with earnest sanity, 'the most complex of all Shakespearian parts'; Jaques, who

---

[1] Cf. F. Fergusson, *The Idea of a Theater* (New York, 1954), p. 116.

is 'halfway to revolt against the world and wants to be a fool';[1] it must include dear old Gaev of *The Cherry Orchard*, a clown because he still retains a faith in himself, and Captain Shotover of *Heartbreak House*, a clown because he has lost such faith in himself as he had; Pirandello's Emperor Henry, who has clowned himself to destruction; Synge's Playboy, clown to his audience but not to himself or Pegeen, and Azdak of Brecht's *The Caucasian Chalk Circle*, clown to himself but not to his audience; Anouilh's General St Pé and Osborne's Archie Rice, so full of doubts that they act the clown to reassure themselves; and the Jimmy Porter of the post-war years, so certain that the rest of the world is a clown that unwittingly he becomes one; and Didi and Gogo, who wait for Godot, fashioned in the shape of clowns the better to symbolize and to satirize every speech and gesture we make ourselves.

The quintessential clown and anti-hero of today's conception even appears stripped of almost all particularity now in Samuel Beckett's plays, and never more concisely than in the pathetic, ludicrous figure who is flung on to the stage for *Act Without Words I*, a mime for one player set to music. On a bright, dazzling stage, a 'desert' of a stage, a single actor is 'Man', alone and open to inspection. A whistle is heard from the right, and he reflects and goes out right, only to be flung back again. 'He falls, gets up immediately, dusts himself, turns aside, reflects.' The teasing whistle is heard next from the left, and the same frustrating performance is enacted again, until he responds no more. This is man being conditioned as Köhler conditioned his apes. But his role as Tantalus son of Zeus has only begun. A little tree descends from the flies to offer a circle of shade, and he is offered scissors with which, perhaps, to cut himself a hat, but he uselessly trims his nails instead and the shadow disappears. A tiny carafe, bearing a large label inscribed 'WATER', is hung just out of reach, together with three cubes on which to stand to reach it, the insatiable whistle still blasting its directions. No sooner has he so arranged the cubes to reach the ·water than the carafe is pulled just

[1] These comments on Edgar and Jaques are taken from J. Isaacs's excellent remarks on the Shakespearian fool in 'Shakespeare as Man of the Theatre' in *Shakespeare and the Theatre* (The Shakespeare Association, 1927).

271

out of reach again. So the torment goes on, his own efforts un-availing, until our protagonist lies there on the stage, the carafe dangling and playing about his face, the whistle imperiously inviting his attention. But 'he does not move'.

The meaning of this little piece is clear enough: man is always to be at the mercy of unremitting, impersonal, unseen forces, despite his own efforts. For all the actor has no words, he assumes the zany character the action lends him. Since he is so mocked, we must laugh at his antics as he tumbles about the stage. Yet when he lies there finally, looking at his hands, wondering at his own impotence, the pathos of his situation is unmistakable.

This and the other dramatic 'clowns'[1] are most serviceable agencies for the playwright to enable us to see in immense variety the mixture of the comic and the pathetic in man. For the audience, the quasi-clown either stands outside the scene as commentator, or else moves towards the middle stage until his state of mind is recognizably our own. Thus Gaev is on the fringe; Uncle Vanya is central. The General in *Ardèle* is an oblique commentary from without, but in *The Waltz of the Toreadors* he is measured instead of measuring others. Hamlet at times is the clown who stands at dead centre of the action in a world that cannot admit clowns.

Perhaps the clown's function is to be seen as an echo, even an extension, of the parody in the traditional sub-plot, A. P. Rossiter's 'shadow-shows', Falstaff in his burlesque of Hotspur, Polonius unconsciously underscoring the father's role of King Hamlet, Thersites debunking the Grecian heroes, and so on. Where these sub-plots mock the serious issues of their plays, the clown mocks himself. The irony of the sub-plot grows bitter; the clown grows melancholy. As we feel and comprehend the relevance of the sub-plot to the main plot, so we understand the schizophrenia of the clown.

---

[1] To the catalogue should be added the farcical puppet heroes of Michel de Ghelderode, and Bummidge, the comic hero of Saul Bellow's *The Last Analysis*, forced to be his own psychiatrist: 'Nearing sixty, he is still eagerly mapping programs and hatching new projects. Half ravaged, half dignified, earnest when he is clowning and clowning when he means to be earnest, he represents the artist who is forced to be his own theoretician' (New York, 1965), p. ix.

Today the force of the sub-plot has been largely replaced by ironies within character. The illumination of an issue from more than one angle is often apparent from the structure of the individual character and the incongruity of the details with which he is built. Characters like Mme Ranevsky are complex because warm-hearted foolishness is complex. She has it in her to be both tragic heroine and fool. That she holds a precarious balance between the two is evident from the ease with which actresses tip her towards one or the other. It is true there is a sub-plotted, reduplicating structure for ironic ends in, for example, Eliot's *The Cocktail Party* and *The Confidential Clerk*, and in *Point of Departure* and the *Ardèle* of Anouilh. These writers, like Chekhov, are nevertheless using several clowns on the stage at a time. Their achievement is to rub two or more together to make them the more comic and the more pathetic. The contemporary hero may be the clown, the broken-hearted clown, wearing the mask-like paint of Pirandello's Henry IV, 'two small, doll-like dabs of colour' on a pallid base, heightened features hiding the grey within.

The broken-hearted clown is a grey hero. How tiresome that Aristotle should have chosen to write,

The objects the imitator represents are actions, with agents who are necessarily either good men or bad—the diversities of human character being nearly always derivative from this primary distinction, since the line between virtue and vice is one dividing the whole of mankind. It follows, therefore, that the agents represented must be either above our own level of goodness, or beneath it, or just such as we are...This difference it is that distinguishes Tragedy and Comedy also; the one would make its personages worse, and the other better, than the men of the present day.[1]

It does not matter whether Aristotle meant good and bad, or high and low, or serious and trivial; the contestable words are 'this primary distinction'. They state a palpable untruth which has misled us when making judgments on dramatic characters from Oedipus and Macbeth to Miss Julie, Halvard Solness, Blanche Dubois and Jimmy Porter.

For us to interpret such complex characters as these on grounds of

---

[1] Aristotle, *On the Art of Poetry*, trans. Bywater (Oxford, 1920), pp. 25–6.

vice or virtue or other moral status is not only to diminish their size, but to misconceive the drama in them. The impulse behind the greater play is rarely a preconceived moral system; rather, the good dramatist starts, proceeds and finishes by an intuitive and honest assessment of experience, if the characters are to convince and come to life, and if the resulting play is to reflect an experience of any value to an audience. The villainous and the virtuous characters spring from what Walter Kerr has recently defined as 'the thesis play'. He asserts rightly that 'it is better to make a man than to make a point'.[1]

'People don't have their virtues and vices in sets! they have them all anyhow', declares Hesione Hushabye of *Heartbreak House*, discussing the mixture in her husband Hector. Dark comedies, grey comedies, encourage subtle and living characters, quite apart from any close psychological portrayal which may also be present, because the pure white or the plain black soul is specifically excluded. The force of *The Wild Duck* lies not in the melodramatic pathos of a little girl's suicide, but in the failure of its hero Hjalmar Ekdal. He is the small man who responds as a small man when he is torn between truth and pretence; he is the normal man who corrupts what he touches when he finds himself caught between his wife's guilt and his daughter's innocence. The force of *The Cherry Orchard* lies not in the melodrama of having your dear old home sold out, but in understanding how a small woman, Mme Ranevsky, may well let such a thing happen. She may loom larger when she suggests that she knows the meaning of love where Trofimov does not, but her capacity to comprehend the world about her and its pressing issues is frighteningly limited. The power behind *Death of a Salesman* is not in the self-evident disease of the society depicted, but in the small man, Willie Loman, who displays his tragedy through a comic obsession. Yet we are not asked to hate these people: if we are not to love them, we are to live with them. 'May you be ordinary', writes Philip Larkin: for we respond to such characters with the understanding and feeling with which we read his ironically named poem, 'Born Yesterday':

[1] W. Kerr, *How Not to Write a Play* (London, 1956), p. 58.

In fact, may you be dull—
If that is what a skilled,
Vigilant, flexible,
Unemphasized, enthralled
Catching of happiness is called.

'Let us not take it for granted that life exists more fully in what is commonly thought big than in what is commonly thought small,' urged Virginia Woolf.[1] The modern movement has been to admit triviality into human stage behaviour, and to make drama of it. The hero of twentieth-century dark comedy is the character who makes the grand speech, but who has to clear his throat and scratch his nose. The dark comic dramatist tends to make special use of the duller elements of human personality in order to extend the content of drama: stupidity, boredom, carelessness, doubt, disappointment, caprice, reluctance, vacillation, bungling, mediocrity—everything that seems paltry in us. All the virtues and all the vices have their commonplace aspects: courage can be accidental, pride can be humiliating, love can be animal, revenge can be spiteful, just as cowardice can be understood, avarice can be pathetic, and selfishness and petty vanity can be amusing. The dark comic dramatist suggests it is a mistake, whether moral or aesthetic, for us to see the trivia of life, the gewgaws and baubles that bedeck the human spirit in public and in private, as unimportant.

However, a real problem remains for the dramatist if he is to show on the stage how important little people and petty behaviour are. The technical difficulty is to dramatize boredom without boring the audience, to demonstrate bungling without bungling the play. This task faced the authors of *Peer Gynt*, *Uncle Vanya*, *Heartbreak House*, *Right You Are*, *The Plough and the Stars* and *Waiting for Godot*. A full account of their success, or partial success, would need to call upon the testimony of many spectators over many years and would be a study on its own; but it would be a study of the great theatrical experiment of our age.

Where is the value in the unpretentious? It is not enough to argue that audiences do not go to the theatre to see mediocrity: do we cease to eat because we have eaten before? The best of these plays are

[1] V. Woolf, 'Modern Fiction', in *The Common Reader*, 1st series (London, 1925).

nourished by the actuality of our experience, as the best plays have always been.

There will be little glory in the unheroic hero. Just as every reader asked himself whether he felt sympathetic towards, or critical of, Emma Bovary when she first made her appearance, in much the same way everyone who saw *Look Back in Anger* questioned his personal response towards Jimmy Porter. We respond with sympathy *and* criticism, both. In detail after detail, Osborne, like Flaubert, ensures that each surge of warm feeling is undermined by a cold current of reality. Osborne moves us to compassion for Jimmy's personal past: 'For twelve months I watched my father dying—when I was ten years old...', then impulsively turns his hero face-about to address his wife in an affected tone of self-mortification: 'I want to stand up in your tears, and splash about in them, and sing. I want to be there when you grovel. I want to see your face rubbed in the mud—that's all I can hope for.'

While Emma and Jimmy have their heads in the air, we remain with our feet on the ground. They are victims of themselves and of society—that is their tragedy, and we feel for them; they are also members of that society—that is Flaubert's and Osborne's comedy, and we criticize them.

The romantic centre of the modern novel and drama, the hero, is replaced by a pattern of feeling, which the central character, if there is one, may not be able to recognize because it is part of him.[1] Only we, the observers, may see the whole pattern. The beetle has a narrow view of the garden; the gardener can observe all his stupid motions, can admire his efforts, laugh at his failures, help him to safety, or crush him with a touch of his toe.

In a letter to Suvorin in 1888, Chekhov wrote:

...Dividing people into successful and unsuccessful means looking at human nature from a narrow and prejudiced point of view. Are you successful or aren't you? What about me? What about Napoleon? One would need to be a god to distinguish successful from unsuccessful people without making mistakes. I'm going to a dance.[2]

[1] Cf. S. O'Faoláin's concept of the 'anti-Hero' in *The Vanishing Hero* (London, 1956).
[2] Chekhov to Suvorin, quoted by R. Hingley, *Chekhov* (London, 1950), p. 211.

The Comic-Pathetic Hero

That is the dark comic attitude. From the troubled and un-successful Ivanov to the confused Mme Ranevsky, whose modest aim for success was a happy love-affair, Chekhov dispenses with a hero. He invites us to look beyond the figure we see standing there, and, especially in *Uncle Vanya*, *Three Sisters* and *The Cherry Orchard*, he does it by placing others with him at the centre. Our eye cannot rest on any one replica of him, but must float between several, resting on none. Thus we find ourselves giving a rarer attention to the distances between them, to the relationships between them as they move in private and public. We watch with psychiatric eye how they affect others in the play. We do not pin any one of them down for anatomical examination: we gladly let them pursue their course. We make use of each in order to estimate the particular climate in which each lives, and measure one against another in order to eliminate divergencies of eccentricity. We may arrive at a just conclusion about the general source of each particular little dream, each show of temper, burst of laughter or silent grief. So the pattern emerges; indeed, the more clearly we see it, the clearer grows the corporeality of the characters who make it up.

Forty years after Chekhov, Brecht returned to the observation of people and their behaviour, in order to arm himself with theories for drama in a very different convention, and with lessons for a very different way of acting. He wrote a poem of 'Everyday Theatre',[1] which, like dark comedy, should be 'serious and gay', yet 'full of dignity', and he addressed it to his actors. 'Artists,' it begins,

> Artists, you who make Theatre
> in great houses, beneath artificial suns of light,
> in front of the silent crowd—go and seek now and then
> the Theatre of everyday,—thousandfold and without fame
> yet so very full of life; Theatre of the earth; Theatre
> fed by the living together
> of people; Theatre played in the streets.

Here a woman imitates her landlord, he goes on; the man there at the street corner 'demonstrates how the accident happened'; but he

[1] Brecht, 'Über alltägliches Theater', trans. W. M. Marckwald (unpublished), from 'Der Messingkauf', *Theaterarbeit*, ed. Brecht, etc. (Dresden, 1952), p. 398.

277

remains only 'a signpost that points', and he himself is not involved. Brecht will put no heroes on his stage, and if he must have a central character, the actor must leave us emotionally free to watch him with detachment. Such, at least, were his intentions. The actor, the character and the spectator were to be on equal terms:

> ...what we do is something universal and human
> which hourly occurs in the busy throng of the streets,
> nearly as dear as eating and breathing is to man.

THE DARK TONE

The Elizabethan audience's ability 'to shift rapidly its modes of attention', as S. L. Bethell has put it,[1] is not essentially an Elizabethan gift, nor is it to be found only in a non-naturalistic drama like Shakespeare's. An assumption by the playwright of some such psychological mechanism is evidently pervasive through much modern drama. There are to be found in audiences only degrees of alertness; the spectator is either awakened or he is not, and the shift between comedy and pathos, and their delicate balance, is one way of startling him into wakefulness.

In the same way, the shift between happiness and misery, or more usually between a little buoyancy and a little melancholy in a variety of degrees, is common to most people's wakeful moments. Some unconscious apprehension of life's vagaries may impel us to weep at moments of great happiness and laugh at times of great anguish. Perhaps in the concentrated and freely responsive atmosphere of the theatre, we are not too different from the child who displays that extraordinary facility for switching his mood from tears to smiles and back again within a moment.

We are so made that we can respond by such extremes if we will, and the nature of existence itself, by which, to echo Dr Johnson, in one home there may be joy while in the next suffering, by which the morning may be shining and the evening overcast, makes this oscillation necessary. From his observation, the reader will be able to multiply examples of this dark, jaundiced comedy of living. It may

[1] S. L. Bethell, *Shakespeare and the Popular Dramatic Tradition* (London, 1944), p. 108.

arise when we see the social ritual which surrounds the dead, while we also contemplate death itself. It may colour international politics where we see the fencing and weaving of the diplomats as we reflect on the momentous issues that concern them. In the theatre many dramatists have recognized the usefulness of this ambivalence. In drama as in life, nevertheless, the impulse to laughter and the impulse to tears sit uneasily together. It is tantalizing, first, that artificial forms like those of tragedy and comedy should admit their opposites, and, second, that a dramatist, knowing the discomfort of juxtaposing two discordant responses, should deliberately exploit the tensions they set up when put together.

Plato, at the tail of his *Symposium*, dropped the explosive hint that has been irking us since, that the tragic poet might also be a comedian: 'Socrates was forcing them to admit that the same man might be capable of writing both comedy and tragedy.'[1] In 1950 Christopher Fry confessed that his idea for a comedy presented itself to him first as tragedy: 'If the characters were not qualified for tragedy, there would be no comedy, and to some extent I have to cross the one before I can light on the other.'[2] This was certainly true of the 'October' comedy, *Venus Observed*, which he had just completed when he wrote this. This presents a man in middle age, the Duke of Altair, who has reached a point in life where he has to make a prodigious decision: not whom he should choose as wife, but rather whether he should allow his remaining years to drift into sentiment for the past, which is the tragedy of age, or grasp his future and marry Rosabel, 'sharing two solitudes'. He chooses Rosabel, but this is no conventionally happy ending, rather an admission that age and the resignation of age may be viewed as comedy. The whole play analyses the Duke's decision, and the experience of the play is to share the comic-tragic embarrassment of life to which the Duke testifies.

Life is still the reference point. Shakespeare would on occasion measure the scale of his tragedy against ordinary life and the simpler

---

[1] Plato, *Symposium*, trans. M. Joyce, in *Five Dialogues* (London, 1938), p. 81.
[2] C. Fry, 'Comedy' in *The Adelphi*, vol. 27, 1 (November 1950), p. 28, quoted by G. Melchiori, *The Tightrope Walkers* (London, 1956), p. 168.

human feelings, but until nearly the twentieth century the ideal of naturalistic representation in the theatre had not complicated the forms that drama might take. The playwrights to discover, through an inimitable observation of people, that powerful meanings could be created in the theatre without resort to the exaggerations, and sometimes distortions, of classical tragedy and comedy were Ibsen and Chekhov, but especially the latter. Chekhov saw that everyday life holds its own incongruities. There he found sufficient to create the comic attitude in the audience, and sufficient to sound the echoes of tragedy at the same time. In seeking a satisfactory form for his new drama, he hit upon what Wilson Knight has called 'a new sublime incongruity' that is neither comedy nor tragedy.[1] This study has tried to show how this form reached perfection in *The Cherry Orchard*, but today the special colouring of this method tinges all manner of drama. Thus in *Look Back in Anger*, when Cliff is bandaging the burn on Alison's arm, the touch is typical, not to say hackneyed:

> CLIFF. . . . What is it, lovely?
> ALISON. Nothing.
> CLIFF. I said; what is it?
> ALISON. You see—(*hesitates*). I'm pregnant.
> CLIFF (*after a few moments*). I'll need some scissors.

But Chekhov's Alison would have called it indigestion, and Chekhov's Cliff would have lost the scissors.

In one way Chekhov and his successors were safely disciplined while ordinary life applied a steady brake to the play. Less assured is the mixture of farce with tragedy, or sentiment with comedy, acted out at some remove from naturalism.

There are moments in Ibsen's largely naturalistic play *The Wild Duck* when the behaviour of Hjalmar and Old Ekdal comes so close to farce as to risk upsetting the balance of feeling in the play. Indeed, the whole business of the ridiculous attic is one of the most daring strokes in this author's repertoire: intended to provoke a degree of laughter at the outset, the significance of the attic grows as the theme of the play emerges. Our first response is turned against us,

[1] G. W. Knight, *The Wheel of Fire* (London, 1954), p. 160.

as the attic symbolizes a whole way of life we recognize to be one we often cherish ourselves. While Eric Bentley says, as we saw, that 'in this play the farce takes its life from the pathos, the pathos from the farce, the whole practical problem being one of controlling the subtle interactions of the two contrary modes',[1] such a problem is capable of a smooth resolution in a convention close to naturalism.

Of a different order is the violent mingling of farce with pathos in the work of Anouilh, Samuel Beckett and Eugène Ionesco. The risk here is that, even if the producer and his actors do hit upon the precise level of playing to keep the balance of the play, there can be no guarantee that they can hold all the audience all the time. Audiences pricked too hard will kick.

Of sentiment in comedy, one can only echo the remarks of critics[2] who have found the sentimental comedy of the eighteenth century an undramatic cheat and a bore. But where in Molière's *The Misanthrope* or in Shaw's *Heartbreak House* and *Saint Joan* the comedy is just as deliberately, but more subtly and dramatically, displaced by motions of sympathy towards the hero or heroine, something more fundamental is happening. Both Molière and Shaw in these plays almost miscalculate the pressure of their situations upon their audiences' feelings. Perhaps they intended to try us with tears and shudders, interested in the peculiar flavour of the resulting mixture. The honesty of Alceste, in love with his coquette, turns a mannered comedy into something closer to melodrama; the comedy of authority in its various guises challenged by Joan the individualist cannot be sustained—the sober dealings of history take charge; the farcical education of Ellie Dunn of its own momentum is driven to a point where it becomes an implied baptism in the terrible. Yet both Molière and Shaw felt the need at particular moments to retrieve their balance and tone—with the comic Du Bois, with Joan's Epilogue, with the explosion over Heartbreak House. In wrenching us back into an objective frame of mind, they gave their comedy that extra touch of ice missing from Farquhar, Steele, Cumberland and

[1] E. R. Bentley, *In Search of Theater* (London, 1954), p. 45.
[2] See L. J. Potts, *Comedy* (London, 1948), pp. 144 ff., and A. Sherbo, *English Sentimental Drama* (London, 1958).

others of the sentimental English drama, and from the *comédie larmoyante* in France.

To the fact that this sentimental tradition is not dead, London's West End and New York's Broadway perennially bear witness. Promising comedies are still maimed in the tearful way, as was John Whiting's early play *A Penny for a Song*. Otherwise an excellent satire on crazy English attitudes towards war, the pathetic love of Dorcas Bellboys for blinded Edward Sterne quarrels incessantly with the dry mockery of the rest of the play. It is not an extension of Whiting's argument that their love should flourish and be doomed, but an interpolation from another play, happily unwritten.

Clashing tears and laughter are uncomfortable companions, but, where in life their reconciliation is necessary if we are to make peace with ourselves, in drama their conflict is serviceable if that peace is to be disturbed. David Daiches argues that 'tragic relief' in comedy would destroy the 'magic circle' in which comedy moves.[1] But reference to modern drama, where this kind of conflict is part of the dramatic philosophy of the serious comedian, will again and again show the dramatist stretching the fabric of his comedy in order to trouble an audience whose expectations have become callous and settled. The new craft of dark comedy, which eventually sours the laughter and redoubles the emotion, is likely to be drama at its most cheerless and uncompromising.

The dramatist who can swing between the extremes of tragedy and farce within the same framework is today the man to sting us. Nevertheless, if he is not to drive his audience to distraction by offering a drama too inharmonious to be acceptable, he must of course have a sense of the unity of his piece.

It is easy to see why critics, standing by the ancients or by their own experience, have thought that a play should leave a single, unalloyed impression, and that this was a virtue in itself. Dryden's Lisideius is to be excused for arguing that mirth and compassion are 'things incompatible' and that 'the poet must of necessity destroy the former by intermingling the latter',[2] because this can happen.

---

[1] D. Daiches, *Critical Approaches to Literature* (London, 1956), p. 237.
[2] Dryden, *An Essay of Dramatic Poesy*, ed. Arnold (Oxford, 1889), p. 43.

The opinions of Diderot, Manzoni, Voltaire and many others who thought that opposites destroy unity must command some respect: in plays from *The Changeling* of Middleton and Rowley to *The Cocktail Party* of T. S. Eliot precisely this happens.

It need not do so. The unity of a play is not to be conceived narrowly as a matter of forms, as unity of 'action', but as a final tone and climate, a 'fourth' unity in which opposites may flourish together in the audience's mind. Indeed, Aristotle himself seemed to be arguing towards this position when he qualified his 'one action' with the gloss, 'a complete whole, with its several incidents so closely connected that the transposal or withdrawal of any one of them will disjoin and dislocate the whole'.[1] The implication that the parts must mutually support each other is Coleridgean. Augustus William Schlegel further insisted that the separate parts must be 'comprehended by the understanding': 'They are all subservient to one common aim, namely, to produce a joint impression on the mind... the Unity lies in a higher sphere, in the feeling or in the reference to ideas.'[2] The fourth unity is possible even where the ingredients are mixed, provided that the author burns with his thesis, has made an accurate assessment of his audience, and can keep it strictly enslaved. It may often depend on a flair for hitting the appropriate note for the time, as with Shakespeare and Chekhov; perhaps, as with O'Casey and Fry, conjuring a unifying mood to subdue us.

Schlegel's is an appeal to the end, an appeal for the serviceableness of the parts, which was Johnson's appeal in his celebrated defence of tragicomedy. As Schlegel saw the unity of tragedy, so we might see a unity in dark comedy. 'We must not suppose', he wrote,

that the order of sequences in a tragedy resembles a slender thread, of which we are every moment in anxious dread lest it should snap. This simile is by no means applicable, for it is admitted that a plurality of subordinate actions and interests is inevitable; but rather let us suppose it a mighty stream, which in its impetuous course overcomes many obstructions, and loses itself at last in the repose of the ocean. It springs perhaps from different sources, and certainly receives into itself other rivers, which

[1] Aristotle, *On the Art of Poetry*, trans. Bywater (Oxford, 1920), p. 42.
[2] See A. W. Schlegel, *Lectures on Dramatic Art and Literature*, trans. Black (London, 1846), pp. 243 ff.

hasten towards it from opposite regions. Why should not the poet be allowed to carry on several, and, for a while, independent streams of human passions and endeavours, down to the moment of their raging junction, if only he can place the spectator on an eminence from whence he may overlook the whole of their course? And if this great and swollen body of waters again divide into several branches, and pour itself into the sea by several mouths, is it still not one and the same stream?[1]

It seems an essential task for the contemporary critic to observe the manner in which a play's contradictory ingredients, while seeming to destroy each other, can be contrived for mutual support. He is today challenged to investigate whatever new unity any particular mixture of opposites may create. He will certainly find himself looking for the common roots of the tangle confronting him. If the elements of a play as kaleidoscopic as *Troilus and Cressida* or *Peer Gynt* do not disintegrate in performance, it is because its pattern was determined by natural pressures and organic processes, reflected in the vitality of the play.

William Empson suggests that 'the drama in England has always at its best had a certain looseness of structure'.[2] Complexity in plotting, contradictions in tone, seem again and again to be reproducing the sensations of life with its complexities and contradictions (in recent times, not only in England). We get the feeling that, in Empson's words, 'the play deals with life as a whole'. From the spontaneous eruption of tomfoolery within the sacred framework of the medieval mystery plays to the contrivances of O'Casey to show his subject from opposed points of view in, say, *The Plough and the Stars*, we are reminded again that the point of reference is life; but if this is true, the looseness is merely apparent and not real.

After the magnificent Shakespearian rhetoric of Henry's 'Once more unto the breach...', which ends, we remember, with an injunction to 'follow your spirit', what better way of having us keep our wits and hear a ring of truth than by dragging on Nym, Bardolph and Pistol immediately?

> BARDOLPH. On, on, on, on, on, to the breach, to the breach.
> NYM. Pray thee Corporal stay, the knocks are too hot...

[1] A. W. Schlegel, *Lectures on Dramatic Art and Literature*, p. 245.
[2] W. Empson, *Some Versions of Pastoral* (London, 1950), p. 27. See especially ch. 2, 'Double Plots'.

Is not the 'looseness' of this bathos perfectly justified in the structure of *Henry V*?

There is a primary urge within us to make sense and to make a whole of the plurality and variegations of life, and to do so without procuring an abortion of the truth by excluding what may not fit. In a play which arises from such motives as these, there may be a conviction of feeling which has nothing to do with consistency of character, the external unity and progression of plot, or the maintenance of the conventions within the play. The dark comedian echoes Goethe: 'It is at bottom better to make a confused piece than a cold one.'

Dark comedy may initially anatomize, but it does it to free us of stereotyped but arbitrary attitudes. It makes elastic those thoughts and feelings grown rigid, in order to offer us a dramatic experience before the parts of that experience are drawn together again. The farcical and the pathetic will flow by imperceptible motions into one another, as they do when life is seen at a distance, as when age reflects on youth; or they will be violently thrown together, as when we stand close at the centre of it. Yet life is still of a piece, and so the play can be.

Affairs in dark comedy rarely conclude: they persist, and their repercussions may be felt to be unlimited.[1] This drama does not make decisions for us, but at the most suggests likelihoods, depicts chanciness and stresses both sides. It stimulates us by implications, and it does not pass judgments—only the spectator may do that, if he feels he has the courage: but, as in life, he may never dare to commit himself so far. In dark comedy we are specifically asked not to be fanatics.

---

[1] In discussing 'The Theater of Commitment', Eric Bentley argues, 'A pessimistic ending tells us that nothing can be done. An optimistic ending tells us that nothing need be attempted: since everything is already all right, we should feel reconciled to the All. It is in fact hard to put an ending on a play that does not have some such conclusiveness, optimistic or pessimistic. Yet an attempt—often known as the bitter ending—has been made from time to time, and it is bitter because it is not a true ending at all, but is open at the end. We associate it with tragicomedy, and it has a special point in activist drama, polemical drama, drama of Commitment, because it says: what happens after this is up to you, the public.' *Commentary* (New York, December 1966), no. 6, vol. 42, p. 70.

I. A. Richards argued that the structure of some poems and plays includes contrasting elements in order to widen experience, the content of the writing deriving from relations between 'the opposite, the complementary impulses', thereby promoting 'a stability and order' possible only when the natural inclusiveness of the mind is satisfied.[1] It is natural, in our better moments, to balance our loves and hates, and sympathize with the villain and laugh at misfortune and forgive the sinner. Such antitheses may shape clumsily in the mind as a grotesque patchwork, or resolve a muddle into an uncommon mood. That such antitheses are valuable for literature is suggested by Empson's fourth type of ambiguity: 'When two or more meanings of a statement do not agree among themselves, but combine to make clear a more complicated state of mind in the author.'[2]

Jean-Paul Richter once confessed, 'In my consciousness, it is always as if I were doubled: as if I were two I's in me. Within I hear myself talking.'[3] The split mind of a writer has always lent him a force and a great appeal, once his reader has been persuaded to identify himself with him. This is easier for a novelist than for a dramatist, who cannot too simply call up a character's thoughts. It accounts for the modernity of the stories of Melville's *Bartleby* and Conrad's *The Secret Sharer*, in which the position is explored where a man can be a stranger to himself. It accounts for the complex sense of truth in the novels of Dostoevsky, where minor characters enact the minds of the major, as Raskolnikov understands himself in Sonia and Svidrigaylov, and Ivan Karamazov in Smerdyakov; or where several contradictory characters complement each other in a pattern which exposes the complete mind of the author, like the brothers in *The Brothers Karamazov*. For this is the writer using his 'third voice',[4] essentially the dramatizing approach to artistic expression. Such dualism permits a fullness of statement: it is inclusive, as the mind is inclusive, of the passionate with the bawdy, the sacred with the profane, the sublime with the ridiculous.

[1] See I. A. Richards, *Principles of Literary Criticism*, 2nd ed. (London, 1926), pp. 247 ff.
[2] W. Empson, *Seven Types of Ambiguity*, 2nd ed. (London, 1947), ch. 4.
[3] Quoted by A. R. Thompson, *The Dry Mock* (California, 1948), p. 66, from Walden, *Jean-Paul and Swift*, p. 53.
[4] See T. S. Eliot, *The Three Voices of Poetry* (London, 1953).

These things we perceive simultaneously; in art it has often been taken as duty to separate one from the other, to clarify the issues, even to simplify for the lay mind. It is comforting to be told that any issue is black or white, and that we have only to know which is black and which is white. But it may take a fine degree of moral courage to admit a grey into our thinking. It is especially daring to send an audience home in a dark mood, and then to try to draw it back into the theatre for similar medicine. Yet to do so is to urge a truth about the nature of people and things. It is no work for the playwright-preacher or playwright-politician: it excludes the overt progapandist. The didactic drama of Georg Kaiser (*Gas*), Ernst Toller (*Masses and Man*), and J. B. Priestley and Graham Greene more recently, does not easily admit the irony of dark comedy.

Like Rickie Elliot in E. M. Forster's *The Longest Journey*, the new playwright suffers from 'the Primal Curse, which is not—as the Authorized Version suggests—the knowledge of good and evil, but the knowledge of good-and-evil'. For this reason he is taking a risk: he may produce a dark entertainment, a cold pudding mixed of antithetical moral ingredients which will not blend but which lie leaden on the stomach. Yet the success of the best plays of Chekhov and Pirandello, for example, tells the story of writers who have explored their medium to its particular limits in order to overcome an intrinsic ugliness in their subjects. Their synthesis of contradictory impressions is managed by a careful anticipation of their interactions. The new playwright must solve Coleridge's gigantic conundrum of the creative imagination and explore the mystery of 'the balance or reconciliation of opposite or discordant qualities'[1]—if, in the theatre, the audience is to find it possible to steady the pendulum.

UNHOLY JOY: ATTITUDES OF DRAMATIST AND AUDIENCE

A casual prophecy by Hazlitt in 1817, that 'the progress of manners and knowledge has an influence on the stage, and will in time per-haps destroy both tragedy and comedy',[2] has been largely fulfilled

---

[1] Coleridge, *Biographia Literaria*, ed. Shawcross (London, 1907), vol. 2, p. 12.
[2] Hazlitt, *Lectures on the Literature of the Age of Elizabeth and Characters of Shake-speare's Plays* (London, 1884), p. 22.

in our time. The reasons for this are as difficult to assess as 'manners and knowledge' are to measure, and the temper of the twentieth century is particularly volatile. Yet no art form is so directly related to the thoughts and feelings of its audience, so sounds its pulse, as drama. Especially does dark comedy, the drama of the split mind, with its seemingly sceptical motives, reflect the mood of the times. In the delightful burlesque of an 'anti-drama' which Anouilh introduces into his *L'Hurluberlu*, the dramatist gives himself away in the mocking stance he adopts:

MENDIGALES. ...The modern theatre has made a great stride forward. The idea that it should offer simple amusement, or relaxation, is out.

GENERAL (*good-humouredly, as he sits down*). Heavens, why? Mustn't we laugh any more?

MENDIGALES. Temporary inhabitants of a planet threatened by atomic destruction, we have no time for amusement. Now it is a question of working to grip the consciousness of man, by man, for man,—and in humanity. Which does not in the least exclude, you will see, metaphysical anguish and a kind of humour of despair.

GENERAL. That promises us a happy evening!...[1]

There follows an account of 'Whizz! Bang!' or 'Julian the Apostate' and the frivolous tone scarcely conceals Anouilh's own instinct for the 'humour of despair' with which he reproaches Samuel Beckett. Troubled himself, the modern dramatist is intent on troubling the spectator, and his handiest device has been to thrust remorselessly together the laughter and tears.

It is a kind of blasphemy that, when Gogo in *Waiting for Godot* prepares to hang himself with the cord that holds up his trousers, we should be compelled to laugh at the abject man whose trousers have fallen about his ankles. Should we not be sobered by the thought of suicide, even supply a degree of admiration? But Beckett wishes us to mock, and so doing touches a willing spring within us. Our impulse to shout aloud in a solemn gathering, to laugh in church, is a human response to restraint. We are restrained in society only by the conventions of society. In art, the artist will dare to do what in life may be impossible if he feels his audience can respond as he

[1] Trans. Miss D. J. Hardy, unpublished.

wants it to. We saw how the Mystery Cycles could jest about what awes man most: life, death and the hope of salvation.

The drama that we have examined is drama that is self-analytical and self-conscious. Through a more finely spun texture it is harder to see the blasphemy against life. Bawdy will show itself if fashion permits; but the motives for domesticating the sublime, and for exalting the trivial, may be hidden.

There may be a simple skirmish between the reason which rejects and the sympathies which are loth to be denied: so Chekhov pricks at his three sisters separately, but adores them together; so Dylan Thomas ridicules the villagers of *Under Milk Wood*, and yet loves the village. It may be the wish of the author to keep tangible and recognizable what is feared as a mystery, to make a chance of destiny, to make a man of God and an animal of man, so that, in Philip Leon's words, 'his blasphemy makes the divine more present than the most solemn of hymns':[1] this is the faith of Shakespeare in the raging of Lear, and perhaps also of Pirandello[2] and Beckett. Or, in reverse, 'hot baths of sentiment' may be followed by 'cold douches of irony', and Irving Babbitt's account of romantic irony aptly fits Anouilh's peculiar taste of tears: 'When disillusion overtakes the uncritical enthusiast, when he finds that he has taken some cloud bank for *terra firma*, he continues to cling to his dream, but at the same time wishes to show that he is no longer the dupe of it';[3] the writer may introduce the tensions of self-mockery as a safeguard *against* mockery, 'a kind of homeopathic treatment'.[4] In each case we see a mask of mockery hiding the passion behind it.

In the twentieth-century drama we have glanced at, there arises another factor. It is the writer's anxiety to counter the glibness of the fixed idea, and to block a too easy response. At its worst, this may appear as a novelty for the sake of shocking us, an attempt to cover a deficiency by taking the audience off guard; at its best, it is a shaking of the bottle before the dose is administered, a skilfully controlled dramatic irony.

[1] P. Leon, 'Holy Nonsense', *The Listener* (London, 29 November 1956), p. 879.
[2] See F. May, 'Drama of Reality', *Drama* (London, winter 1954), p. 22.
[3] I. Babbitt, *Rousseau and Romanticism* (Boston and New York, 1919), p. 264.
[4] Cf. D. Daiches, *Critical Approaches to Literature* (London, 1956), p. 161.

It is possible to identify loosely some of the attitudes implied in the playwrights we have discussed. Their drama is that of a culture in which man, rightly or wrongly, has placed himself at the hub of the world. He has no sure God to leap to, or else he will not leap without first arguing the point. It is a drama of human vanity in which 'hell has no vastness'. It is a drama which must exclude tragedy while there is no apparent virtue in rising above the sordidness of the human condition or in trying to reach a decisive conclusion about its problems. As Shaw wrote in his preface to *Three Plays by Brieux* in 1911, you do not leave a modern play with the feeling that the affair is finished or the problem solved for you by the dramatist: 'The curtain no longer comes down on a hero slain or married: it comes down when the audience has seen enough of the life presented to it to draw the moral, and must either leave the theatre or miss its last train.'[1] If on his way home the spectator is not still talking, he feels that the characters are.

For ours is also a disputatious drama, making an argument of itself, taking nothing on trust. Bertolt Brecht adopted the term 'dialectical' to describe his theatre;[2] nor was he borrowing the word from Marxism. He was drawn to the Hegelian dialectic, as was Shaw to the Socratic, and he understood Hegel's contradictions of thesis and antithesis in order to apprehend the nature of the real world. Brecht wrote that Hegel

had such a sense of humour that, for example, he could not even conceive of, say, order without disorder...He denied that one equals one, not only because everything that exists is continually turning into something else, namely its opposite, but because generally nothing is identical with itself.[3]

This very neatly reflects the tragicomic sense with its dramatic ambivalence; it reflects the friction and contrariety of Pirandello's *Umorismo*.

Dialectical writing stands less chance of suffering from disease by decadence: it may indicate disillusion and pessimism behind the

[1] Shaw, *op. cit.* p. xvii.   [2] See Brecht, *Die Dialektik auf dem Theater* (1957).
[3] Brecht, 'Flüchtlingsgespräche', *Aufbau* (E. Berlin, February 1958), pp. 181–2, quoted in M. Esslin, *Brecht: A Choice of Evils* (London, 1959), p. 129.

façade of laughter, but in remaining relativist it is not passive and it does not drift. Pirandello was much taken with Machiavelli's confession: 'If at times I laugh and sing, I do it because this is the only way I have to provide an outlet for my painful tears.'[1] To feel about experience in this way suggests at least an activity of spirit alive to the variety of life, and perhaps not far removed from Keats's poetical character:

It enjoys light and shade; it lives in gusto, be it foul or fair, high or low, rich or poor, mean or elevated—It has as much delight in conceiving an Iago as an Imogen. What shocks the virtuous philosopher delights the camelion [*sic*] Poet.[2]

Yet the spectator may shuffle his feet at all this. The electrifying incongruities made possible by the non-naturalistic methods of the later dramatists repeatedly risk the accusation of writing in 'bad taste'; but when our barriers are down and the vitality of the conception compels a synthesis in the mind, we are left in a glow of new experience. This drama is the modern tragicomedy finding its way and coming to maturity. It offers the shock tactics Shaw noticed in Tolstoy's *The Fruits of Enlightenment*, his 'terrible but essentially comedic method'[3] applied with more deliberation and a wider sense of stage convention. Bad taste is of the essence of every rebellion, and rebellion is of the essence of artistic vitality.

It is understandable that critical estimates of the dark comedy are so much at odds: audience ratings can never apply to such plays. The critical assumptions of the audience are challenged and their critical passions laid bare. Says one, 'Don't we go to the theatre for pleasure, not to be improved? Discomfort is not entertainment.' 'Pleasure', 'entertainment'—these are the shovel-words of a vexed spectator. Says another and rarer bird, 'Isn't each new play properly an experiment in the uses of the imagination? We go to the theatre to feel afresh and to think again.' The B.B.C.'s Audience Research Department reported that Beckett's radio play *All That Fall* had an

[1] Quoted in D. Vittorini, *The Drama of Luigi Pirandello* (New York, 1935), p. 89.
[2] Keats, *Letters*, ed. M. B. Forman (1935), p. 245.
[3] Shaw, *London Mercury* (May 1921), reprinted in his preface to *Tolstoy, Plays*, trans. Maude (London, 1923).

appreciation index of 58, a below-average figure, the result of an amusingly wide distribution of ratings: A+ 17%, A 34%, B 22%, C 17% and C− 10%. The Head of Audience Research commented, 'Fascination, revulsion, cynicism, boredom—and even abuse—were all evident in the comments of listeners.'[1] In gaining complexity and integrity, dark comedy must inevitably lose the popular market. If, as perhaps in the cases of Brecht, Anouilh and Tennessee Williams, the dark comedian strains to win gratuitous affection, a peculiar sensationalism may disturb the balance of feeling, and, as we have seen, contradictory impressions within the mind of the spectator may fail to blend.

What of dramatic criticism? In spite of Dr Johnson's defence of tragicomedy there has always been some critical unease in the presence of, for example, the parodying heroics in drama by Falstaff and Parolles and their kind. We can understand Dryden's anxiety for the spectator who may be 'confounded' by the mixture of the ingredients of comedy and tragedy. It was a similar distrust, in this case justifiable, that set the more astute dramatists and commentators against that special brand of tearful comedy of the eighteenth century, and equally a distrust of the sentimentality that made short-lived the comedy of Wilde (except in *The Importance of Being Earnest*) and Barrie and Bridie. But academic criticism often tends to be anxious for a fallacious purity of tone and a clarity of purpose in drama: it wants to separate the masque from the anti-masque, the tragedy from the comedy, the tears from the laughter. As Mary Lascelles said of *Measure for Measure*, 'any hasty interpretation..., or any which hardens into a formula, is likely to approach misconstruction'.[2] The best dialectical montage of scenes must always defy verbal exegesis in the end: the paradox of the spectator who is implicated in his own detachment can never be resolved in the study. Today we have moved closer to another of the frontiers of drama: this is the originality of the modern movement.

[1] B.B.C. Audience Research Department News Letter no. 205 (March 1957).
[2] M. Lascelles, *Shakespeare's Measure for Measure* (London, 1953), p. 164.

DIDACTICISM AND DESPAIR

It is apparent that the drama we are discussing is often unashamedly didactic. The simple disguises of satire, the imaginary worlds of Lilliput and Brobdingnag, of Evelyn Waugh's *The Loved One* and Aldous Huxley's *Ape and Essence*, devised temporarily to deceive while we coolly pass judgment on ourselves—these are mission-school parables compared with the hoaxes and snares of Chekhov and Pirandello and their disciples. With these dramatists we torture ourselves with the agonies we witness on the stage, because the methods of dark comedy invite our warm immersion in the experience of the creatures of the play, where literary satire must keep us cool and critical. Hence the danger is always present in the new comic theatre that we accept melodrama, sentimentality and easy cynicism in disguise. Satire dare not make us suffer until after the event, lest we revolt too soon; dark comedy will drag us passionate through the mud.

It is a modern morality drama. The simple medieval play form was of life as a journey on a narrow path between the forces of good and evil, with its stage a simple symbol of the World set between Heaven and Hell,[1] though a certain delightful raciness broke in from time to time. Its abstract characterization was on the whole fixed and dull and incapable of development. In an age of faith, a simple hero binds the medieval play, a justifiable symbol for a universal view, but still an Everyman without individuality.

Since those times, the journey has grown more complicated, the symbols less definite. The freedom that expressed itself before in racy characterization, in humour and the pursuit of side issues, has more and more taken charge of the drama. We have seen thin little Everyman grow dramatically robust in his passage to Faustus and Hamlet, and on to Peer Gynt and even Jimmy Porter. This is of course not necessarily a mark of artistic 'progress', but in an age of doubt simplicity is hardly admissible; there may be no blatant preaching, and the sermon must be muffled. The sophisticated of the twentieth century, like the judicious of the seventeenth, resent

[1] See R. Williams, *Drama in Performance* (London, 1954), ch. 2.

it if they are over-persuaded by the sentiment of melodrama, or find the satire cynically over-exaggerating its object of contempt. The early Anouilh (of *L'Hermine* and *Jézabel*) makes his forces of good and his forces of evil too blunt and artless. Beckett's *Endgame* is so negative that only those in the audience who admit no positives will look on with more than clinical interest. Brecht, too, can under-estimate his audience when in *The Caucasian Chalk Circle* his Grusha is just another girl with a baby pushed out into the snow, and his drunken monk is there to make a parasite of the whole church. We are right to resent sentimentality and cynicism in drama, since both must simplify what is complex. Bad drama cuts off the loose ends; good drama ties them up.

Nevertheless, the drama remains a metaphor, the good dramatist a whole man with an involuntary attitude and therefore willy-nilly a man with a 'message'. No apology is needed for a suspect term, for today the disguises for didacticism are many. First, there is the drama that looks like life, but is not: the coterie of *The Cocktail Party* stripped to reveal tentative religious implications, the elaborately rigged choice between religion and 'psychology' in Graham Greene's *The Living Room*. Secondly, there is the generalizing of human experience willingly conceded behind a screen of myth, in plays like Giraudoux's *Tiger at the Gates*, Christopher Fry's *The Firstborn* and Anouilh's *The Lark*. As in Greek tragedy, the repetition of a known plot distracts attention from the credibility of the story and places a convenient emphasis on its values; and where the disguised naturalist stands in danger of making his character a puppet, the downright allegorist can devote his whole attention to making his puppet human. Thirdly, there is the vast field of deliberate fantasy, from the dream plays of Strindberg, Maeterlinck and Pirandello to wilder extravaganzas like *Under Milk Wood*, *Waiting for Godot* and *The Chairs*. In this genre, we may resent the unbalanced simplifications of Priestley's *They Came to a City*, but be duped into accepting the partiality of Beckett. The didactic level of the play may lie shallow or deep; or we may be blinded by technique.

The play most likely to succeed in any of these disguises is the play which works through our experience. *Waiting for Godot* perhaps needs to pull few punches because there is enough of recognizable life in Didi and Gogo; even more in their cheerless Micawber situation—who dare answer No to the query, 'Aren't you waiting for something to turn up?'? Nevertheless, complete honesty must be the quality that makes the symbolism in these plays viable, and in a questioning age like ours it is understandable that dramatists should take up an apparently safe position and join with Chekhov in saying, 'You would have me, when I describe horse-thieves, say, "It is wrong to steal horses." But that has been known for ages without my saying so. Let the jury judge them; it is my job simply to show what sort of people they are.'[1] Yet only the pedagogue would choose to describe a horse-thief.

The drama of the modern theatre is an earnest and didactic drama because it is a drama of dismay and sometimes of despair. Like the Elizabethans, our writers all express the fascination of horror; and the blend of laughter and tears this essay has been examining is expressly the kind of ambivalent gesture made towards what is deeply repulsive. Nevertheless, the mixture of grief and embarrassment and pity and derision, if spicy and rarely dull, is in the end melancholy and dispiriting. It demonstrates disillusion; it rarely incites to action. It can therefore fairly easily become comfortable, self-pitying and morbid.

This is not to say that dark comedy need leave us complacent; but the time has passed when we can respond to the sick despair of the post-1945 theatre with the moving account Shaw wrote after seeing *The Wild Duck* in 1897:

To sit there getting deeper and deeper into that Ekdal home, and getting deeper and deeper into your own life all the time, until you forget that you are in a theatre; to look on with horror and pity at a profound tragedy, shaking with laughter all the time at an irresistible comedy; to go out, not from a diversion, but from an experience deeper than real life ever brings to most men, or often brings to any man: that is what *The Wild Duck* was like last Monday at the Globe.[2]

[1] Chekhov to Suvorin, quoted by W. H. Bruford, *Chekhov and his Russia* (London, 1948), p. 18.
[2] Shaw, *Our Theatres in the Nineties*, vol. 3 (London, 1932), p. 138.

This fairly describes our response to the naturalistic techniques of Ibsen and Chekhov—we are moved to feel a unique dismay, even disgust, but never despair. We remain in partly insulated detachment which leaves us free to understand a passionate experience. We do not laugh as sceptics, but as participants who share an insight.

Today, there is no forgetting we are in a very much more strongly demonstrative theatre: we are more frequently bludgeoned, not wooed, into an attitude of cynicism, sometimes of nihilism. In post-war plays like *Endgame*, *The Entertainer*, *Cat on a Hot Tin Roof* and *The Birthday Party* dismay has sunk into despair; the characters are sick where Chekhov's ineffectual drifters were only ailing.

It is the sickness of Hamm whose hope for life ranges between the inaccessible window, love for a broken toy dog and the security of a dustbin with the comfort of a dog-biscuit to suck. It is the sickness of Archie Rice, who has ceased to fight. Or of Jimmy Porter, racked with emotional doubts, shrieking at society and religion in the person of his wife, a man for whom life is dirty and moreover not worth cleaning up: 'There aren't any good, brave causes left.' It is also the mortal sickness of Big Daddy's 'little spastic condition' he deceives himself into accepting, and the moribund hypochondria of Dan Rooney's reply in *All That Fall* when Maddy asks whether he is 'not well':

Well! Did you ever know me to be well? The day you met me I should have been in bed. The day you proposed to me the doctors gave me up. You knew that, did you not? The night you married me they came for me with an ambulance. You have not forgotten that, I suppose? (*Pause.*) No, I cannot be said to be well. But I am no worse. Indeed I am better than I was. The loss of my sight was a great fillip. If I could go deaf and dumb I think I might pant on to be a hundred.

It is the self-tormenting sickness of a Nathalie in Anouilh's *Ardèle* who moans with delight on the discovery of sex, and next morning wishes to kill herself from disgust. Or the sickness of blind credulity in Willie Loman, riding for a fall on a shoe-shine and a smile.

'A neutral tone is nowadays preferred', writes the poet of the 'fifties with grim understatement.[1] And we have called ours the comedy of despair. But at least these dramatists are aware of the ambiguities and uglinesses of life, and are not afraid to speak. They are not blind, and the contemporary theatre insists upon offering more than a diversion and an escape.

In a troubled century, writing a play which can daringly hold a balance between the emotions of melodrama and the detachment of comedy may be described as artistic tightrope-walking. Indeed, 'funambulism' has been used as a vivid term by Giorgio Melchiori to describe a characteristic of our time:

I think it is as good a term as any to express the sense of danger—or should we say with Auden, anxiety—and precariousness so vividly reflected both in the form and in the content of the artistic and literary works of the first half of this century. And since a work of art cannot be such if (even expressing uncertainty and doubt) it does not achieve a temporary balance, funambulism seems indeed to convey also that: the achievement of the true artist in our age, who, like the successful acrobat, succeeds in keeping step by step, moment by moment, his balance, while being aware of the void or turmoil around him.[2]

The satisfaction of dark comedy, when it arises, lies in watching the playwright keep this balance; the significance of it lies in his finding it important to do so.

There would be a cowardice in remaining on ground level, drabbling in self-pity. This is not the appropriate time for desertion into outmoded forms of comedy: one could argue that the criticism of the earlier comedy is ineffectual, its detachment an escape, its field of social observation a limitation. A renaissance today of the comedy of Congreve and his contemporaries or the confident comedy of Goldsmith, Sheridan and Oscar Wilde would be an affront to the dignity of the atomic-age audience. *The Cherry Orchard*, Pirandello's *Henry IV*, the *pièces brillantes* and *grinçantes* of Anouilh invite anguished experience; their ironies can sicken; their flavour can be acrid and nauseous—but they may be the only

---

[1] D. Davie, 'Remembering the 'Thirties' in *New Lines*, ed. Conquest (London, 1956), p. 70.
[2] G. Melchiori, *The Tightrope Walkers* (London, 1956), p. 8.

dish we could find savoury. Far more appropriate is the pain of Pirandello's *umorismo*, where 'every feeling, every thought, every impulse which rises in the humorist unfolds itself suddenly in its opposite'.[1]

Today it can be a mature drama, and it can be a positive experience, which accepts the pain and yet keeps the balance. To walk the tightrope is probably to evolve by hard practice a relevant philosophy of tolerance, one which does not strike poses or make rhetorical gestures, but which deals in the honest problems of *l'homme moyen sensuel*.

We should not therefore be too inclined to think that this drama is unhealthy. Although it is implicitly didactic, it is encouraging that there is sometimes a reluctance on the part of its authors to deliver explicitly their implicit sermon: at its best it is merely humble before the facts. At its best it does not approve, yet it will not readily place blame or condemn wholesale: it will not draw hard and fast lines. It flinches when it feels the urge to preach, or it is careful to flirt with us. Thus Chekhov puts his words of positive hope, 'Humanity is advancing towards the highest truth, the greatest happiness that it is possible to achieve on earth, and I am in the van!', in the mouth of Trofimov, the immature, the eternal student. It is his self-confessed failure Vershinin who prophesies that 'in two or three hundred years life on this old earth of ours will have become marvellously beautiful'. We are left guessing. Pirandello offers us a romantic finale in *Henry IV* and the hero kills the villain, but only to find that he has condemned himself to absolute imprisonment within his own masquerade. At the end of *The Waltz of the Toreadors*, General St Pé is advised by his doctor that 'life should be led like a cavalry charge', and in this way he prepares himself to lead it with a 'Take aim! Steady! Fire!' only to be surprised into his habitual inconsequence by the curtain entrance of pretty little Pamela, the new maid. 'The writer must be as objective as a chemist,' declared Chekhov.[2]

[1] Pirandello, *L'Umorismo*, 2nd ed. (Florence, 1920), p. 196. The original reads, 'Ogni sentimento, ogni pensiero, ogni moto che sorga nell'umorista si sdoppia subito nel suo contrario.'

[2] Quoted by W. H. Bruford, *Chekhov* (London, 1957), p. 24.

If we are lucky, we read between the lines of a life as it should be lived; but it is a drab morality that is being advocated and demonstrated. Yet whether wistful or passionate in complexion, it remains rather uncertain, with all the irony of a lucky Jim.

It can be healthy, too, in being scrupulous and self-aware, as Shakespeare's Lear is self-aware when he discovers his humility, or as Dostoevsky's Mitya Karamazov is aware as he leaps between his divine vision and his animal lust, discovering the angel and the insect inseparable within himself. 'Yes, man is too broad, too broad, indeed. I'd have him narrower.' His effort is to understand why beauty is so terrible; to admit that God sets us nothing but riddles, and that all contradictions exist side by side; to know that in the little dark back-alleys behind the main road—there one finds precious metal in the dirt.

The laceration of making such discoveries is felt implicitly in the best of the drama we have discussed. When Fry declared he must look for tragedy before he could find his comedy and to some extent cross the one before he could light on the other, he added, 'In a century less flayed and quivering we might reach it more directly; but not now unless every word we write is going to mock us.'[1] The pure and tragic impulse may have been a symptom of a rocklike civilization, and shown man's wish to see his place among the angels. The shifting sands of this century enjoin each man to build alone. Through each new play he writes, the dark comedian is saying with William Blake, 'I must create a system or be enslaved by another man's.'

[1] C. Fry, 'Comedy' in *The Adelphi*, vol. 27, 1 (November 1950), p. 28, quoted by G. Melchiori, *The Tightrope Walkers* (London, 1956), p. 168.

READING LIST

Abel, L., *Metatheatre* (New York, 1963).

Artaud, A., *The Theater and Its Double*, tr. M. C. Richards (New York, 1958).

Aylen, L., *Greek Tragedy and the Modern World* (London, 1964).

Babbitt, I., *Rousseau and Romanticism* (New York, 1919).

Bentley, E. R., *Bernard Shaw* (London, 1950).

—— *In Search of Theater* (London, 1954).

—— *The Life of the Drama* (New York, 1964).

—— *The Modern Theatre: A Study of Dramatists and the Drama* (London, 1948), earlier *The Playwright as Thinker: a Study of Drama in Modern Times* (New York, 1946).

Bergson, H., *Laughter: An Essay on the Meaning of the Comic* (London, 1921).

Bethell, S. L., *Shakespeare and the Popular Dramatic Tradition* (London, 1944).

—— *The Winter's Tale: a Study* (London, 1944).

Boas, F. S., *Christopher Marlowe: A Biographical and Critical Study* (London, 1940).

Bogard, T. and Oliver, W. I., *Modern Drama: Essays in Criticism* (New York, 1965).

Bradbrook, M. C., *English Dramatic Form: a History of its Development* (London, 1965).

Brown, J. R. and Harris, B. (eds.), *Contemporary Theatre* (London, 1962).

Bruford, W. H., *Chekhov* (London, 1957).

—— *Chekhov and his Russia: A Sociological Study* (London, 1948).

Brustein, R., *The Theatre of Revolt* (Boston, 1962).

Chayefsky, P., *Television Plays* (New York, 1955).

Chekhov, A. P., *The Selected Letters of Anton Chekhov*, ed. L. Hellman (London, 1955).

Chiari, J., *The Contemporary French Theatre* (London, 1958).

Clark, B. H., *European Theories of the Drama* (Cincinnati, 1918).

Clinton-Baddeley, V. C., *The Burlesque Tradition in the English Theatre after 1660* (London, 1962).

Coe, R. N., *Beckett* (Edinburgh, 1964).

—— *Ionesco* (Edinburgh, 1961).

Daiches, D., *Critical Approaches to Literature* (London, 1956).

Daniels, M., *The French Drama of the Unspoken* (Edinburgh, 1953).

Reading List

Donoghue, D., *The Third Voice: Modern British and American Verse Drama* (Princeton, 1959).

Downs, B. W., *Ibsen: The Intellectual Background* (Cambridge, 1946).

—— *A Study of Six Plays by Ibsen* (Cambridge, 1950).

Dryden, J., *An Essay of Dramatic Poesy*, ed. T. Arnold (Oxford, 1889).

Dürrenmatt, F., *Problems of the Theatre*, tr. G. Nellhaus (New York, 1958).

Eliot, T. S., *On Poetry and Poets* (London, 1957).

—— *Poetry and Drama* (London, 1951).

—— *Selected Essays* (London, 1932).

—— *The Use of Poetry and the Use of Criticism* (London, 1933).

Ellis-Fermor, U. M., *The Frontiers of Drama* (London, 1945).

—— *The Irish Dramatic Movement* (London, 1939).

—— *The Jacobean Drama* (London, 1936).

Empson, W., *Seven Types of Ambiguity*, 2nd ed. (London, 1947).

—— *Some Versions of Pastoral* (London, 1950).

Esslin, M., *Brecht: A Choice of Evils* (London, 1959).

—— *The Theatre of the Absurd* (London, 1962).

Fergusson, F., *The Idea of a Theater* (Princeton, 1949).

Findlater, R., *The Unholy Trade* (London, 1952).

Freud, S., *Wit and its Relation to the Unconscious* (London, 1906).

Frye, N., *Anatomy of Criticism* (Princeton, 1957).

Gardner, H., *The Art of T. S. Eliot* (London, 1949).

Garten, H. F., *Modern German Drama* (London, 1959).

Gassner, J., *Form and Idea in the Modern Theatre* (New York, 1956).

Gerhardi, W., *Anton Chehov: A Critical Study* (London, 1923).

Ginestier, P., *Le Théâtre contemporain dans le monde* (Paris, 1961).

Gray, R., *Brecht* (London, 1961).

Grossvogel, D. I., *The Self-conscious Stage in Modern French Drama* (New York, 1958).

Guicharnard, J., *Modern French Theatre from Giraudoux to Beckett* (Yale, 1961).

Guthke, K. S., *Modern Tragicomedy: An Investigation into the Nature of the Genre* (New York, 1966).

Harvey, J., *Anouilh: A Study in Theatrics* (Yale, 1964).

Hazlitt, W., *Dramatic Essays* (London, 1895).

Henn, T. R., *The Harvest of Tragedy* (London, 1956).

Hingley, R., *Chekhov* (London, 1950).

Hobson, H., *The French Theatre of Today* (London, 1953).

Hogan, R., *The Experiments of Sean O'Casey* (New York, 1960).

Hoy, C., *The Hyacinth Room: An Investigation into the Nature of Comedy, Tragedy, and Tragicomedy* (New York, 1964).

Reading List

Ibsen, H., *Letters and Speeches*, ed. E. Sprinchorn (New York, 1964).

Inskip, D., *Jean Giraudoux: The Making of a Dramatist* (London, 1958).

Ionesco, E., *Notes and Counter Notes* (London and New York, 1964).

Johnson, S., *Johnson on Shakespeare*, ed. W. Raleigh (London, 1908).

Jones, D. E., *The Plays of T. S. Eliot* (London, 1960).

Kerr, W., *How Not to Write a Play* (London, 1956).

Kitchen, L., *Mid-Century Drama* (London, 1960).

Kitto, H. D. F., *Greek Tragedy: A Literary Study*, 3rd ed. (London, 1961).

Knight, G. W., *The Wheel of Fire: Interpretations of Shakespearian Tragedy* (London, 1949).

Koestler, A., *The Act of Creation* (London, 1964).

Krause, D., *Sean O'Casey: The Man and his Work* (London, 1960).

Kronenberger, L., *The Thread of Laughter* (New York, 1952).

Krutch, J. W., *American Drama since 1918*, 2nd ed. (London, 1957).

Lamm, M., *Modern Drama*, tr. K. Elliott (Oxford, 1952).

Langer, S. K., *Feeling and Form* (New York, 1953).

Lascelles, M., *Shakespeare's Measure for Measure* (London, 1953).

Lavrin, J., *Aspects of Modernism from Wilde to Pirandello* (London, 1935).

—— *Ibsen: An Approach* (London, 1950).

Lawrence, W. W., *Shakespeare's Problem Comedies* (London, 1931).

Lewis, D. B. W., *Molière: The Comic Mask* (London, 1959).

Lucas, F. L., *Tragedy in Relation to Aristotle's Poetics* (London, 1928).

Lumley, F., *Trends in Twentieth Century Drama: A Survey since Ibsen and Shaw* (London, 1956).

MacCarthy, D., *Shaw* (London, 1951).

Magarshack, D., *Chekhov the Dramatist* (London, 1952).

Mander, J., *The Writer and Commitment* (London, 1961).

Marowitz, C., Milne, T. and Hale, O., *The Encore Reader* (London, 1965).

Marsh, E. O., *Jean Anouilh: The Poet of Pierrot and Pantaloon* (London, 1953).

Matthiessen, F. O., *The Achievement of T. S. Eliot*, revised ed. C. L. Barber (London, 1958).

McMahon, J. H., *The Imagination of Jean Genêt* (Yale, 1963).

Melchiori, G., *The Tightrope Walkers: Studies of Mannerism in Modern English Literature* (London, 1956).

Meredith, G., *On the Idea of Comedy and the Uses of the Comic Spirit* (London, 1903).

Moore, W. G., *Molière: A New Criticism* (London, 1959).

Morgan, M. M., *A Drama of Political Man: A Study in the Plays of Harley Granville Barker* (London, 1961).

Mortensen, B. M. E. and Downs, B. W., *Strindberg: An Introduction to his Life and Work* (Cambridge, 1949).

Murray, G., *Euripides and his Age* (London, 1913).

Nicoll, A., *The Theatre and Dramatic Theory* (London, 1962).

—— *The Theory of Drama* (London, 1931).

Norman, C., *The Muses' Darling: The Life of Christopher Marlowe* (London, 1947).

Northam, J. R., *Ibsen's Dramatic Method: A Study of the Prose Dramas* (London, 1953).

O'Faoláin, S., *The Vanishing Hero: Studies in Novelists of the Twenties* (London, 1956).

Palmer, J., *Comedy* (London, 1948).

Peacock, R., *The Art of Drama* (London, 1957).

—— *The Poet in the Theatre* (London, 1946).

Pirandello, L., *L'Umorismo*, 2nd ed. (Firenze, 1920).

Poirier, M., *Christopher Marlowe* (London, 1951).

Potts, L. J., *Comedy* (London, 1948).

Praz, M., *The Hero in Eclipse in Victorian Fiction* (London, 1956).

Price, A., *Synge and Anglo-Irish Drama* (London, 1961).

Priestley, J. B., *English Humour* (London, 1929).

Pronko, L. C., *Avant-Garde: The Experimental Theater in France* (Berkeley, 1962).

Richards, I. A., *Principles of Literary Criticism*, 2nd ed. (London, 1926).

Robinson, L., *Ireland's Abbey Theatre: A History, 1899–1951* (London, 1951).

Rossiter, A. P., *English Drama from Early Times to the Elizabethans* (London, 1950).

Sartre, J.-P., *Jean Genêt, comédien et martyr* (Paris, 1952).

Schlegel, A. W., *Lectures on Dramatic Art and Literature* (London, 1846).

Sedgewick, G. G., *Of Irony, especially in Drama* (Toronto, 1934).

Shaw, G. B., *Our Theatres in the Nineties* (London, 1932).

—— *The Quintessence of Ibsenism* (London, 1932).

Sherbo, A., *English Sentimental Drama* (London, 1958).

Sprigge, E., *The Strange Life of August Strindberg* (London, 1949).

Stanford, D., *Christopher Fry: An Appreciation* (London, 1951).

Starkie, W., *Luigi Pirandello* (London, 1926).

Steiner, G., *The Death of Tragedy* (London, 1961).

Styan, J. L., *The Elements of Drama* (Cambridge, 1960).

Taylor, J. R., *Anger and After* (London, 1962).

Tennant, P. D. F., *Ibsen's Dramatic Technique* (Cambridge, 1948).

Thompson, A. R., *The Dry Mock: A Study of Irony in Drama* (Berkeley, 1948).

Thomson, J. A. K., *Irony: An Historical Introduction* (London, 1926).

Tillyard, E. M. W., *Shakespeare's Problem Plays* (London, 1950).

Toumanova, N. A., *Anton Chekhov* (London, 1937).

Tynan, K., *Curtains* (London, 1961).

Valency, M., *The Breaking String: The Plays of Anton Chekhov* (New York, 1966).

Van Druten, J., *The Playwright at Work* (New York, 1953).

Verrall, A. W., *Euripides the Rationalist* (Cambridge, 1895).

Vittorini, D., *The Drama of Luigi Pirandello* (New York, 1935).

Watt, I., *The Rise of the Novel* (London, 1957).

Welland, D., *Arthur Miller* (London, 1961).

Wellwarth, G. E., *The Theatre of Protest and Paradox* (New York, 1964).

Wellek, R., *A History of Modern Criticism, 1750–1950*, 2 vols. (London, 1956).

Willett, J., *Brecht on Theatre* (London, 1964).

—— *The Theatre of Bertolt Brecht* (London, 1959).

Williams, R., *Drama from Ibsen to Eliot* (London, 1952).

—— *Modern Tragedy* (London, 1966).

Wimsatt, W. K. (ed.), *English Stage Comedy* (New York, 1955).

Worcester, D., *The Art of Satire* (Cambridge, Mass., 1940).

INDEX

Index

Index

Index